THE PRIMER
OF OBJECT
RELATIONS

THE PRIMER OF OBJECT RELATIONS

Second Edition

Jill Savege Scharff
David E. Scharff

Jason Aronson
Lanham • Boulder • New York • Toronto • Oxford

Published in the United States of America
by Jason Aronson
An imprint of Rowman & Littlefield Publishers, Inc.

A wholly owned subsidiary of
The Rowman & Littlefield Publishing Group, Inc.
4501 Forbes Boulevard, Suite 200, Lanham, Maryland 20706
www.rowmanlittlefield.com

PO Box 317
Oxford
OX2 9RU, UK

British Library Cataloguing in Publication Information Available

Library of Congress Cataloging-in-Publication Data
Scharff, Jill Savege.
  The primer of object relations / by Jill Savege Scharff and David E.
Scharff—2nd ed.
    p.   cm.
  Includes bibliographical references and index.
  ISBN 0-7657-0347-5
  1. Object relations (Psychoanalysis) 2. Psychotherapy. I. Scharff, David E.,
1941– II. Title.
  RC489.025S34 2003
  616.89'14—dc21   2003040319

Printed in the United States of America

⊚™ The paper used in this publication meets the minimum requirements of
American National Standard for Information Sciences—Permanence of Paper
for Printed Library Materials, ANSI/NISO Z39.48-1992.

CONTENTS

FIGURES AND TABLES

Figures

Tables

PREFACE

It's more than ten years since we wrote *Scharff Notes*, reprinted as *The Primer of Object Relations Therapy*. Object relations theory was on the fringe at that time. Since then it has gained in acceptance. Once excluded from discussion, it is now featured at both psychoanalytic and family therapy meetings. In the Sexton, Weeks, and Robbins *Handbook of Family Therapy*, it was listed as one of five traditional approaches! It is time for a second edition of the *Primer*, expanded to include revisions, clarifications, and advances in object relations theory and practice and now called *The Primer of Object Relations*. The *Primer* is written to stand alone, in the same accessible format for the ease of use of the same readership, from undergraduate student to psychotherapy teacher. If you want to go into object relations in greater depth, you might look up citations given in endnotes for each chapter, or dip into the reading lists, or study more comprehensive texts also listed in the reference section.

Object relations theory continues to develop under the influence of new knowledge in related disciplines and paths of clinical inquiry. Clinical adaptations used in brief therapy, attachment research extended to adults and couple relationships, studies of neurological development and affect regulation, clinical insights on physical, sexual, and societal trauma, and contemporary Kleinian ideas have validated and enriched

object relations therapy. Principles of chaos theory dealing with nonlinear dynamic systems are pushing object relations theory toward a para-
digm shift. The effects of these advances are evident in object relations
therapy today.

We have extended our description of the technique of object relations
therapy with individuals, couples, and families with young children, and
we've given more examples, including work with dreams. We have
added a description of the Group Affective Model, an innovative
method for learning theory and technique, internalizing it, and applying
it in therapy. We have included our new guide to the geography of the
transference. Also new to this edition, we've added chapters on brief
therapy, attachment theory and its clinical application, and chaos theory,
explaining advances in our clinical thinking.

We want to reach undergraduate students who are learning the fun-
damentals of theory and therapy as well as graduate students in psychology, social work, or marital and family therapy. We hope to interest
first-year residents in psychiatry and interns in psychology, social work,
marital and family therapy, and pastoral counseling. We think that the
book will be useful for trainees in occupational therapy, art and other expressive therapies, and psychiatric nursing. And finally, we hope that the
primer will be a compact, convenient resource text for the teachers of
these various undergraduate, graduate, and postgraduate students, and
for the experienced clinician who wants to integrate the unfamiliar perspective of object relations theory into an existing approach.

Mental health professionals from remote parts of the United States
and from other countries have no access to object relations theory other
than through textbooks. When puzzled, they have no colleagues to turn
to for help. Although they may have enjoyed our more complex books,
they want simplification and clarification of some of the ideas and further
discussion of how the concepts apply in their clinical situations. The content of this volume derives from these students' most frequently asked
questions at national seminars, together with our responses. Through our
lecture, discussion, and dialogue format, we re-create the seminar for
them and for you, in order to take you beyond the forbidding aspects of
theory and technique and give you access to object relations theory and
therapy as a sensible way of thinking and working that is easily understood and immediately applicable to clinical practice.

We've continued to learn from teaching students and colleagues at national and international workshops and seminars. But the greatest boost to our understanding has come from working with students, faculty, and distinguished guests at the International Psychotherapy Institute, which we founded in Chevy Chase, Maryland, to provide a learning community for students and faculty who are otherwise isolated from object relations training. That's where we refined the Group Affective Model for teaching and learning object relations theory and practice, using a modular design so they could commute to join in workshops. In addition to attending lectures and clinical case presentations, participants meet in small affective learning groups for integrating intellectual and emotional understanding through discussion, personal and group experience, and clinical application. This has given us access to difficulties that interfere with understanding and has led to insights and changes that prove the value of the concepts. We hope to include you in the learning community by sharing our new ideas in this second edition of *The Primer of Object Relations*.

We are grateful to Jason Aronson for his commitment to publishing texts on object relations theory and practice—especially for supporting our idea of an affordable paperback primer—and to the staff at Rowman and Littlefield for their editorial and promotional work.

We have reinvented the identities of the subjects of our clinical descriptions so as to preserve a personal context for their universally observable dynamics without betraying their confidentiality. To those individuals, couples, and families, we give special thanks. We gratefully acknowledge the intellectual stimulation and encouragement received from mental health professionals at our seminars, where their questions continually provoked further thought and challenged us to be clear and concise. This book is for them and for you, mental health professionals and students who are curious about the object relations approach.

HOW TO USE THIS PRIMER

In the interest of readability, we do not break the flow to pause for references in the body of this text. When we use a concept or an author's name with which you may not be familiar, we cite it briefly in the chapter notes that follow each chapter. In chapter 24, we offer a guide to further reading both for the beginner and for the advanced student of object relations theory. To satisfy our concern for attribution and accessibility to reference materials, we do give a complete bibliography at the end of the book. The bibliography is divided into ten categories to simplify the advancing student's search for more to read in a particular category of interest. The categories are: object relations theory of individual and group; application of object relations theory to couple and family therapy; integration of object relations theory with other approaches; American object relations theory; transference and countertransference; self psychology theory applied to individuals and couples; Freudian theory; attachment theory; chaos theory; other relevant contributions.

With this design, you can read uninterruptedly and take in the material as a whole the first time through. You can skip the references altogether, look at them at the end of reading each chapter, or wait until you have finished the book. Those of you who want to track down sources will search for author and date in the chapter notes at the end of each chapter, and then find the full annotation in the relevant category of the formal bibliography at the end of the book. We hope that this primer format will bring object relations theory to you clearly and easily.

The primer may be used as the only text on object relations theory for the eclectic therapist. It serves as an introduction and guide to reading our more advanced texts. It also leads to wider recommended reading in object relations theory and therapy.

I

OVERVIEW OF THE CONCEPTS OF BRITISH OBJECT RELATIONS THEORY

THE SELF AND ITS OBJECTS

WHAT IS BRITISH OBJECT RELATIONS THEORY?

British object relations theory is a theory of the human personality developed from study of the therapist-patient relationship as it reflects the mother-infant dyad. The theory holds that the infant's experience in relationship with the mother is the primary determinant of personality formation and that the infant's need for attachment to the mother is the motivating factor in the development of the infantile self. It is an amalgam of the work of British analysts Ronald Fairbairn, Donald Winnicott, Harry Guntrip, and Michael Balint of the British Independent group, augmented by that of Melanie Klein, and others of the Kleinian group. Although Independent group and Kleinian group theories are quite distinct from each other, and differ in the ways that they each diverge from Sigmund Freud's theory of the mind, they are similar in focusing on the importance of the infant's experience of the mothering relationship. The Independent group followed Freud's use of the psychosexual stages of development, but disagreed that the inevitable progression of these stages was based on the primacy of the instincts. They proposed instead that the need to be in relationship to a caregiver was the fundamental driving force and that

the characteristic kinds of relatedness seen at various ages were determined by shifting dependent needs, not by instinctual loading of
the erogenous bases. The Kleinians stayed true to Freud's view of the
primacy of the instincts and elaborated upon the death instinct, but
they revised his psychosexual timetable. They described their ideas of
how the infant uses unconscious fantasy to effect the release of tension from the instincts and how the processing of fantasy creates psychic structure. Both Independent group and Kleinian theorists developed theories of personality formation and psychic structure different
from Freud's, and different from each other. Nevertheless, the theories can be integrated because of their commonality in focus on the
first three years of life—in analytic theory referred to as the pre-
oedipal period of development—and their emphasis on psychic structure arising from the infant's experience of the mother-infant relationship.

WHAT ARE OBJECT RELATIONS?

Object relations is an inclusive technical term that spans the intrapsychic
and interpersonal dimensions. It refers to the system of in-built parts of
the personality in relation to each other inside the self. These parts are
expressed in the arena of current relationships by which the original intrapsychic representations of object relations are further modified. Internal objects and other parts of the self are reciprocal with outer objects so that, in any relationship, the personalities are mutually
influenced by each other. Our external relationships are in interaction
with our internal psychic structures.

WHAT IS AN INTERNAL OBJECT?

An internal object is a piece of psychic structure that formed from the
person's experience with the important caretaking person in earlier life,
captured in the personality as the trace of that earlier relationship. Not
a memory, nor a representation, it is a part of the self's being.

HOW IS THE INTERNAL OBJECT DIFFERENT FROM THE EXTERNAL OBJECT?

The external object refers to the significant other with whom the person is in relationship. It might refer to the early significant other or the present significant other. It bears a relationship to the internal object in that the internal object is based on the experience with the original external object and is expressed in the present choice of an external object. The internal object is also modified by its relationship with the present external object.

WHAT FACTORS MAKE THE INTERNAL OBJECT MORE THAN A DIRECT, INTERNAL RECORDING OF EXPERIENCE WITH THE EARLY EXTERNAL OBJECT?

There are several factors. During the early relationship to the mother, the baby has a limited capacity to understand what the mother is feeling or expressing or to separate this from what the baby feels. The baby's limited cognitive capacity distorts the view of the mother, so that already the internal object does not accurately reflect the external object. Later on, as the baby grows and develops, new issues at the forefront of development change what the baby thinks is happening with the external object. So the baby creates a contemporary version of the internal object to internalize. For instance, when the child is at a point where autonomy and control are at the leading edge of development, the child's capacity to hold on to, and let go of, the external object reshapes the internal object's organization. In summary, previous experience with the external object at all stages of development is cumulatively internalized. When child, adolescent, and adult meet new people, they will expect the new relationships to be like those they have known. Even if they are not really like that, the new figures may be experienced as though they were, in order to reaffirm that new experience is familiar and will not create a demand for change in the internal object relationships. Pressure from healthy, new external objects to maintain their integrity reverses this trend. Then, new relationships can afford both partners the opportunity for further modification of their internal object worlds.

DOES THE HUMAN PERSONALITY CONSIST ONLY OF A COLLECTION OF OBJECTS?

No. Objects are only part of the personality. Infants are born with their own potential personality. At birth, there is a self ready and prewired to relate to the external objects that the infant will find in the environment. In relation to these external objects, the self then grows and develops and builds upon its experience with the objects to create psychic structure.

WHAT IS THE SELF?

The self refers to the total personality growing through the life cycle. At first it is a pristine, unformed self, gradually becoming enriched by experience with the objects. According to infant researcher Daniel Stern, the baby is organized from the beginning to acquire experience in order to build a personality and a sense of self. The self comprises: (1) the old-fashioned concept of the ego as an executive mechanism that modulates self-control through its control of motility, sphincters, and affect states, and mediates relations with the outside world, (2) the internal objects, and (3) objects and parts of the ego bound together by the affects (feelings) appropriate to the child's experiences of these object relationships.

We've used the term *self* to refer to the combination of ego and internal objects in a unique, dynamic relation that comprises the character and gives a sense of personal identity that endures and remains relatively constant over time.

WHAT IS THE RELATIONSHIP BETWEEN SELF AND OBJECT?

The self is the unique psychic organization that creates a person's identity. The external object is what the whole self relates to when it interacts with another person. The internal object is one of the substructures of the self. Also inside the self are various other internal objects and parts of the ego that correspond to them. The ego and its parts moderate operations and feelings that are identified with the self, organized in subcategories of the ego. These broad subcategories relate to corresponding internal objects. These categories of the self and their relevant objects are bound together by the emotion or affect that characterizes the object relationship. Different kinds of internal object relationships arise during different affect states.

CAN YOU DEFINE AN
INTERNAL OBJECT RELATIONSHIP?

Internal object relationship is a term for the relationship between part of the ego and its object bound together by the feelings that are experienced by the ego in relation to that object. The internal object relationship becomes an enduring, but potentially modifiable, part of the self that may remain in consciousness or may need to be pushed out of consciousness if it provokes intolerable anxiety.

We now have a view of the self as consisting of conscious and unconscious parts. Object relations theorists hold that the unconscious is part of the ego, in contrast to Freud, who described the unconscious as separate from the ego, located in a part of the personality that he called the "id"—a seething mass of impulses seeking discharge and governed by irrational thinking processes.

HOW DOES THE INTERNAL OBJECT RELATIONSHIP
FORM IF THE MOTHER IS NOT RAISING THE CHILD?

At their time of writing, the theorists were thinking of the influence on the child of mothering by the actual mother, the woman who had borne the child or who had undertaken to raise the child. Fairbairn and Winnicott noticed the reality of the holding and handling of the child, but also noted the influence of the mother's personality on the mother-infant relationship, whereas Klein was more concerned with the infant's fantasies about the relationship. All of them underemphasized the father's contribution to the child's experience, except as the mother's partner.

Nowadays, with fathers taking a more active part in the raising of their children and mothers working outside the home and the advent of two-mother and two-father families, we use the term *mother* to refer to the person who is centrally responsible for the daily care of the child. This person might be the actual mother (biological or adoptive), the father (or partner), an older sibling, the family housekeeper, or more likely a combination of them. The impact of family dynamics on the individual development of the older child has been described by Roger Shapiro and John Zinner. We need more studies of the effect that sharing of the mothering function has on the infant's development to be more precise about its impact on personality, but for now we can say that the infant integrates experience with multiple external objects to arrive at composite internal objects. All of these significant people are in relationship to each other. The relationship between these external objects affects the integration of composite internal objects and their internal dynamic relation.

WHY WOULD IT NOT BE BETTER TO CALL THE THEORY "SUBJECT RELATIONS THEORY"?

Some people find the term *object relations theory* rather cold and impersonal. They might feel happier calling it *subject relations theory*. We stick to Fairbairn's original "object relations" terminology, which was developed from its base in Freud's theory. Freud used the word *object* to refer to the target that the drives aimed at and looked to for gratification in the person of the caretaker. In his view, the object of the drives was not personal, because the drives were an impersonal force seeking discharge.

For us, however, the object is not an impersonal matter. Our view stems from Fairbairn's original assertion that what is primary is the need for a relationship (not the need for instinctual tension release) and that the person in whose care the child is growing is vitally important as an object of attachment (not of drive gratification).

WHY NOT CALL THIS APPROACH "PERSONAL RELATIONS THEORY"?

This does sound more human, but it does not do justice to the history of the development of the ideas, and it colloquializes what is really a technical matter. We reserve the term *object relations theory* precisely to highlight the technical aspects of the theory and its clinical application.

NOTES

For an excellent, concise overview of the contributions of Fairbairn (1944, 1952, 1954, 1958, 1963), Winnicott (1951, 1956, 1958, 1964, 1965, 1971), Guntrip (1961, 1969, 1986), and Balint (1986), we suggest the review article, "The British Object Relations Theorists: Balint, Winnicott, Fairbairn, Guntrip" (Sutherland 1980). For an easy approach to the theories of Klein (1935, 1946, 1948, 1952, 1955, 1957, 1975), see Segal (1964) and Klein and Riviere (1967). The work of Freud is summarized for the beginner in Freud's introductory lectures on psychoanalysis (Freud 1910a) and for the advanced reader in his final published paper (Freud 1940), written at the age of eighty-two. The contribution of infant research to the development of the self is found in Stern (1985) and Schore (1994). Papers by Shapiro (1979), Zinner (1989), and Zinner and Shapiro (1972) are reprinted in *Foundations of Object Relations Family Therapy* (Scharff 1989b).

2

BASIC FREUDIAN CONCEPTS

Before we look at Ronald Fairbairn's scheme of the endopsychic structure of internal object relations in chapter 3, we must review Sigmund Freud's topographic and structural theories and his basic psychoanalytic concepts of (1) the unconscious; (2) the ego, the id, and superego; and (3) resistance and defense.

THE TOPOGRAPHIC THEORY

Freud's most outstanding contribution was to show that human behavior is determined by factors outside conscious awareness. From his study of associations to dreams and slips of the tongue, he concluded that some of a person's feelings and ideas could be separated off from conscious thought in response to trauma in infancy. Such trauma might include a frightening event, a childhood seduction, a hospitalization, loss of a parent, and so on. He found that the working of the unconscious was not governed by logic and reason, but by primitive, impulse-ridden thinking called *primary process*. Freud's idea of analysis was to trace the patient's associations to the manifest content of dreams and slips of the tongue in order to reestablish the forgotten connections. In this way, he made the unconscious conscious, subjected it to the conscious form of thinking called *secondary process* governed by rules of reason, and so relieved the infantile neurosis. Freud originally described the mind as being divided into conscious, preconscious, and unconscious areas. This first tripartite theory is known as the topographic theory.

STRUCTURAL THEORY

Many years later, Freud postulated another tripartite theory of the mind. In this theory he ascribed a structure to cope with the unconscious. He now called the unconscious the *id*, envisioned as a seething cauldron of aggressive and sexual drives. To mediate between the unruly id and the demands of external reality, the *ego* emerges out of the mess of the id. The ego is constructed as a structure mainly (though not entirely) engaged in preconscious and conscious functioning. The ego comprises (1) the set of executive functions or mechanisms that mediate between the id and the outer world and (2) the set of accumulated identifications with the lost objects of the drives, all of which culminate in a personal identity. After the resolution of the oedipal period of development when the child gives up the wish to possess one parent and kill the rival, the third structure, called the *superego*, develops, based on selective identifications with the forbidding, critical qualities of the parents and reaction formations against these. The superego has both conscious and unconscious elements and guides the child toward moral responsibility. The topographic and structural theories cannot be superimposed exactly upon each other, but coexist as useful ways of viewing the mind.

THE THEORY OF PSYCHOSEXUAL DEVELOPMENT

Freud held that the human infant is motivated by two opposing instincts. At first, Freud saw these as the *sexual instinct* (also called libido), for getting on with life and enjoying sexual pleasure and the *self-preservative instinct,* for repressing the sexual instinct in order to face reality. Later, he saw opposition to the sexual instinct more in terms of the *death instinct*, of which the manifestations were harder for him to see but which he thought was diverted into the external world in the form of destructiveness and aggressiveness. These instincts, or *drives* as they are now more commonly called, have the *aim* of gratification by the *object* that they fall upon. Their *source* is the pool of instincts, impulses, or drives seething untamed in the unconscious part of the mind that Freud called the *id*. These instincts have to be tamed in order not to lose the love object. The infant takes inside successive versions of the love object that have to be given up at each stage of development, and out of these introjections are formed the child's *ego* (the conscious, executive part of the self) and *superego* (the critical, forbidding, guiding part of the self, based on the selective internalization of the parental functioning). Freud's case histories make it clear that he was well aware of the mother's holding and handling of her infant, but in the formulation of his theories he underemphasized the quality of the relationship. Instead, he focused on the structure and function of the child's mind in relative isolation and developed for this task a model of the mind based on science. The organism seeks (1) discharge of instinctual tension, (2) repetition of tension-reducing behavior so as to return to a state of *homeostasis*, or (3) *narcissistic* retreat into the self, where needs either do not disturb or their satisfaction can be imagined as vividly as if it were occurring.

THE PSYCHOSEXUAL STAGES OF DEVELOPMENT

The instincts go through a series of *psychosexual stages of development* that unfold in a predetermined, universal sequence.

Pre-oedipal Development

At first predominantly *oral* in nature, the instincts propel the infant to suck—both for survival through being fed and for pleasurable, libidinal gratification—and later to bite and spit as a way of releasing aggression. When the mouth gives way to the *anus* as the dominant *erogenous* zone, the child gains pleasure from the feces and from the control the anus can exert over holding on to or letting go of them. In the *phallic* stage of development, the child is now aware of and seeks genital sensations, often confused with the urethral sensations of urination. As always, the drives seek objects to gratify their expression. Naturally, the mother is training her child to gain control over these impulses, and so she becomes forbidding as well as gratifying of her child's wishes. Aware of differences in the genitalia between the sexes, the female child imagines that the more obvious penis affords the boy greater pleasure than she enjoys. This is a source of unhappiness and sometimes shame and poor self-esteem. The sequence now moves on to the *oedipal phase*.

Oedipal Development

The little girl develops the fantasy of getting a penis for herself: the best and biggest is the one that she seeks, namely her father's. The child does not want to admit that this is her mother's territory and imagines that she may have to get rid of her Mommy so as to have her Daddy, and any babies that he might give her, all to herself. The girl is then afraid of an angry mother who will kill her or her unborn babies. The boy notices that his mother is interested in his father and assumes that her interest has to do with her wish for his penis. Size comparisons notwithstanding, the boy hopes that his mother will find his penis more attractive than her husband's. If not, the boy imagines, he may have to kill his rival, the father, who, if he should find this out, might angrily retaliate by killing the boy (or at least might cut off his penis to punish him for wanting his mother). Freud called the boy's fear of retaliation *castration anxiety*. The girl was thought to have a *castration complex*, in other words to be upset that she had already been castrated.

Freud thought that the girl's feminine identity forms as a result of her castration complex, namely, her sense of inferiority at not having a valued penis like a boy. His view of feminine identity as a deficit state has been successfully challenged by observational infant research, feminist psychology, and child analysis. We now know that girls have as strong a sense of sexual identity as do boys, long before the phallic period of development. Boys and girls alike envy each other's different sexual characteristics. Excessive signs of castration complex and penis envy in the girl occur when possessing a penis is imagined to make up for an inner sense of deficit or loneliness. Envy of the procreative power of the female body leaves the boy feeling inadequate. One defense against this is to devalue women and aggrandize phallic competence—which tends to drive the penis envy of women and so divert attention from the womb envy of men.

In both sexes, images of the forbidding parents are internalized as a part of the mind called the *superego*, which operates as a conscience and matures in its capacity for maintaining altruistic as well as moral values. Capable now of more complex thinking, the child realizes that there is no way of having everything and gives up forbidden sexual longings to possess one parent and murderous wishes to kill the other, in favor of being the child of two parents who are together. The Oedipus complex is more or less resolved and the child moves on into the latency stage, where ego and superego defenses against regression are strengthened and issues of autonomy and skill-building come to the fore. If unable to master the challenges of a particular developmental stage, a child may become *fixated* there or even *regress* to an earlier developmental stage inappropriate to chronological age.

The nature of the *resolution of the Oedipus complex* determines the character structure by seven years of age, with one qualifier: the Oedipus constellation comes up for reworking during the sexually energized phase of adolescence. Its state of resolution by that time determines the ego's degree of disengagement from the old incestuous objects, which, in turn, determines how free the young person is to develop age-appropriate, sexually experimental love relationships with peers. The mate who is eventually selected will offer attraction and passionate attachment powerful enough to defeat the tie to the old objects and yet similar enough to inherit the transference to them.

Based in object relations theory, our ideas about the organizational boundaries of the unconscious differ from those of Freud. Nevertheless, we continue to view his concepts of unconscious motivation and unconscious organization as basic to any psychodynamic approach. Similarly, although we disagree with Freud's view of the instinctual basis of psychosexual development in which the sexual instinct cathects the erogenous zones in a preset sequence that then determines psychosexual development, we do find that the sequence occurs as Freud described it and that the child uses the oral, anal, urethral, phallic, and eventually genital routes for the experience of arousal and discharge of sexual and aggressive feeling. But we think that these feelings originate within the relationship to the caretaker as it evolves through the various stages of child-rearing, from the nursing, lap-baby stage, the toilet-training toddler stage, to the nursery-school stage of separating from the mother and exploring the wider world of friendships and sexual difference.

As Erik Erikson pointed out, when he reviewed the eight stages of man, there is a dilemma to be solved at each stage. At the oral stage, the task is to establish trust and find a balance between taking in and putting out. At the anal stage we are concerned with holding on and letting go of our parent as well as our body products. At the phallic-urethral stage we want to be admired more than our rivals or else we feel ashamed and sometimes defective. At the genital level we are ready to give and receive love in a faithful, free way, no longer bound by a rivalrous obsession to possess the opposite-sex parent. Fairbairn regarded the stages of psychosexual development as reflecting the child's use of techniques of relating appropriate to the caretaker's attempts to train the dependent child.

According to Freud, the oedipal child wants to possess the opposite-sex parent and kill the rival to secure this goal. Fairbairn thought that the conflicts of the oedipal phase represented the child's attempt to simplify the following problem: In the pre-oedipal stage, the child had two ambivalently held relationships, one with the mother and the other with the father, each of them contributing elements to both the internal exciting and rejecting object relationships. In the oedipal phase, the child attempts to solve the ambivalence by making the relationship with one parent attractive and the other rejecting, at first possibly selecting the same-sex parent for the positive relationship, but at the height of the oedipal phase the attractive relationship is usually with the opposite-sex parent.

CAN YOU SAY MORE ABOUT THE ID?

In Freudian theory, the id comprises the sexual and aggressive instincts bursting to express themselves and find gratification. The organism wants to discharge the energy from these drives so that it can return to a state of nonexcitation. The id is organized by primary process, a disorganized, primitive way of connecting ideas in a chaotic matrix. In the unconscious, troublesome thoughts and feelings get separated from the impulses in which they originated, and might then connect through primary process with some unrelated thought. Freud invented free association, a technique of saying whatever comes to mind—even if the thoughts do not seem to follow naturally—to retrace these random connections and so derive meaning from apparent non sequiturs that could not be arrived at by formal inquiry.

HOW IS THE EGO DIFFERENT FROM THE ID?

Freud wrote that the ego is organized according to secondary process thinking characterized by logic and reason rather than by unmitigated feelings and impulses under the pressure of instinctual tension. Secondary process is better suited to carrying out the executive functions of the ego, such as managing affect states, integrating whole object experience, identifying with object qualities, tolerating ambivalence, and relating to the outer world.

WHY DO WE CARE ABOUT CONSCIOUS AND UNCONSCIOUS LEVELS OF ORGANIZATION?

They are useful clinically, as we conceptualize the treatment process. The task of treatment is to analyze the chaotic and confusing signals from the unconscious so as to free the ego for dealing with reality. Freud said simply that where id had been, the ego would be. In other words, we work toward substituting conscious and more rational understanding for previously irrational behavior stemming from the primary process of the unconscious. Freud said that the goal of treatment is to make the unconscious conscious.

WHAT ARE RESISTANCE AND DEFENSE?

Freud described resistance as a function of the patient's unconscious organization that tends to prevent unconscious things from becoming conscious. It goes against the patient's conscious wish to cooperate and get better, and it operates against the therapeutic effort and often against the person of the therapist. Much later, Sigmund Freud and his daughter Anna Freud described the personality as consisting of many defenses that are ego mechanisms for structuring and controlling unconscious impulses. Today we think of defense as an intrinsic part of character structure. Patterns of defense occur not so much to keep unconscious forces at bay as to structure the expression of deep-seated needs, affects, and conflicts, while protecting the vulnerabilities of the individual. All of this we now think of as happening within the context of the individual's need for primary relationships. Thus, defenses such as projection, denial, displacement, sublimation, reversal of affect, and reaction formation can all be seen as ways of structuring relationships.

NOTES

Freud's psychoanalytic theories appear in the *Standard Edition* of his work as follows:

Topographic theory, the unconscious, primary process, the preconscious, consciousness, secondary process (1915c).

Repression (1915a, 1915c).

Structural theory, ego, id, and superego (1923).

Identification (1917a, 1923).

Dream theory (1900).

Slips of the tongue or parapraxes (1901a).

The sexual instinct, the self-preservative instinct, psychosexual stages of development (1905b).

The death instinct (1920, 1930).

The Oedipus complex and its resolution (1910a, 1910b, 1924).

Resistance, repression (1917c).

Defense (1895).

For elaboration on the mechanisms of defense, see A. Freud (1946).

For the first extension of Freud's theory to a relational context, see Erikson (1950).

3

FROM FREUD TO
OBJECT RELATIONS THEORY

WHAT DID FREUD MEAN BY THE OBJECT?

Sigmund Freud introduced the term *object* as a technical term to describe the location where the drive energy (the libido) could expect to be gratified. In Freud, the internal object represents the *object of the drives*. That's a difference from object relations theory, which deals with the *object of attachment*. In Freudian theory, at first there is no external object. The libido finds its object inside the infant, and the infant is in a self-involved state of primary narcissism.

HOW DOES THE NARCISSISTIC OBJECT FORM?

With experience of satisfaction at the breast the infant takes the mother's nurturing as the object of the libido. Suffering from the loss of this gratification when the breast is absent, the infant hallucinates the breast and finds the missing oral satisfaction in its own body, and is turned inwardly now in a state of secondary narcissism, only gradually coming to recognize that the object exists outside the self. As the main erogenous zone moves from oral through anal and phallic to genital areas, the infant connects the experience of physical stimulation in each area with the attention given at each stage by the person who administers care.

HOW DOES THE LOST OBJECT LEAD TO PSYCHIC STRUCTURE?

Studying people in love and those who lost a loved one by bereavement, Freud noticed that actual loss of the object leads to a division in the self as one part of the self identifies with the lost object. From this he got the idea of psychic structure forming from the internalization of the libido's experience with objects. Identification with the renounced and forbidding objects of the oedipal phase leads to the formation of the controlling, conscience-guiding superego. The instincts were still important to his ideas, but now Freud had a theory of regulatory psychic structures able to experience and resolve conflict as well as oppose the immature or unacceptable aims of instinctual energy.

WHAT DID FAIRBAIRN THINK OF FREUD?

Ronald Fairbairn admired Freud's classical theory, studied it closely, and taught it faithfully, but he found himself in theoretical and practical disagreement with its most basic tenets—that the infant is driven by instinctual energy to seek gratification and that there is no ego at birth, only an id. The concept of the id was too impersonal for him and didn't fit the facts of his academic and clinical experience.

WHY DID FAIRBAIRN DEVELOP OBJECT RELATIONS THEORY?

Fairbairn's study of philosophy and psychology and his clinical psychoanalytic experience treating children who were being sexually and physically abused, military personnel with war neuroses, and patients with schizoid defenses against trauma and loss, led him to alternative conclusions about human motivation and development. Freud focused on the intrapsychic life of his patients, but Fairbairn studied the relationship between his patients' internal worlds and their experiences in childhood with each parent and in treatment with the analyst. Nevertheless he was highly respectful of Freud's contribution, and so he built his modifications and revisions, keeping the words object, libido, and ego.

NOTES

Scharff, J. S. (2002). In *The Freud Encyclopedia*, ed. E. Erwin. London and New York: Routledge.

4

ENDOPSYCHIC STRUCTURE

Ronald Fairbairn described three main categories of internal object relationship, one in the conscious part of the self and the other two repressed in the unconscious: (1) the ideal object relationship (in the conscious part of the self), (2) the exciting object relationship (in the unconscious part of the self), and (3) the rejecting object relationship (in the unconscious part of the self). Fairbairn's model of psychic organization is summarized in figure 4.1.

HOW DID THESE REPRESSED
OBJECT RELATIONSHIPS DEVELOP?

Sorting and ordering of the internal psychological organization occurs through the mechanism of splitting paired with repression. Fairbairn thought that the infant found even the good mother to be rejecting at times; for instance, when she could not be there the instant that her infant wanted comfort or food. To cope with the intolerable feelings of anxiety and abandonment, the infant held on to her by taking the image of her as this rejecting object inside, in a process called *introjection*. In Fairbairn's theory, introjection is the ego's first defense against unbearable pain and separation from the object. (In our view, however, infants internalize all aspects of the mothering relationship and sort them according to the quality of the experience. Out of this elementary coding of experience, they form psychological structure and become capable of separate functioning.)

WHERE DO SPLITTING AND REPRESSION FIT IN?

In Fairbairn's view, following the introjection of the bad object, the infant now has a sense of dissatisfaction inside the rudimentary infant self. To retain undisturbed an ideal image of the mother in consciousness, the infant's ego deals with the pain of rejection by repressing the whole image of the unsatisfying object into unconsciousness. There the *rejected object* is further sorted into two categories, (1) the *rejecting object*

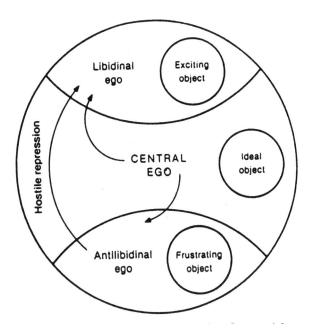

Figure 4.1. The Endopsychic Situation. Reprinted from *The Sexual Relationship: An Object Relations View of Sex and the Family*, courtesy of Routledge and Kegan Paul. Copyright © David E. Scharff, 1982.

and (2) the *exciting object*. However, an internal object cannot be split off and repressed by itself. The part of the ego that has to relate to that painful object has to be split off with the object, along with the affect that characterizes this painful relationship. In the case of the rejecting object, the relevant affects are anger, frustration, and sadness. In the case of the exciting object relationship, the affects are ones of craving and painful longing.

CAN YOU DESCRIBE THE REJECTING OBJECT RELATIONSHIP?

The rejecting object relationship consists of the antilibidinal ego, the rejecting object, and the affects of anger, rage, and sadness. Fairbairn originally called the part of the ego that was repressed with the rejecting object "the internal saboteur" because it threatened to return to consciousness and there spoil defensive idealization. Later Fairbairn changed the name of this part of the self to the *antilibidinal ego*. The rejecting ego supports the central ego in further repressing the exciting object relationship. This sabotages the possibility of the central ego being invested with a good level of excitement about anticipating and seeking pleasant, vital relationships.

CAN YOU DESCRIBE THE EXCITING OBJECT RELATIONSHIP?

The other class of bad object relations—bad because painful, not morally bad—is the *need-exciting object relationship*. A good mother can excite need in her infant by being too attentive. She might anxiously hover near her infant or feed him too readily before he can feel his lust for food, comfort, and connection. Fairbairn's term for the object that excites need and desire is the *libidinal object* and for the part of the ego that related to it, the *libidinal ego*. He chose these names to follow classical usage of the term libido to describe the sexual drives, which were thought by Freud to be the seat of all desire, but any correspondence is quite inexact. The affects that characterize the libidinal object relationship are ones of unsatisfiable longing, anxious arousal, and desperation.

CAN YOU GIVE AN EXAMPLE OF THE EXCITING AND REJECTING OBJECT RELATIONSHIPS?

Mrs. Constable, a beautiful and appealing woman, had been in therapy with me (JSS) for two years at the hospital outpatient clinic. By this time, we both knew that she carried the burden of an exciting object relationship derived from her infantile experience of prolonged and suddenly terminated breast-feeding with her mother. She perpetuated this object relationship with her own babies, at one point storming the hospital nursery to demand her sleeping newborn. She realized that she wanted the excitement of feeding her child because she felt lonely and scared in her hospital room. In later years her eldest boy developed a habit of letting his tongue hang out. Mrs. Constable felt revulsion at this habit and became quite phobic of his mouth in order to avoid the anger that she felt toward him. As treatment progressed, she understood that she was also avoiding her own feelings of emptiness, hunger, and neediness that his open mouth evoked in her. Here, a rejecting object relationship defended against the stimulation of the more painful and therefore more repressed exciting object relationship.

The constellation came to light in the transference in a vivid and violent way. Mrs. Constable missed her appointment time, which was the last one before I had to go to another job. Arriving at my office twenty minutes after the end of her session time, she coyly peeped around my half-open door and told me that she was sorry to have mistaken the time. Even though she could see that I was collecting my things to leave, she sweetly asked if I could see her. When I told her that I had to go to another appointment, Mrs. Constable pleaded with me seductively. When I said that we would have to miss this time and meet as usual in two days' time, Mrs. Constable became enraged. She told me that I was cold and uncaring. She proceeded to hit me until she was restrained in the corridor by two male nurses who heard the commotion through the open office door. Seeing me apparently available had excited her need for me. When the exciting object relationship could not be gratified in relation to me, the rejecting object relationship was expressed in full force. When she arrived too late for me to see her, she had hoped to repress the inevitable activation of the rejecting object relationship by attempting to recruit me to the exciting object relationship where I would need to see her as much as she needed to see me and more than I needed to keep my next appointment. After this episode, she idealized the male nurses as strong men who really knew what she needed, while I was experienced as a horrible, weak, and unsatisfying woman. In her transference to me, the rejecting object relationship had to be worked on for months before she could experience me as helpful once more.

Thomas Ogden has suggested another term for the libidinal object relationship, namely the *craving self* that longs for a *tantalizing object*. Harry Guntrip pointed out that excessive activity of the libidinal part of the self may serve to cover over a dreadful sense of deadness at the center of the self, suggesting to him an even more deeply repressed part of the self.

IS THERE A MORE REPRESSED PART OF THE SELF THAN FAIRBAIRN KNEW ABOUT?

Fairbairn's original theory did not account for a part of the self more deeply repressed than the libidinal internal object system. Harry Guntrip proposed that in schizoid states, a further subdivision occurs. Part of the already repressed libidinal ego is repressed and split off into a remote, deadened part of the self where it is sheltered against the expected danger of empathic failure and the desperately frightening experience of a void within the core of the self. Fairbairn accepted Guntrip's important addendum to his theory. Michael Balint discovered a similar phenomenon in his regressed patients. They described a feeling of something missing at the core of the self. He called this *the basic fault*. These deficit states arise from a poor mother-infant relationship in which the infant does not feel cared for, loved, and lovable. Object relations theorists recognized that their discoveries had implications for technique. As Guntrip put it, therapy had to offer a challenge to the closed system of parts of the personality and present a context for rebirth and regrowth in the therapeutic relationship as an alternative to regression.

WHAT IS THE OBJECT RELATIONSHIP OF THE CENTRAL SELF IN CONSCIOUSNESS?

Late in his theory-building Fairbairn described the object of the central self, discovered during his study of hysterical states. He called it the *ideal object*. In the hysterical state, it is an object shorn of excessive excitement or rejection. The hysterical person seeks in the lover a bland object so as not to be unbearably upset or excited.

In the normal state, we think of the ideal object as an internal object that is satisfactory. We might call this the good-enough object, or simply, the good object. Nowadays, the terms *ideal, good,* and *good enough* are used interchangeably. The ideal object is the object of the central ego and is connected to it by positive feelings in the full range of human affects, and it remains in consciousness because it is satisfying. The ideal object relationship in the central, conscious part of the self is available for interaction with ideal objects in other personalities. Being in consciousness, the central ego in association with its ideal object is free to grow and open to being modified because it is not harbored secretly inside the self, as the repressed exciting and rejecting object relationships are. Nevertheless the good object tends to be absorbed or metabolized by the central self. The ideal object relationship suffuses the entire personality rather than standing out as a discrete, recognizable piece of psychic structure.

In the case of Mrs. Constable, the good object in relation to the central self gave rise to a central ideal object relationship that was expressed in her capacity to be an energetic mother and homemaker, a sought-after committee person, and a patient with the capacity to sustain a therapeutic alliance despite the assault of the return of the repressed bad object relationships in the transference.

Paradoxically, although it is in consciousness, the ideal object relationship is less observable than the repressed object relationships that are expressed in the interpersonal field—and especially in the transference—in the form of unsatisfying relationships that call attention to them.

CAN YOU SUMMARIZE THE OBJECT RELATIONSHIPS IN ACTION?

The human personality is a system of conscious and unconscious object relationships in dynamic relation. The central ego actively represses the rejecting and exciting constellations. The antilibidinal ego further represses the exciting object constellation, and the libidinal ego further represses the rejecting object constellation. A further split may occur in which an endangered part of the libidinal ego is further repressed and becomes deeply withdrawn. Now we can summarize the endopsychic situation as follows: (1) *in consciousness*, the ideal object relationship, consisting of the central ego, the ideal object, and feelings of satisfaction and goodness; (2) *in unconsciousness*, the *rejecting object relationship*, consisting of the antilibidinal ego, the rejecting object, and feelings of frustration and rage; and the *exciting object relationship*, consisting of the libidinal ego, the exciting object, and feelings of frustration and painful longing.

COULD YOU ELABORATE ON THE SELF?

The self is the original psychic structure at birth. It develops by building into it traces of important and formative relationships. As it does this, the self becomes the encompassing structure that includes not only its original potential for structure but also a sense of identity based on all the internal object relations within it. The ideal, exciting and rejecting objects, the central, libidinal, and antilibidinal parts of the ego in relationship to these objects, respectively, as well as the whole collection of corresponding affects are all in an internal dynamic relationship to one another. This dynamic relation between parts of the self follows the universal system of the endopsychic situation that Fairbairn described, but the precise balance of forces is unique to each person.

HOW IS IT THAT INTERNAL OBJECT
RELATIONSHIPS ARE IN DYNAMIC RELATION?

Fairbairn described how one part of internal structure represses another part directly and indirectly. The central ego represses both the exciting and rejecting object constellations directly. Then the rejecting object constellation (that is, the internal saboteur and the rejecting object
together) lies on top of the libidinal object like a blanket keeping it out
of awareness of the central ego. Fairbairn said that repression happens
in this direction rather than the reverse, because it is much more painful
to be aware of an unrequited longing than to have an angry relationship.
On the contrary, we find that it is equally common for the libidinal or
excited object relationship to repress rejecting object relations. We see
this in a person who has a seductive attitude toward others, as a defensive way of repressing aggression or feelings of rejection. We see it in
married partners who seduce each other to be sexually intimate in order
to avoid angry feelings that cannot be expressed.

When Fairbairn described the secondary repression of the libidinal
by the antilibidinal constellations inside the self, he opened the door for
us to understand that internal object relationships inside the self are in
dynamic relationship to each other, so that at one point one constellation will be the controlling or ascendant organization, and at another
point another will come to the fore. This is a crucial discovery that informs the clinical approach to patients. We find that we are dealing with
various parts of the patient's self and that we are being used to re-create
now one object relationship and now another.

IS THE SELF THE SAME AS THE EGO?

Not in our view. Some people have said that the self is the more modern term for the old-fashioned term *ego*. Guntrip used the term *self* that
way and John Sutherland in his teaching was inclined to follow Guntrip's
usage. In our lexicon, *self* is an overall term for that continuing sense of
uniqueness that a person carries. We think that the term *self* includes
ego, that is to say, the executive relating function and both its conscious

and unconscious aspects, the objects that the parts of the ego relate to, and all the feelings that arise between the parts of the ego and the parts of the object.

DO YOU USE THE WORD EGO, THEN, FOR THE MORE MECHANISTIC PART OF EACH OF US THAT PERFORMS CERTAIN EXECUTIVE FUNCTIONS BUT IS NOT CAPABLE OF RELATING AS A WHOLE PERSON?

Yes, the ego is an executive subset of the self. Only the self can relate as a whole person.

DOES FAIRBAIRN'S THEORY OF PATHOLOGY APPLY TO NORMAL DEVELOPMENT?

The prevalence of dissociation in the psychic functioning of Fairbairn's hysterical patients prompted a theory designed to explain the development of hysterical neuroses and schizoid personality. His theory draws attention to the ubiquity of splitting in the full range of personality types. With slight modification, we have applied Fairbairn's theory of the endopsychic situation shown in figure 4.1 to the understanding of normal development. See figure 4.2.

In healthy development, having less need of repression, the internal object relationship components of personality communicate freely. Within the context of basic relatedness, there is the normal pull of need and desire for others at the libidinal pole (pathological only when there is excessive excitement of need leading to intense longing or craving) and the normal need for separateness or autonomy (pathological only when there is an excessively tenacious tie to, or avoidance of, the bad object leading to self-hatred, self-destructiveness, and violence). The elements in figure 4.2 represent these poles of normal relating rather than pathological organizations. At the core of personality in health is the central ego—an overarching, complex, integrative organization that monitors self-awareness, maintains identity, and manages the executive

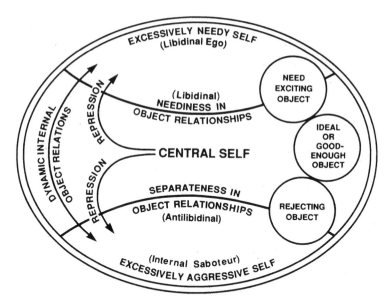

Figure 4.2.   Amplification of Fairbairn's Model of Psychic Organization.
Neediness and separateness are aspects of the central self. Exciting and rejecting objects partly communicate with the ideal object and are partly repressed. All aspects of self and objects are in dynamic relation. Reprinted from *Refinding the Object and Reclaiming the Self*, courtesy of Jason Aronson. Copyright David E. Scharff, 1992.

functions of the self—connected to the good-enough object. (Only in pathology such as hysteria is this good object called ideal, that is to say shorn of imperfections.) The good-enough object in this model of health is based on experience with the good mother who does not have to be perfect, but only good enough for the baby to love and to feel completely satisfied with from time to time.

This model stresses the normal functions of (1) the splits in personality formed by the pulls toward and away from object relating; (2) the tendency toward integration of personality aimed at by the central self; (3) the communication between poles of personality in health; and (4) the flexibility and interaction between parts of the self, which is not found in neurosis, psychosis, personality disorder, and trauma. Trauma provokes the most severe splits in personality, resulting in voids alternating with encapsulated fragments of self and object. See chapter 10 on the effects of trauma.

HOW DID FAIRBAIRN VIEW THE PROGRESSION OF NORMAL DEVELOPMENT?

Development proceeds from the absolute dependence of the child on its caretaker to the mature interdependence of adult partners. The move from infantile to mature dependence is marked by the use of *transitional techniques of relating*, which are strategies based on unconscious fantasy. They are not pathological structures, unless they are overused to the exclusion of personal flexibility over time. Fairbairn summarized these strategies according to whether the good and bad internal objects were unconsciously understood to lie inside or outside the self (see table 4.1).

WHAT ARE THE TRANSITIONAL TECHNIQUES OF RELATING?

Fairbairn thought of obsessional, phobic, hysterical, and paranoid character formations as the result of techniques for dealing with good and bad objects. In obsessional and paranoid techniques, the person imagines that the good object resides inside. In hysterical and phobic techniques, the good object is thought to be outside the self. In hysterical and obsessional techniques, the bad object is internal to the self. In phobic and paranoid techniques, the bad object is kept external to the self. These unconscious fantasies about the quality and location of internal objects determine strategies for relating to others, depending on whether the person seeks or avoids the good or the bad object.

Table 4.1.   Transitional Techniques of Relating

Technique	Accepted (Good) Object	Rejected (Bad) Object
Obsessional	Internalized	Internalized
Phobic	Externalized	Externalized
Paranoid	Internalized	Externalized
Hysterical	Externalized	Internalized

WHAT DO YOU MEAN BY INTERNALIZATION OF RELATIONAL STRUCTURES?

We have described Fairbairn's view that in development, young children take in aspects of their experience with each caregiver and create internal objects in connection to the corresponding parts of the self. They do the same with siblings and other family members. Beyond that, children take in aspects of the relationship with each caregiver and each family member and re-create them in internal object relationships. Not only that, they recognize and take in the relationship between their caregivers and other family members, influenced by their capacities for perceiving at different developmental stages.

The child is also taken in as a new object for each parent. This happens in two major ways. The child arises from and is a representative of the sexual coupling of the parents. As a person in his or her own right, the child is an object of affection, interest, and hate for the couple. The installation of the growing child as a new internal object significantly reorganizes the parent's mind and the couple's relationship.

WHAT DO YOU MEAN BY OBJECT SORTING, CONSTRUCTION, AND ELIMINATION?

Building on the internalization of experience with individuals, dyads, and groups in infancy and especially in the oedipal period, the human personality continues to grow in adulthood. Falling in love, marrying, giving birth to children, remarrying, and mourning the losses of infertility, illness, and death, the self *sorts* experience into internal object relationship categories, internalizes it, matches it to prior models, and puts together new constructions based on changing life experiences, increasing brain development, and social understanding as development proceeds. The self progressively integrates changing aspects of its internal object relationships to maintain its cohesion, flexibility, and vitality.

Internal housekeeping goes on as the personality matures. The self reevaluates the internal object constellations and sorts them according to their value. Some continue to enhance the self and some become irrelevant. Others that take up space and "crowd out" good, new experience must be eliminated. For instance, deeply problematic parental objects may crowd a teenager's mind and prevent reaching for new experiences with the wider social group and the academic body of knowledge. The teenager may remain controlled by these objects and construct new objects in their image. Or the teenager may reject the actual parents while excluding the corresponding internal objects. In object exclusion, the object is mourned and eliminated from the internal space. The excluded object loses its dynamic importance and no longer has any special meaning or relationship to the self.

NOTES

Fairbairn (1963) condensed his verbal description of intrapsychic organization on one page. His key concepts of internal object relations appear as follows:

The internal saboteur (1944).
The libidinal and antilibidinal ego (1954, 1963).
The ideal object (1954, 1963).
Fairbairn's papers are collected in Fairbairn (1952) and Scharff and Birtles (1994).
Others have elaborated on these ideas:
The craving self and the tantalizing object (Ogden 1986b).
The withdrawn libidinal ego in schizoid states (Guntrip 1969).
The self (Guntrip 1969, Sutherland 1980).
The internal couple (J. Scharff 1992).

5

PROJECTIVE AND INTROJECTIVE IDENTIFICATION AND CONTAINMENT

AFTER INTROJECTION OF THE OBJECT, SPLITTING, AND REPRESSION, WHAT ARE THE OTHER IMPORTANT MECHANISMS OF UNCONSCIOUS ORGANIZATION AND COMMUNICATION BETWEEN PERSONALITIES?

The mechanisms of projective and introjective identification were described by Melanie Klein in 1946, later clarified by Hanna Segal, and elaborated by Thomas Ogden, Joseph Sandler, and Jill Scharff. Projective and introjective identification are psychic mechanisms that serve communicative, defensive, and organizational functions. They begin in the earliest months of life, when infants are struggling with great anxiety stemming from fears about surviving. They worry that the force of their feelings will overwhelm the caretakers on whom they are totally dependent. In projective identification the infant exports these anxieties in the form of fantasies of putting dangerous parts of the infant self into the mother for control of aggression. The mother is then identified with these projected, or displaced, parts of the self. This is the first phase of the projective identification process. The infant then fears that feelings that might have overwhelmed the infant self had they remained within will now return in the haunting form of a mother who has been infused with these frightening feelings. The mother is then seen as a re-taliatory object. This is the second phase of the projective identification process. Now the infant takes in this view of the mother through intro-jective identification, which is the third phase of the projective identifi-cation process. The infant now becomes more like the frightening mother and has even more fearsome feelings to get rid of. The good-enough mother, however, is able to metabolize these worrisome feel-ings, to cope with them, and to return a view of her infant as not overly damaging or endangered. Wilfred Bion described the mother's process as *containment* of her child's anxieties.

The infant also projects into the mother valued aspects of the self for safekeeping of the good. The mother is also suffused by the warmth of the infant's good feelings toward her and returns her sense of the child as loving and gratifying. Putting out and taking back appreciated good-ness and detoxified badness is the infant's way of building a relationship and forming a durable personality.

Projective and introjective identification are reciprocal processes in-side the self and also between the self and the external object. Projec-tive identification originates from the mother as well as the baby. The mutuality of the projective and introjective identificatory processes be-tween mother and child is shown in figure 5.1.

CAN YOU SAY MORE ABOUT THE INTROJECTIVE IDENTIFICATION SUBPHASE OF PROJECTIVE IDENTIFICATION?

Introjective identification is also to be regarded as a process in its own right. We have found that it tends to be overlooked because it happens inside the ego. It is easier to see how the object is being affected than to detect internalizations that are integrated into the self. Putting out is more visible than taking in. In introjective identification, infants take in that modification of earlier feelings that the mother has pro-vided. They take in the experiences and build them into a more ma-ture view of themselves. If the mothers are not able to contain their infants' worries, the babies then receive a view of themselves that con-firms their poor sense of themselves as unmanageable. When the

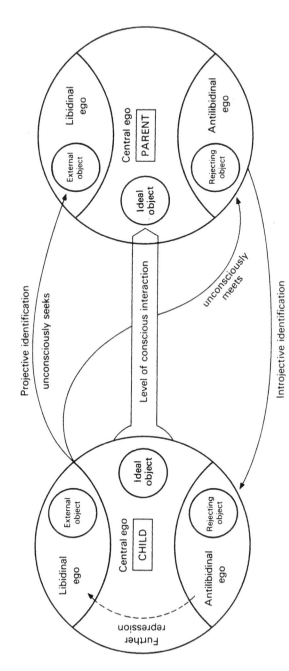

Figure 5.1. **Projective and Introjective Identification in the Mother-Infant Relationship.** The mechanism here is the interaction of the child's projective and introjective identifications with the parent as the child meets frustration, unrequited yearning, or trauma. The diagram depicts the child longing for needs to be met and identifying with similar trends in the parent via projective identification. The child who meets with rejection then identifies with the frustration of the parent's own antilibidinal system via introjective identification. In an internal reaction to the frustration, the libidinal system is further repressed by the renewed force of the child's antilibidinal system. Reprinted from *The Sexual Relationship: An Object Relations View of Sex and the Family*, courtesy of Routledge and Kegan Paul. Copyright © David E. Scharff, 1982.

mothers are good enough, the infants take in the mother's good containing function and then become able to manage themselves and their feelings, now and in the future, in a progressively more competent and reliable way.

CAN YOU SUMMARIZE THE STEPS OF THE PROCESS OF PROJECTIVE AND INTROJECTIVE IDENTIFICATION?

These steps are amplified in *Projective and Introjective Identification and the Use of the Therapist's Self*. We can reduce them to their main components, summarized in table 5.1:

Table 5.1.   The Steps of Projective Identification

1. Projecting or getting rid of a part of the self
2. Finding it in the object, that is, experiencing the other person as embodying that part of oneself, whether the person happens to be like that or not
3. Taking in and becoming like the object that was projected into

WHAT IS MUTUAL PROJECTIVE IDENTIFICATION IN COMMITTED RELATIONSHIPS?

Intimate partners tend to view each other through the lens of their own experience of themselves. This is a two-way street. The partners choose each other because there is a degree of fit between their personalities that permits each of them equally to discover lost parts of the self in the partner. These may be cherished or denigrated parts of the self, and the partner is then treated accordingly. Interacting closely like this over time, the couple creates a joint personality that functions as a unique identity, a source of strength, support, and modifying influence for the selves of the individual partners. This joint personality is a culture medium for the nourishing of individual part-egos and objects as the partners continue to mature.

Look back at figure 5.1. Imagine that the two side-by-side images of Fairbairn's endopsychic situation now represent two partners in a couple relationship, instead of a mother and an infant. We make this transposition in figure 5.2 to see how marital partners communicate unconsciously over time and affect each other's growth and development.

> Figure 5.2 traces one example of how an internal object may be modified when a rather inhibited husband repeatedly craves attention silently from his attractive, lively, busy wife. He hopes she will long for him as he does for her, but she is engaged with her friends and her projects, and pushes him away. His exciting object relationship seeks to emerge from repression by identification with her exciting object relationship, but instead it is repressed by her rejecting object relationship with which he now introjectively identifies, and he withdraws. When his rejecting object relationship is reinforced in this way, the unconscious secondary repression of his exciting object constellation increases, and he does not approach her again. If interactions like these dominate a marriage, the husband constructs an augmented version of a rejecting object and a crushed exciting object. In the healthy marriage, when the rejecting pattern is not regularly reinforced, the husband will construct ameliorated versions of his rejecting and exciting objects, and these will be more conducive to his appealing successfully to his wife. Adapted from *Object Relations Individual Therapy*, courtesy of Jason Aronson. Copyright © Jill S. Scharff and David E. Scharff, 1988.

WHAT IS THE INTERNAL COUPLE?

The idea comes from integrating the theories of Klein and Ronald Fairbairn. The internal couple is a psychic structure formed from the child's experience of the caregivers as a team of parents taking care of the child and as a couple of intimate life partners whose commitment to taking care of each other and sharing pleasure is a source of security and bounty and, at the same time, an object to be cherished and defended— or maybe attacked out of greed and envy. The child's internal couple is based on the parental couple as perceived by the child at various developmental stages and modified when the child gets to know other couples. The internal couple has many layers. The internal couple laid down in the early months is seen as a feeding pair; in the toileting years, the couple seems to be engaged in a battle for control; and in the oedipal phase it is an object filled with all the excitement and awe of the primal

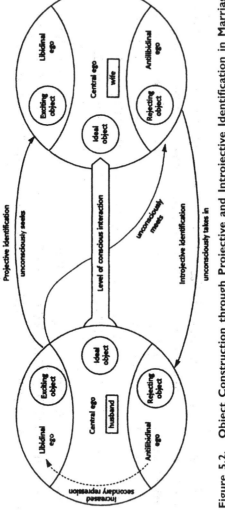

Figure 5.2. Object Construction through Projective and Introjective Identification in Marriage.
Reprinted from *Object Relations Individual Therapy*, courtesy of Jason Aronson. Copyright Jill Savege Scharff and David E. Scharff, 1998.

scene and sometimes filled with the child's destructive rage at being excluded. Children may greedily devour the internal couple to possess its goodness for themselves. One child may fear its power and exclude it from consciousness. Another child may try to split the couple into its component parts and form a replacement couple by pairing with the image of one parent. Coming to terms with the fact of the parents' relationship and the child's exclusion from it is essential to developing a sense of the self as separate and capable of independent thinking.

Insight about our own internal couple is crucial to therapists' effectiveness, nowhere more obviously than in couple therapy. This helps the couple therapist tolerate exclusion from the couple's relationship, bear the guilt of being let in on their intimacy, form working couples with each partner in turn as well as with the couple, avoid being drawn into feeling partial to one or the other's point of view, and maintain the capacity to observe, reflect, and process the experience.

CAN YOU SAY MORE ABOUT CONTAINMENT?

Containment is a term introduced by Wilfred Bion. It refers to the mother's ability to hold her baby's needs in her mind. Bion thought that this ability belonged to the realm of thought, but we think of containment as an integrated emotional and cognitive process. The baby has various unmanageable anxieties that, in the Kleinian way of looking at things, stem from the "death instinct," or, in our own way of thinking, from aggression and its excesses. The baby, not able to manage these anxieties, puts them into the mother who "contains" them in her maternal state of "reverie" and is not destroyed by the force of the aggression. Through a transformation of the disorganized elements of baby experience into thought made possible by this state of reverie, the mother can then feed back to the infant the unthinkable anxiety in a more manageable, tolerable form. Bion used the term *contained* for these originally overwhelming anxieties that the mother then helps the infant to manage. He referred to the mother as the container.

Taking off from Bion's idea, we think that containment occurs through resonance with the mother's own internal object relations. Through normal projective identification, she matches her child's anxieties with her own partly repressed internal object relationships, and then, by being able to bear or even appreciate her own and her child's anxiously viewed parts herself, she gives them back safely to her infant, along with her capacity for tolerance.

NOTES

Klein's concept of the unconscious processes of introjective and projective identification has revolutionized our conceptualization of therapeutic action. These processes deserve study both in the original and in the following expositions:

Projective and introjective identification (Klein 1946, Segal 1964, Ogden 1982, Sandler 1987a, b, J. Scharff 1992).
Containment and reverie (Bion 1962, 1967).
The internal couple (J. Scharff 1992, J. and D. Scharff 1998).

6

THE HOLDING ENVIRONMENT

The mothering function is addressed from a different vantage point by Donald Winnicott. He referred to the quality of the actual relationship offered by the mother to her infant in which the infant could expect a secure and stable relationship with an attentive need-satisfying mother. Winnicott was referring not to an internal processing function but to a physical caretaking relationship characterized by "primary maternal preoccupation" and devotion to her infant. He used the term *holding environment* to describe this process, within which the mother provides a *holding relationship*. Winnicott thought that the mother's capacity to provide this secure holding relationship in her role as the *environment mother* was what let the infant become a separate self. Then, the infant self could relate to the mother as an object of love and aggression, *the object mother.*

WHAT ARE SOME OF THE OTHER CONCEPTS THAT WINNICOTT CONTRIBUTED TO CLINICAL WORK?

Winnicott gives us several other concepts that are both theoretically and clinically useful: the centrality of the mother-infant relationship, the object mother, the environment mother, the psychosomatic partnership, the transitional space and transitional objects, and the fit between true and false self.

WHAT DID WINNICOTT MEAN BY THE PHRASE "THERE IS NO SUCH THING AS AN INFANT"?

Winnicott meant that without maternal care the infant cannot survive. The mother's devotion is essential to the vitality of the baby. The baby cannot grow without her love. The mother-infant relationship is the context in which the baby becomes a person. We do not mean to suggest that a person is fully formed during the pre-oedipal relationship to the mother. People continue to be modified by new relationships throughout life, but primary relationships always exert a continuing influence on personality structure. Winnicott showed how the mother-infant relationship is re-created in the transference.

WHAT IS THE DIFFERENCE BETWEEN THE OBJECT MOTHER AND THE ENVIRONMENT MOTHER?

Winnicott described two important aspects of relating in the mother-infant relationship. In the first aspect, the mother formed the context for the baby's growth and development. This he called the *environment mother*. Providing an "arms-around" relationship, the environment mother holds the baby in her arms, sets the conditions for keeping the baby fed, clothed, warm, and safe, and takes care of the physical and emotional environment for the baby. If all goes well, the baby takes the environment mother for granted and just "goes on being."

Within the envelope provided by the environment mother, the mother offers the baby a direct object relationship. Winnicott called this aspect the *object mother*. This mother is the object of the baby's love, hate, interest, and desire. It is apparent that both parts of the mother are always present and are represented in therapy. We can distinguish which of these functions the mother is fulfilling at a certain time and which are being evoked in the therapeutic relationship. Within the envelope provided by the environment mother, the baby is free to find a separate self. In the relationship with the mother as an object, the baby is provided with the stuff from which to build internal objects. From experience of the relationship between the environment mother and the object mother, and that between the whole mother and the infant, the infant develops internalized object relationships and a sense of self.

WHAT IS THE PSYCHOSOMATIC PARTNERSHIP?

Winnicott also contributed the idea of the *psychosomatic partnership*. The earliest relationship to the mother is completely physical, when the fetus lives literally inside the mother. At the moment of birth, a physical and emotional interface develops across which the mother and baby then have to relate. The baby becomes psychologically organized through sorting of the experience of physical holding and handling.

WHAT ARE THE TRANSITIONAL SPACE AND TRANSITIONAL OBJECT?

Over the first few months, this physical relationship gives way to a progressively larger psychological relationship. It does so with the creation of what Winnicott called the *potential space* between mother and baby. We tend to refer to this as the *transitional space*. In this space, the baby relates to the mother across a growing physical distance. Here, the baby is free to discover the things that the mother is offering, as though the baby had been the one to invent or create them. Winnicott says that we must never challenge the baby to resolve the paradox of whether something was offered by the mother or invented by the infant. We maintain respect for the infant's illusion of separateness as the basis for true autonomy and for the creative potential of the transitional space. In this space, the baby has *transitional objects*, such as a favorite blanket or teddy bear, which belong to the baby entirely and are used and abused, held and thrown, loved and hated as the baby's own, and yet they represent the mother. By interacting with the transitional object, the baby can act as if in full control of the object mother.

In figure 6.1, we can see that the transitional space is a blend of inner and outer experience. It is in communication with the holding provided by the mother just as it is in communication with the direct object relationship to the mother that provides the material of the baby's growing internal world. Winnicott noted that this is also the locus of creativity.

WHAT IS WINNICOTT'S CONCEPT OF TRUE AND FALSE SELF?

Winnicott thought that each of us has an inner core that stems from our biological givens. He called this the *true self*. The false self is a caretaker part of the self that protects the core and enables the self to accommodate to the needs of others. It is not false in the sense of being fake or untrustworthy. It is simply cover for the true self. When child-rearing emphasizes the needs of others at the expense of the self, there is then a discrepancy between the false self and the true self. A denial of the true self results, and the cover appears to be untrue to the true self. In pathology, the false self becomes false in the sense of being somewhat fake. In health, the false self is not so split off from the true self. It successfully enables us to preserve our selfhood while negotiating with others. As Christopher Bollas notes, good fit between false self and true self is essential to the maintenance of personal vitality and integrity.

HOW ARE THE TERMS *CONTAINMENT* AND *HOLDING ENVIRONMENT* DIFFERENT?

Winnicott's terms *holding* and *handling* are visible elements of an external process that is observable, whereas Wilfred Bion's term *containment* describes an internal process in the realm of thought. Winnicott's term is dealing with the interpersonal aspect, Bion's with the intrapsychic dimension of the two individuals. Holding and handling is concerned with the management of the space between the mother and the baby, whereas containment is referring to the space inside the mother in which she processes her baby's anxieties.

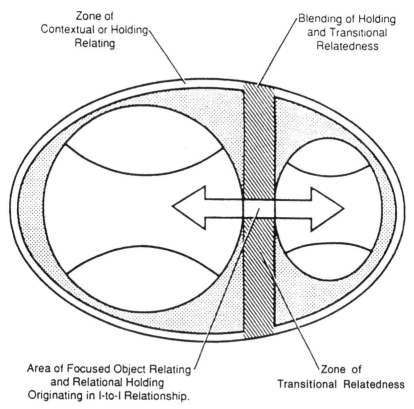

Zone of
Contextual or Holding
Relating

Blending of Holding
and Transitional
Relatedness

Area of Focused Object Relating
and Relational Holding
Originating in I-to-I Relationship.

Zone of
Transitional Relatedness

Figure 6.1. Winnicott's Organization of the Mother-Infant Relationship. The psychosomatic partnership begins with a physical holding-and-handling relationship between mother and infant. The oval envelope drawn around mother and infant signifies the environmental function provided by the mother's holding—the *arms-around* relationship. Within this envelope, mother and infant have a direct object relationship—the intense I-to-I relationship, communicated in words, gestures, gaze, and physical exchange—out of which the infant constructs internal objects. Reproduced from *Refinding the Object and Reclaiming the Self,* courtesy of Jason Aronson. Copyright © David E. Scharff, 1992.

Now we have two contributions that need to be put together to constitute the whole process. We stress that the mother holds the baby in the physical and emotional sense. According to Winnicott, as the object mother she provides an intimate relationship for her baby, and as the environment mother she takes care of the environment so that the baby can feel safe and is able to "go on being." At the same time, a psychological process is going on inside herself in which she absorbs and transforms, or in Bion's word, *contains*, those anxieties that the baby inevitably faces. It is the process outside, namely the holding environment, which sets the stage for the internal process, namely containment, to occur inside the mother and later to be taken in by the baby. Both internal and external processes have to occur at the same time for the baby to handle anxiety well and so have a maximal chance of undisturbed development.

WHO IS BOLLAS?

Christopher Bollas is an American by birth, but he studied in Britain with Winnicott and is arguably the leading British object relations theorist. Finding his own language for describing the formation and functioning of the self, Bollas writes that one's personal idiom is built from being in touch with the unconscious, projecting parts of the self into important objects, and experiencing the self again through those objects. The resulting object relationships continue to change and grow over time as they interact with others. Bollas took the concepts of projective and introjective identification to new lengths when he described the processes of *interjection*, in which a parent inserts a part of the self into the child, and *extractive introjection*, in which a person steals a part of another person's mind.

WHAT IS AN INTERJECT?

Sometimes the actual behavior of the parent and the force of the unconscious fantasies that govern the parent's behavior are so intrusive that the infant's usual defensive process of introjection is overwhelmed. In other words, there is no memory trace and no ego involved in splitting and repression to protect the self. There is only a hugely unpleasant, unfathomable feeling state. If it could be repressed, the feeling would be separated from the idea that caused the pain, and the feeling would remain though the cause of it would be forgotten. When it is too awful, the feeling and its source have to be erased by dissociation from the new object; therefore, it does not become integrated in the dynamic system of parts of ego and objects. It lives on in a state of primal repression as a not-me part of the self. Bollas calls this an *interject*.

To put it simply, an interject is a part of the parent that has jumped in, overwhelmed the usual defenses, and taken over an area of the self.

A foreign object fills some of the space inside the child's self. This happens when there is both a defect in the holding environment provided by the "contextual mother," a direct intrusion into the child by the "object mother," and a collapse of the transitional space. This situation arises most obviously from interaction with psychotic, violent, and sexually abusing parents, including parents who totally overstimulate their children by exposing them to their sexual interaction. More subtle parental projections also become interjects.

CAN YOU GIVE AN EXAMPLE OF AN INTERJECT?

A bright, engaging mother became noticeably depressed when her children went to elementary school. A thwarted academic, she withdrew into books, sitting for hours reading and ignoring her daughters. The daughters suffered the loss of a good mother even before she died when they were young adults.

The younger daughter became a mother herself. Unlike her mother she was an active woman and she had chosen an ambitious, physically energetic husband. She took good care of him, their home, and the children. She was the boss, as his mother had been when he lived at home. He worked long hours, and at home he liked to relax with a book. Always cleaning, cooking, planning, and volunteering herself, she found jobs for him to do so that he didn't have time to read. This was a source of strain but he admired her energy and appreciated her direction, and so it was not unmanageable. Their marriage was a success.

As a mother, she was ever-present. She had high standards for performance. She kept her children busy studying and playing tournament tennis. As long as they were engaged with her, busy, and achieving, she felt accomplished as a mother. In therapy, she worked on her need for activity as a defense against dying prematurely like her mother, and feeling the loss of her companionship growing up. When her high-achieving children left home, they were lost without her daily involvement and all three of them withdrew into self-destructive drug abuse.

She wanted to fix everything for every one of them, but she couldn't. To get better, they had to withdraw from her and decide their own courses of action. The woman was devastated. The children had taken in a disavowed part of her, a parental projection of withdrawal and inactivity that was unbearable and had to be obliterated by drug use, which only led to more withdrawal and inactivity. To recover from the using habit they had to return the disavowed projection and reintroduce withdrawal and inactivity in their relationships with their mother before being able to separate from her more successfully and ultimately find their own energy.

CAN YOU ILLUSTRATE EXTRACTIVE INTROJECTION?

Let's say a woman who studied hard is distraught to learn that she has failed an exam and complains that she has been treated unfairly. Her husband is full of sympathy for her situation, but instead of comforting her, he rails against the teachers, the administration, and the examiners so loudly and so long that she loses her own outrage. The husband has overidentified with her outrage, has emptied her mind of it, and has taken away from her the energy she needed to present her case. That is a single instance of extractive introjection. When a parent does this over time, it has a weakening effect on the child's self.

NOTES

Winnicott's concepts, derived from his experience as a pediatrician and analyst of the mother-infant relationship, are to be found in the following papers or books:

Primary maternal preoccupation (1956).
Holding environment, holding relationship, holding and handling, and the centrality of the mother-infant relationship (1960).
Environment mother and object mother (1945, 1963a, 1963b).
Psychosomatic partnership (1971).
Potential space and transitional objects (1951).
True self and false self (1965, and Bollas 1989b).
For a thorough overview of Winnicott's concepts, see Phillips (1988) and Grolnick (1990).
Interjection and extractive introjection (Bollas 2000).

⑦

THE CONCEPT OF POSITIONS

WHAT WAS MELANIE KLEIN'S CONCEPT OF *POSITIONS?*

Melanie Klein described two fundamental positions, the paranoid-schizoid position and the depressive position. These offer an alternative or parallel view to Sigmund Freud's psychosexual stages of development. Klein arrived at her ideas from study of the infant-mother relationship, re-created in the transference. Her ideas are vivid both in clinical supervision and in discussion of direct observation of mother-baby couples.

The *paranoid-schizoid position* occurs during the first few months of life, when the infant faces a maximal amount of anxiety with a minimal cognitive processing apparatus. Gradually learning from experience and maturing cognitively, the infant becomes capable of more advanced functioning typical of the depressive position.

In the paranoid-schizoid position, the infant's relationships are dominated by splitting and repression with projection of aggression. The resulting object relationships are therefore part object relationships, characterized by all-or-none qualities. The mother is seen by the infant as good or bad, or more precisely as a good or bad breast, in keeping with the part object ascendancy at this stage. She is perceived as having been spoiled in fantasy by angry oral, urethral, or anal outpourings. Part of her is loved, and another part hated, but she cannot be loved and hated at the same time, because the infant is not capable of seeing her as a whole person. It is in this position that splitting and pathological degrees of projective identification dominate, as ways of defending against anxiety and as modes of relating.

The *depressive position* is a major development that begins by about three or four months of age. The maturing baby periodically moves beyond splitting, projection, and the resulting all-or-none quality of early relationships, toward a state of concern for the object. The child becomes cognitively capable of a more complete image of the mother as a whole person who is capable of embodying good and bad, loving and rejecting qualities. The new capacity for holding in mind the good, present mother and the absent or bad mother at the same time means that splitting is no longer the only option for dealing with pain. Pain can now be borne by reliance on the internalized good object. Once it is reliably inside the self, the infant becomes able to tolerate ambivalence, to experience guilt about being responsible for the way that the object has been treated, and to repair the harm done. Early aspects of envy that were prominent in the paranoid-schizoid position are in the depressive position modified by guilt, concern for, and gratitude toward the object, and the wish to make up to or "repair" the relationship with the object. Working through of depressive and persecutory anxieties continues through the first few years of childhood.

IS THE PARANOID-SCHIZOID POSITION ONE THAT A PERSON GROWS OUT OF AND THEN MATURES INTO THE DEPRESSIVE POSITION ?

Once these positions come on line they are present through the rest of the life cycle. We do not totally grow out of the paranoid-schizoid position into the depressive position, but the more mature person functions more often in the depressive end of the range. Both positions are potentially operative, both normally and pathologically. As adults, we continue to move between them. Both of them are positions from which to deal with the world, and each has its assets and liabilities. The paranoid-schizoid position is the basis of psychosis but also promotes an inquiring and sometimes suitably untrusting approach to the outer world. The depressive position enables us to have concern for others, to empathize, to make up for having harmed others who are important to us, and to accept loss and reality. The depressive position need not imply the presence of a depressed mood. It refers to a capacity to tolerate depression due to guilt and loss, and to experience concern for the object.

Klein also described "the manic defense." A person who cannot bear guilt and yet who has progressed beyond paranoid-schizoid functioning may jump over the depressive position in order to avoid the painful realization of damage done to the object, which comes with the depressive position. Instead of feeling concern for the harmed object, the person controls the object contemptuously and denies its separateness, its suffering, and the ambivalence that it evokes. Concern for the object may be mimicked in a manic repair attempt that covers over the effect on the object and serves to avoid responsibility for one's effect on others.

ARE THESE THE ONLY POSSIBLE POSITIONS?

These are the two that Klein described. More recently, Thomas Ogden studied the work of Esther Bick, Donald Meltzer, Frances Tustin and several other contributors and integrated their work with his own to come up with an even earlier position that he calls the *autistic-contiguous position.*

The autistic-contiguous position stems from the baby's need to be next to an object, the edge of which provides definition of the boundary of the baby's self. Babies use object proximity to the physically well-defined edges of their caretakers in order to define both the physical body self and the internal psychological contours. Like the other two positions, the autistic-contiguous position remains throughout life.

As children and as adults, we move among these three positions along the continuum from primacy of self to concern for objects. We are preoccupied at our most anxious times with development and cohesion of the self (*autistic-contiguous position*), and at more mature times with the care of our whole, ambivalently loved object (*depressive position*). Between times, we struggle against feared retaliation from split-off, repressed bad part-objects (*paranoid-schizoid position*) (see figure 7.1).

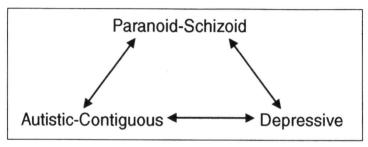

Figure 7.1. The Continuum of Endopsychic Positions. Reprinted from *Object Relations Individual Therapy*, courtesy of Jason Aronson. Copyright © David E. Scharff, 1998.

NOTES

Klein studied unconscious fantasy and communication between infant and mother. She found that because of destructive anxiety, the infant relates to the mother as a part-object and only later becomes capable of keeping the mother as a whole object in mind and feeling concern for her. The two states of mind persist throughout life as potential ways of relating. They are discussed in the following works:

The paranoid-schizoid position and the depressive position, splitting and projection (Klein 1946).

The manic defense, concern, and repair (Klein 1935).

Ogden integrated the earlier work of Bick (1968, 1986), Tustin (1981, 1984, 1986), and Meltzer (1975) to arrive at his concept of the autistic-contiguous position (Ogden 1989).

ATTACHMENT THEORY

WHO INTRODUCED ATTACHMENT THEORY?

John Bowlby, a researcher with a background in analysis and ethology, studied our biological "givens" and our need to be in nurturing relationships as infants—true for humans and other mammals. He contributed attachment theory, the basis for much of the modern research into infant development and the mother-infant relationship. He took an ethological (animal behavior) approach and made a convincing argument that the infant in the human species needs a relationship to the mother for survival. Then he viewed behavior in terms of anxiety about nearness to and separation from the mother.

Bowlby emphasized that human infants need a reliable figure on whom to depend when they are under threat. The caregiver's empathic, consistent responses to fear and protest are calming and reassuring. The experience of this *secure base* is taken inside as a capacity for secure attachment with a good ability for self-soothing. This makes play, exploration, and self-reflection possible. If the caregiver has been inconsistent, the infant's attachment to that figure will be insecure, and this will lead to insecure attachment capability and inhibition affecting creative thinking, communication, and sense of adventure. Children develop *internal working models of attachment as secure or insecure*, which influence the way they relate as adults as intimate partners, as parents, and as patients in psychotherapy.

Bowlby found that issues of attachment and loss are central and that the nature of their resolution determines personality development and psychopathology. His work establishes the primacy of problems of separation from and loss of a parent in the development of most psychopathological conditions.

DOES ATTACHMENT THEORY HAVE MORE TO TEACH?

Following Bowlby's seminal work, Mary Ainsworth and Mary Main extended the reach of attachment research. Ainsworth showed that infants show specific patterns of behavior with particular family members when they seek comfort after the stress of separation (see table 8.1). Some infants reconnect easily and show that they feel secure. Others feel insecure, but in different ways: Some of them avoid the attachment figure and reject offers of comfort; some cling to the attachment figure, at the same time resisting comfort; others are totally disorganized by separation and reunion. The attachment style is profoundly influenced by the attachment style of that caregiver and is specific to interactions with that person. However, attachment is not simply a dyadic occurrence. The different attachment styles with the various family members influence the formation of the child's internal objects, and that in turn affects the grown child's choice of partners.

Table 8.1.   Classification of Infant and Adult Attachment Types

Infant Types	Adult Types
Secure	Autonomous/secure
Insecure/avoidant	Avoidant/dismissive
Insecure/resistant	Resistant/preoccupied
Disorganized	Disorganized/unresolved

Reprinted from *Object Relations Individual Therapy*, courtesy of Jason Aronson. Jill Savege Scharff © 1998.

DOES THE INFANT'S ATTACHMENT STYLE CORRESPOND TO THE PARENT'S?

Main and Ruth Goldwyn measured attachment styles in adults and found that they too may be secure, autonomous, and freely expressive. Or they may be insecure in various ways: preoccupied with and dependent on close relationships; dismissing of the need for closeness and compulsively self-reliant; or downright fearful of rejection. Secure and preoccupied adults view their intimate partners positively whereas dismissing and fearful adults tend to have more negative views of their partners. The concept of attachment style helps us to view the family members' behaviors upon entering treatment as attempts at creating a secure base or avoiding re-creating an insecure one.

HAS ANYONE STUDIED ATTACHMENT BEHAVIORS IN ADULTHOOD AS WELL AS IN INFANCY?

Main noticed that the infant's attachment strategy tends to correlate with the adult caregiver's. Peter Fonagy showed that the parent's capacity for *mentalizing* (reflecting on, thinking about, and understanding) the infant's experience is the factor above all that determines the type of attachment. Secure adults with a coherent sense of their own histories, autonomy from their parents, and a good capacity to reflect on what their children feel tend to breed securely attached children. Avoidant/dismissive adults who repress emotionality, deny negativity, and idealize past experience raise children who tend to be insecure and avoidant of their need for attachment. Resistant/preoccupied adults who are incoherent about their childhoods, enmeshed with their parents, and flooded with feelings can expect their children to be insecurely clinging and resistant to comfort. The parent who is in the disorganized/unresolved category can't regulate feelings or behaviors (as a result of being dealt with in highly unpredictable, traumatizing ways in childhood) and tends to have children who can't organize their feelings and show bizarre, confused responses to that parent.

WHAT DOES ATTACHMENT THEORY HAVE TO DO WITH OBJECT RELATIONS?

British object relations theory and attachment theory have in common the belief that human beings are motivated not by instincts but by the need to be in relationships, that a person can't be understood separate from the social context, and that the inner sense of security derives from the experience of early care. So both theories make a connection between inner and outer worlds. Attachment theory deals with internal reality as a collection of internal working models; object relations theory deals with a self as a system of internal object relationships in dynamic relationship. Attachment theory uses systematic observation and narrows its focus to the research study of separation and reunion behavior; object relations uses free-form observation and intuition to study and interpret complex, subtle shifts in behavior in the therapeutic relationship. Both theories focus on observable behavior and take account of defense, anxiety, and motivation. Object relations theory adds the concepts of unconscious fantasy and unconscious communication by projective and introjective identification to elaborate on the connection between internal and external reality. Attachment theory has followed suit by showing that the mother's capacity for mentalizing influences the child's attachment style.

Many psychoanalysts rejected attachment theory as antianalytic in that it diverted attention from the power of unconscious fantasy and instinctual drive during development and refocused it on the external reality of childrearing experiences. But object relations analysts accepted Bowlby's findings from research because they fit with ideas emerging from clinical practice about how the infant took in experience to build the structures of the self.

ATTACHMENT THEORY IS NOT THERAPY; SO HOW IS IT USEFUL CLINICALLY?

Attachment theory changes the way we listen in therapy, and how we interpret the transference. We listen for inconsistencies and breaks in the flow of the patient's narrative. We notice whether the patient's memories are given in words (stored in the left brain indicating explicit memory from a time after speech is acquired or memory that has been put into words by a sensitive parent) or in images (stored in the right brain indicating implicit memory of early experience or trauma that a parent could not detoxify). Knowing that internal working models influence the way that patients relate to their therapists, we prepare ourselves to function as a secure base from which they can embark on exploration. The patient's need for safety and consistent proximity informs the way we design the frame of therapy with regular sessions of predictable length and helps us to detect and then interpret the contextual transference as we provide a therapeutic relationship that has echoes of early childhood caregiving. Mentalizing, a term taken from research, describes quite well the activity of the therapist who, like a secure parent caring for a child who needs attention, senses, imagines, and understands the patient's experience. When a patient tells his story with pauses and slips, instead of assuming that he is revealing or suppressing the intrusion of drive material, we may wonder if, as a child, he suffered from unthinkable anxiety due to lapses in maternal mentalizing.

Attachment theory and research provides a secure base for psychoanalysis but it is not sufficient in and of itself to understand the internal object relationships that form in the infant. It does not explain how the object relationships are modified at various developmental stages as the constitution and temperament of the infant (and later the child and the adult) interact with the various attachment styles of the parents, grandparents, other children in the family and then spouses and children, as they all face unpredictable challenges along the path of life.

CAN ATTACHMENT RESEARCH FINDINGS BE EXTENDED TO COUPLE AND FAMILY THERAPY?

Internal working models of attachment influence how we experience our partners in intimate relationships. Let's take the example of a woman with secure attachment: she views herself and her partner positively. If the woman is classified as preoccupied and resistant to attachment, she views her partner positively but sees herself in a negative light. A woman who is avoidant/dismissive because she prefers to rely on herself views herself positively and her partner negatively, but if she is avoidant of intimacy because she feels afraid, she views herself negatively as well.

Each possible couple forms a *complex attachment* in which each partner depends on and supports the other. In the ideal case, the partners recognize the couple relationship as an entity larger than either of them, a secure base to which they each contribute equally and from which they gain confidence. The strongest, most stable bond occurs between two autonomous/secure adults. Also stable is that between avoidant men with anxious/ambivalent women, but anxious/ambivalent men and avoidant women do not create lasting relationships. Insecure partners take up rigid roles, defensive positions, and interact by domination and submission. Secure partners enjoy reciprocity, flexibility in role differentiation, equality, and respect.

NOTES

Attachment research with infants (Ainsworth et al. 1978).
Secure base (Bowlby 1969, 1973, 1980).
Attachment research with adults (Main and Goldwyn in press).
Clinical application of attachment theory (Slade 1996).
Attachment theory and psychoanalysis (Fonagy 2001).
Mentalizing (Fonagy 2001).
Complex attachment in couple relationships (Morrison et al. 1997a, b; Fisher and Crandell 1997; Clulow 2001).

NEUROBIOLOGY AND AFFECT REGULATION

HOW DO RECENT FINDINGS IN NEUROSCIENCE SUPPORT OBJECT RELATIONS THERAPY?

Object relations therapists have always believed in providing emotional holding and containment of anxiety. They hold that it is important to establish a safe relationship attuned to unconscious communication, foster the transference/countertransference exchange, and then interpret what is happening in the here-and-now and how it reflects the internal object relations set and its connection to personal history. Therapists have measured the therapeutic action resulting from these processes in terms of improved behavior, affect regulation, and the capacity to self-analyze. Now neuroscience gives us confirmation that these processes actually promote brain growth.

Findings in the neurosciences are accumulating rapidly to create a biology of mental processes, an achievement that Sigmund Freud had imagined; but he had to abandon his own effort in that direction because he didn't have the technology to support it and because he wanted to devote his attention to unconscious processes, psychosexual development, and the formation of psychic structure, in order that psychoanalysis could progress. Now neuroscientists working with brain imaging are bringing neurobiology and psychoanalysis together. Their findings show the neurological underpinnings of personality development, unconscious communication, and therapeutic action. Neurobiology confirms the tenets of object relations theories that emphasize the importance of relationships for child development and for psychotherapeutic action.

WHAT IS THE EVIDENCE?

There is now ample evidence from brain imaging research that the infant's brain grows best when the infant is nurtured in a warm, reciprocally responsive relationship with a well-attuned mother or other caregivers. From infancy until age three, the right orbital frontal cortex (the part of the brain over the right eye) grows rapidly and is the dominant part of the brain at that time. The right brain is built to process interaction with the mother quickly and repeatedly. It is responsible for the infant's ability to generate single words (Mamma, Dadda, Yes, No), all of them expressing emotion and connection to important relationships. It integrates and oversees the functioning of other parts of the brain (the amygdala, thalamus, and limbic system that process input from the mother's face, eyes, voice, and touch).

The right frontal lobe specializes in reading the emotions of others, and in expressing emotion. The right brain is the executive center for processing emotional information, and it remains so throughout life.

The left frontal lobe specializes in understanding and expressing through language. The left brain enables the development of linear and logical thinking and fluid verbal communication. It is not until age three that growth of the left frontal cortex catches up. Then the toddler moves from using single words to constructing sentences.

The baby's brain grows in the culture medium of the mother's brain. In partnership, mother and infant read each other's minds at levels far below conscious awareness and far more quickly than two adults can understand one another's words. The frontal lobes retain a capacity for change and growth throughout life. Just as you can still learn new facts or a new language in adulthood (even while losing neurons with aging), you can learn new emotional patterns throughout life, mediated by neuronal patterns and neurochemical change in the brain.

WHAT ARE SOME OF THE FACTORS THAT LIMIT BRAIN GROWTH AND DIFFERENTIATION?

At birth, the baby's brain is already rich in neurons but not yet in the rich connective networks that experience builds. The brain is constitutionally built to be affected by its environment. Of course its development is interfered with by chemical toxicity and malnutrition destructive to neurons. Object relations theorists have always thought that the brain is shaped by social experience. Neuroscience now has ways to prove this. Object relations therapists have long noticed that interpersonal neglect and trauma interfere with the development of the mind. Neuroscience shows that this happens by inhibiting the growth of connectedness between neurons and subunits of the brain. Brain scan studies show that severe trauma also leads to neuropsychological disconnection between functioning subunits that normally function in an integrated way. In subjects who do not feel, or who dissociate, scan studies show a poverty of activity in areas of the right thalamic-limbic area and their connection to the right orbitofrontal cortex. In subjects who show post-traumatic stress disorder, scan studies of brains of people who suffer from fearful flashbacks show increased activity in the right amygdala, where fear responses begin. Brains of those who suffered severe neglect and trauma show more rigid patterns of brain function, less overall right brain growth, and less neural network interconnectivity.

HAS NEUROSCIENCE LOCATED THE UNCONSCIOUS?

The right orbitofrontal cortex is the seat of the unconscious, or at least it is the hardware and software for unconscious processes. It houses implicit and procedural memory, and connections between bodily and social experience. It processes the reciprocal emotional interactions with others through projective and introjective communications in a continuous unconscious communication. This happens between parent and child, between intimate partners, and between therapist and patient. The process is mutual, consisting of rapid interactions of mutual emotional exchange, right brain to right brain, almost entirely below the levels of conscious awareness. Studies of the motor cortex of monkeys reveal the presence of mirror neurons that are activated when one monkey watches another monkey make movements. Perhaps the neuroscientists will discover similar mirror neurons in the parts of the right brain that record facial expressions and tone of voice. Applying this to humans, we would have a neurological basis for the mental mechanism of introjective identification with the emotional experience of the significant other.

This unconscious transmission has major effects on development. In long-term relationships each person affects the other's state of mind and their actual brain organization. Through interaction over time, one mind structures another.

HOW ARE AFFECTS COMMUNICATED?

The face is the lead organ of affective expression. Scientists can show that the face is rich in neuromuscular construction to give rise to various emotional expressions, some of them universal (like smiling or showing disgust) and others more nuanced in specific circumstances. Rich facial expression is accompanied by a richness of vocal inflection. The capacity to express emotion is proportional to the level of activity of the right brain, which is devoted to reading other people's emotional expression rapidly and accurately. When you perceive the emotions of another person you experience a resonant psychological state in yourself, presumably through the action of mirror neurons like those in the motor parts of the brain.

WHY IS THIS IMPORTANT?

In the course of our evolution, we have become able to sense one another's feelings by reading facial expressions. At the most basic level, this promotes our survival: we can detect an enemy's intentions and we can work in synchrony with a friend. Intelligence enables the human race to develop strategies to survive and dominate the planet, but emotional intelligence is the basis for relationships and civilization.

The capacity to understand and regulate our emotions is crucial to the growth of a self. The mother uses her capacity to read her infant's mind and bodily experience so as to help the infant regulate body states, mental states, and feelings. The two of them in partnership co-construct the child's emotional reality. This means that the principal importance of their attachment relationship is to provide the platform from which to teach the infant to regulate affects and states of mind. Affects, states of mind, and the capacity for regulation are the core of the progressive development of the self.

HOW IS THE SELF BUILT FROM AFFECT?

Affect is regulated at first by the mother. The mother marks the newborn's expressions by mirroring them exactly and the infant feels understood. Peter Fonagy calls this *contingent marking*. But slightly older infants prefer a gap between their own expressions and those of their mother. Fonagy calls this *noncontingent marking*. The mother makes an expression similar enough to convey that she has received the message but different enough to modify the original affect, for instance by turning its volume up or down. Thus she not only marks the affect but begins to regulate it. She may mark a slight difference and vary the degrees of difference or randomly lengthen or shorten the interval before she responds each time, teasing the infant until a game develops between them.

In many such interactions, mother and infant collaborate on regulating affect, then increasingly the infant takes over the self-regulation function as the ego interacts with internal and external objects. This process and these internal objects form the units that collectively constitute the self. Over time, the baby develops a growing sense of self. The first self is a bodily self, becomes a self that causes things to happen, then one that is more driven by wishes or intentions for things to happen, and later is a self with a capacity for narrative. The final and most sophisticated quality of self is the self-reflective sense of an autobiographical self, which begins at about the age of four or five, by which time children can tell their own stories and reflect on how it was to live them. Once each aspect of self comes on line, it continues to coexist with all the others for the rest of life.

The emotional components and early memories are housed in the right cortex, while the verbal aspects are housed predominantly on the left. Integration and cross-fertilization of the two ways of thinking are required for optimal growth.

HOW DOES NEUROSCIENCE HELP PSYCHOTHERAPY?

We think of psychotherapy as "the talking cure," but how does talking help? It helps to share the problem and get it off your chest, but the real value lies in putting words to experience to arrive at conflict resolution, mastery, and understanding. Giving voice to an interpretation is helpful because it demonstrates emotional understanding. Even so a therapist's main influence comes through unconscious communication—right brain to right brain. The coregulation of affect between patient and therapist leads to new self-regulation and self-growth. The lifelong plasticity of the right orbitofrontal cortex enables it to change and grow connections that promote emotional maturation. The left frontal cortex supports verbal understanding to promote review and self-reflection. Scan studies of the brain show permanent changes in the brain as a result of long-term psychotherapy.

NOTES

Contingent and noncontingent marking (Fonagy, P. et al. 2003).
Facial expressions (Tomkins 1995).
Neurological development (Siegel 1999).
Neurological development and affect regulation (Schore 1994, 2003).
Neuroscience and psychotherapy (Cozolino 2002).

⑩

TRAUMA

WHAT ARE THE MAIN EFFECTS OF CHILDHOOD PHYSICAL AND SEXUAL TRAUMA ON DEVELOPMENT?

Physical and sexual trauma are causes and effects of an insecure family holding environment. The distortion of the normal holding environment is illustrated in figure 10.1. First review figure 6.1, a diagram of the holding environment in the healthy family, and then compare it to figure 10.1.

Figure 10.1 shows the effect of trauma to the holding environment when the parent (or other adult) controls and invades the child emotionally and physically instead of offering security and facilitation. The transitional zone of relatedness is collapsed. The adult imposes on the child without the usual interplay that facilitates optimal growth. The adult breaks through the physical and emotional defensive barriers the child uses to protect the integrity of body and mind. Instead of being available to the child for use in building internal objects, the adult shatters the process of building mental structure, splitting the self into parts that cannot then grow together.

Children who experience trauma rarely defend well against the abuse. The more traumatic the experience (even in adulthood), the more likely

Zone of Transitional Relatedness
crumbles, obliterated by physical
invasion of child's body.

Child's Internal Structure
disrupted, with failures
of repression,
memory, sorting
of experience.

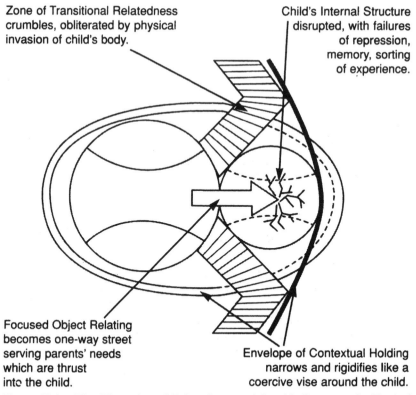

Focused Object Relating
becomes one-way street
serving parents' needs
which are thrust
into the child.

Envelope of Contextual Holding
narrows and rigidifies like a
coercive vise around the child.

**Figure 10.1.   The Distortion of Relatedness and Psychic Structure in Physical
and Sexual Abuse.** Reprinted from *Object Relations Therapy of Physical and Sexual Trauma.*
Courtesy of Jason Aronson. Copyright David E. Scharff 1994.

it is that the experience will be stored as though it were in a sealed capsule that could be buried and forgotten. The central self may be aware of
the gaps in the psyche, or fragments of the self may operate with separate noncommunicating banks of memories.

The thinking of severely traumatized patients is often concrete, expressed not in words but in physical·complaints, like those of Sigmund
Freud's hysterical patients whose pain, paralysis, or cough had converted an unbearable emotional response to trauma into a painful but
bearable bodily symptom. We now realize that conversion reactions
like these symbolize unbearable internal object relationships. Traumatized patients may carry out repetitive, seemingly meaningless behaviors like hand-washing to draw attention to the trauma and try to wash

Table 10.1.   Effects of Physical and Sexual Trauma on Development

* Encapsulation of traumatic nuclei
* Dissociation and gaps in the psyche
* Splits in the self with awareness
* Splits into multiple selves with separate memory banks and a noncommunicating consciousness
* Impaired capacity for fantasy elaboration and symbolization
* Thinking that is literal, concrete, and sometimes nonverbal
* Defensive preoccupation with the mundane
* Preoccupation with bodily symptoms
* Implicit memory behaviors that repeat the trauma

Reprinted from *Object Relations Therapy of Physical and Sexual Trauma*. Reprinted courtesy of Jason Aronson. Copyright Jill Savege Scharff © 1994.

it away without actually bringing it to mind, or they may dwell repetitively on mundane matters to protect them from becoming aware of deep emotional pain. We summarize these responses to trauma in table 10.1.

ARE THERE SPECIAL ASPECTS OF TECHNIQUE FOR WORK WITH SURVIVORS OF CHILDHOOD TRAUMA?

The defensive preoccupation with mundane details of daily life maintains a continuity of self despite the trauma that continues to attack from inside the self. As therapists, we value this capacity to *go-on-being* and we respect the split-off encapsulated aspects of the self and its internal objects. We move carefully between the roles of supporting the holding context for the therapy and being available as a projection screen for the patients' internal objects. We function both as an actively present object, representing figures from the past who helped and who hurt, and as a quiet absence representing the caretakers who were not there at crucial times. As we carry out this painstaking work, we need to hold a balance between work with the trauma and with the going-on-being, because this allows the patient to develop a new sense of safety. This process enables us to slowly recreate a transitional zone where the patient can begin to convert implicit memories contained in bodily symptoms or symptomatic behaviors into explicit thoughts and fantasies. We support the growth of "genera," healing nuclei that gather good experience, so as to repair and replace the traumatic nuclei of injury and self-destruction. We work over time to recover images of a patient's inner world through joining in a transference-countertransference exchange. We put the images and themes into a narrative that allows meaning to emerge. All this helps the patient rediscover a self that is also its own object, that is, a self that can be explored, experienced, loved, and understood. Table 10.2 summarizes some special aspects of therapy after trauma.

CAN YOU ILLUSTRATE THE EFFECTS OF CHILDHOOD SEXUAL TRAUMA ON A WOMAN?

Freda first came to therapy because of abdominal pain for which there was no physical explanation. She readily accessed memories of seeing her parents having intercourse when she was a very young child, but it took several years to remember that her father forced fellatio and intercourse on her from the time she was seven or eight years old. At the same age, Freda's menstruation began, and, to explain where the blood came from, her father put his fingers inside her vagina. She remembered hiding from him on the floor of her closet where she played at mutilating her dolls by cutting them between their legs with scissors,

---

Table 10.2.   Technique of Object Relations Therapy for Trauma

- Welcome going-on-being
- Relate to splits
- Re-create the transitional zone of fantasy
- Monitor the holding environment
- Move between context and focus
- Translate body communications
- Hold a neutral position equidistant between trauma and going-on-being
- Recover images in the transference-countertransference
- Put images into narrative form
- Refind the self as its own object
- Be there as both object and absence
- Transmute trauma to genera

Reprinted from *Object Relations Therapy of Physical and Sexual Trauma.* Reprinted courtesy of Jason Aronson. Copyright Jill Savage Scharff © 1994.

and pouring tomato sauce on the wound. As an adult, Freda was able to have sex with her husband, whom she loved and trusted, only by dissociating.

Once therapy began, Freda feared the reemergence of trauma from inside herself. Then she felt that sex with her husband, and therapy itself, threatened to retraumatize her. In response to this fear, she avoided sex with her husband and spent many sessions with her therapist focusing on the domestic details of her daily life—her job, driving her children, the weather—rarely dreaming and only occasionally diving into painful areas for a few minutes. In these brief forays into traumatic material, she might be taken over by a split-off childlike aspect of her personality, looking fearfully around her as if cowering in the closet lest her father find her.

Over many years of slow and painstaking work, listening to mundane material, the therapist worked with Freda to establish a sense of safety. This allowed her to put her dread into words, move from bodily and behavioral representation of trauma to a narrative, diminish the dissociative gaps in her memory banks and traumatic nuclei, and replace many of the aspects of trauma with genera.

HOW IS CHILDHOOD TRAUMA DIFFERENT FROM LOSS OF IMPORTANT FIGURES IN CHILDHOOD?

The term "childhood trauma" has been used to refer to stressful early experiences such as separation, fright, loss of a parent. These experiences lead to psychological strain, and sometimes to later life symptoms such as depression, unless the experience is put into words, actively mourned, and worked through. We do not mean to suggest that early parent loss is not traumatic, but it is not a secret, and there are community supports the child can turn to. We reserve the term *trauma* to refer to psychological challenges of a single shock or cumulative nature that overwhelm the self, either because the trauma is severe or because the self is weak, and because the child is helpless to change what is happening. In practice, of course, the distinction may not be so neat.

WHAT ABOUT TRAUMA IN ADULTHOOD?

Studies of traumatic war neurosis in World War II, post-traumatic stress disorder after the Vietnam War, and the histories of victims of the Holocaust, showed that physical and psychological stress can overpower the best defenses of the mature personality and result in severe splitting and encapsulation of trauma as a way of managing emotional pain and the fear of disaster striking again. Trauma resonates with any preexisting loss or trauma, so that damage that the person coped with reasonably well originally is aggravated by current trauma and compounds it.

ARE THERE INDIRECT EFFECTS OF TRAUMA ON OTHER FAMILY MEMBERS?

Trauma to one family member will generally have an indirect but significant effect on other members of the family. This occurs, first, because the other family members are affected by the changes to the traumatized person. Second, trauma from the past is often transmitted from one generation to another despite the wishes of parents to spare their children. This happens because they pass on the internal object relations of trauma in unknowing, unconscious ways.

After major trauma, the mind may dissociate from the pain, drive the traumatic material into a sequestered place, and wall it off behind a tough capsule. It is a primitive way of dealing with overwhelming anxiety so that the person can get on with life. The capsule may thicken and stiffen in time and block unconscious communication between parts of the self. This leads to a rigid personality. If it weakens, traumatic material threatens to escape, and then the person may panic or try desperately to avoid stress. Maintaining a tight boundary around the capsule may seem to be effective in preventing activation of trauma. Nevertheless, it may drive the trauma by projective identification into members of the next generation, and they may then become symptomatic.

For instance, parents who are survivors of childhood sexual abuse may bend over backwards to be nontraumatizing, and yet convey their terrible anxiety that sexuality will damage their children. Their vocal inflections and anxious eye movements send a message of fear to their children, even though their words do not.

CAN YOU GIVE AN EXAMPLE OF ADULT PHYSICAL TRAUMA AND ITS EFFECTS ON THE FAMILY?

Tony and Theresa had been married for twelve years and had three children. They were all traumatized when Tony suddenly lost his right arm and shoulder by amputation. His arm had become infected after he received an injection to relieve an asthma attack. Trying desperately to treat the overwhelming sepsis, the doctors told Theresa they had to amputate to save Tony's life. She had no choice but to agree.

After the surgery, Tony became severely depressed, unable to relate to the family, and unwilling to train himself in the use of an electronically operated prosthesis. Tony and Theresa shouted at each other, but Tony denied that he was angry with her. He said that Theresa had done her best and he was grateful. He was only angry with himself. In therapy, the couple realized that they had been avoiding each other to avoid the anger that they could not deal with because they had always dealt with anger by diverting it, a technique that had worked for them until the trauma.

Tony grew up with an alcoholic father who abused him and his mother. Tony's role was to protect his mother and sisters by taking the abuse for them. Theresa's role was to draw fire away from her four older sisters. On one occasion, her mother hit her with an iron skillet on the head, which created a wound that required ten stitches. When they married, Tony and Theresa vowed never to hit each other or their children. Instead, they hit the walls of their house with their bare fists to the point of breaking skin and knucklebones. For disciplining their children, they invented a technique they called "hold-a-wall." They taught the children to go stand with their head against the wall until they could behave.

In therapy, Tony and Theresa were tentative about exploring their issues beyond the trauma. They were inhibited by an unconscious fear of the therapist (himself a doctor), which reflected their lack of safety both with parents while growing up, and with doctors after Tony's recent disastrous experience with the doctor who treated his asthma. As they began to trust him, the therapist was able to show them how their use of walls, which protected them from repeating direct trauma on each other, had formed a wall between them across which they could not communicate. Therapy with the couple involved the same tolerance of mundane daily stories as with individual trauma patients while creating a context of safety in which to rebuild the capacity to go-on-being to-gether.

CAN YOU SEE THE INDIRECT EFFECTS OF TRAUMA IN A CHILD'S PLAY AND DREAMS?

Tony and Theresa's middle child, Tony Jr., was a nine-year-old at the time of his father's amputation. In a session with the whole family, he sat silently while his older sister and younger brother talked easily with the therapist about what had happened and how afraid they were that their father had died. The therapist asked to see Tony Jr. alone for further evaluation when the parents said that his schoolwork had fallen off and that he seemed depressed at home.

In the individual session, Tony was again largely silent. Although he did not seem angry or oppositional, he was unable to play with action figures, draw, or speak beyond a few cryptic and unrevealing answers to direct questions. Finally, the therapist suggested they play the "squiggle game," a technique invented by Donald Winnicott for evaluating children. The therapist drew a wavy squiggle and asked Tony to make it into a picture. Then he suggested that Tony draw a squiggle for the therapist to expand into a picture. As they took turns, Tony came to life, and moved from drawing simply lines shadowing the therapist's line to making images that were more and more revealing of the trauma he had internalized. As the game progressed, Tony Jr. spoke about a recent dream. He and his brother were with their parents in the family van with his father driving as he had before the accident. They were on their way to their family home in Mexico for a great vacation, but his sister was not with them. The dream showed an idealized image of the family being together on life's voyage, perhaps sacrificing the older sister instead of the father's arm.

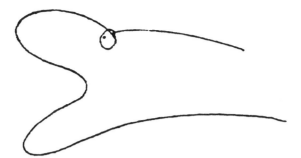

Figure 10.2. Dinosaur Squiggle. Tony Jr. now dares to express eagerness, curiosity and aggression. Reprinted from *Object Relations Therapy of Physical and Sexual Trauma*. Reprinted courtesy of Jason Aronson. Copyright Jill Savege Scharff © 1994.

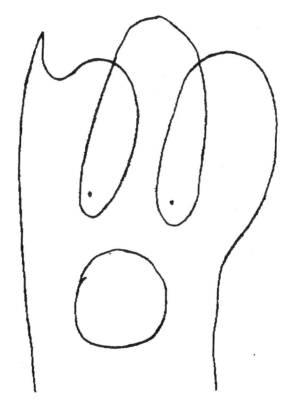

Figure 10.3. Scary Ghost. Tony Jr. is now able to address horror and fright. Reprinted from *Object Relations Therapy of Physical and Sexual Trauma*. Reprinted courtesy of Jason Aronson. Copyright Jill Savege Scharff © 1994.

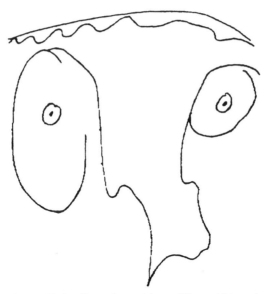

Figure 10.4. Face Scared by a Ghost. Ultimately, Tony Jr. reveals his fragmentation in response to the scary ghosts of trauma. Reprinted from *Object Relations Therapy of Physical and Sexual Trauma.* Reprinted courtesy of Jason Aronson. Copyright Jill Savege Scharff © 1994.

Reviewing the drawings, Tony Jr. said figure 10.2 was a dinosaur. It featured an open-mouthed animal like a snake or dinosaur, but it also resembled the part of the bone of the arm that attaches to the shoulder. Figure 10.3, his next drawing, was a "scary ghost," but it also looked scared itself, as if it had seen a ghost. Figure 10.4, his final drawing, was of a person who is scared by the ghost.

In reality, Tony Jr. had become so sad and frightened by what had happened to his father, and so unable to express it, that his ability to work in school was damaged. In his dream, he created a family that had not suffered and a father who was not damaged. In his play, he was totally blocked until the therapist related to him in ways that bypassed words. When the loss of the father's right arm was such a trauma to the boy, it was helpful to draw and discover that it was okay to use his own right arm effectively.

CHAOS THEORY

HOW DOES CHAOS THEORY EXTEND OBJECT RELATIONS THEORY?

Chaos theory is a set of principles concerning dynamic systems that operate with continuous feedback. These have been studied by scientists working in the area of overlap between mathematics, meteorology, physics, and biology. The behavior of these systems—such as weather, whirlpools, art, biological organisms, human personality, and life in general—is too chaotic to be predictable, and the equations that govern them are too complex to solve, but when the scientists used advanced computer technology they found a way to deal with them by "iterating the equation."

Iterating the Equation

To iterate the equation, scientists solve for x, take that as the starting point for the next run through the equation, and repeat this millions of times, the value for x always slightly different each time as conditions change. The results plotted on a graph yield a visual trace of the system. As the equation is repeated many, many times, a recognizable pattern emerges.

Sensitive Dependence on Initial Conditions

After many iterations, exceedingly small alterations in the starting numbers or conditions of a dynamic system will produce unpredictably large changes in the system.

CAN YOU GIVE AN EXAMPLE OF SENSITIVE DEPENDENCE ON INITIAL CONDITIONS?

Biological systems work on the basis of operating principles designed to provide feedback to the organism, which then adapts by adjusting to the feedback. This occurs over and over. Growth and development in life and in therapy can be said to iterate the equation. For instance, tiny changes in factors producing weather in one place will make unexpectedly large changes in weather in another location. Theoretically, the flap of a butterfly's wings in Brazil could begin a chain of meteorological events that would eventually cause a thunderstorm in Texas. Drawing from this theoretical possibility, the principle of sensitive dependence on initial conditions has been given the nickname of the *butterfly effect.*

CAN YOU DEFINE SOME MORE TERMS FROM CHAOS THEORY?

Tuning Force

The tuning force is the amount of pressure a force exerts on a system moving it toward change. The current interactions of family members and their family history recorded in their internal object relations exert a tuning force on the personality patterns of the group as a whole and on the personalities of each individual family member. Some members of the family may have a relatively greater effect than others. For instance, a mother's internal object relations exert a large tuning force on her children, while a daughter who has left home may exert a relatively weak tuning force on her siblings. Within the mind of the individual, internal objects exert a tuning force on one another and on the person's internal state of mind, as well as exert a force on the pattern of interaction with others.

Self-Organizing Systems

At the edge of chaos, the seeming confusion of a chaotic system takes on a discernible pattern: it self-organizes in relation to a less chaotic system in its environment. For instance, at the shore, the land organizes the turbulence of the sea, and the sea sculpts and patterns the land.

Fractals

Fractals are self-similar patterns that occur across differing orders of scale. Fractal scaling is seen when, at various parts and at different levels of magnification of a system, patterns repeat. They show self-similarity but not exact sameness. For instance, the pattern of veins in a leaf has a rough similarity to the pattern of leaves on a branch and to the branch pattern of the tree. A shoreline is reflected in the shape and distribution of rocks that make up that shoreline, and in the microscopic arrangement of crystals that make up the rocks. Art follows nature in using fractals to create a pleasing whole. For instance, in esthetically pleasing architecture the small features of a building echo the form of the overall structure.

WHAT ARE ATTRACTORS?

Fixed, Limit Cycle, and Strange

A fixed attractor appears to move a system predictably toward rest at a single spot (like a gravity-controlled pendulum). A limit-cycle attractor appears to move a system through a fixed pattern continuously (like an electrically powered pendulum). A strange attractor appears to move a system through a complex, apparently random pattern and pulls it toward an organized pattern. All attractors *appear* to be the force that *organizes* the system, but they are actually *organized by* the dynamics of the system. When the organizing principle governing a complex biological system runs the system over and over, the system does not repeat exactly, but it does eventually produce a recognizable pattern called a *strange attractor*. For instance, a whirlpool seems to pull water into the whirl, although it is actually the flow of the water that produces the whirl.

Basins of attraction are those areas in which the strange attractor seems to exert an especially strong pull on the system. For instance, there is a region of water beyond the influence of a whirlpool, but as objects there move with the flow, they are more likely to be swept into the pattern of the whirl.

CAN YOU GIVE AN EXAMPLE OF A BASIN OF ATTRACTION?

Patterns of family life attract family members into repetitions of actions, and its members will often report that the closer they get to the family group (the closer they get to the family's basin of attraction) the more they get swept up in the family's pattern. At the same time, individual repetitive behaviors join together to create the group dynamics of the family system.

HOW DO YOU DEFINE A SADDLE POINT, BIFURCATION, AND CASCADE?

A *saddle point* is a place where a nonlinear system comes under the influence of conditions that impel it to break up into two directions of flow, thus creating a *bifurcation*. Mathematically, the equations for these systems suddenly have two solutions that take divergent paths. Continuing sensitivity to those conditions creates further bifurcations that double each of the two subsystems, creating four, eight, sixteen subsystems and so on in a *cascade* of doubling until the whole system fragments into chaos. Then at the edge of chaos, the system may meet conditions that influence it toward reorganization once more.

HOW DO YOU RELATE CHAOS THEORY TO OBJECT RELATIONS THEORY?

In human life, strands of experience may diverge and realign or end up in chaos. A young man's experimentation with alcohol may increase on weekends, resulting in two patterns—(1) the weekday pattern of studying and enjoying a beer, and (2) the weekend of heavy drinking—until adult responsibilities create the conditions that curtail his habit to occasional, moderate drinking. His friend's drinking may diverge into continued alcohol and drug abuse until unreliability gets him fired from his first job, and only then is he amenable to help. Alternatively, his friend may be unable to reorganize and continue into the chaos of alcohol addiction.

In Fairbairnian theory, the ego bifurcates (or splits) experience into two strands—rejecting and exciting—depending on the nurturing conditions that the young ego meets in the early years. This splitting of the internal object exerts a further splitting force for a second split or bifurcation into libidinal and antilibidinal parts of ego and object related to each other. If experience exerts further pressure, these original splits may cascade into fragmentations of ego and object that do not relate to each other in a patterned way but lead to psychotic confusion.

In Kleinian theory, the conditions exerting a force on the child's system are called the life and death instincts. The splitting processes (bifurcations) repeated over many iterations of experience create internal object relationships each of which functions as a subsystem or bifurcation of the original infant personality system. Viewed in the light of the internal object relationships, new experience in the first few months of life tends to cluster in the general categories of good or bad (the paranoid-schizoid position). More opportunities for learning in relation to the more developed mind of a good-enough mother modify the infant's perceptions and encourage the systems to converge again to a more integrated view of the object (the depressive position). If not, the projection of goodness or

badness into the caregivers tends to get set in place and evokes confirm-
ing behaviors in them, leading to a cascade of projections until all is lost
in fragmentation of the other and the self, a pattern that Wilfred Bion
called *bizarre objects*.

HOW DO YOU APPLY THESE IDEAS TO FAMILIES AND INDIVIDUALS?

Family and individual life, like all biological systems, is a set of complex
iterated equations. Life's exquisite feedback is accomplished through
many repetitions governed by biological and psychological operating
principles. The family as a group and family members individually use
the family's operating equations to live and work, but these can be
changed by experience, as the family expands, as gene mutations interact with the organism's experience over time, and as psychological learning and growth produce new solutions. The individual and the family
show *sensitive dependence on initial conditions* as they apply operating
equations to the next set of life challenges. Small differences in the beginning of a day can affect the next weeks or even the life course in unpredictable ways, while something that seems to loom large may turn
out to be inconsequential. A major illness may stop development, or, in
other circumstances, may motivate change for the better. This is an example of the butterfly effect.

   Dysfunctional families get stuck doing the same ineffective thing over
and over, following the *selfsame pattern* of a limit-cycle attractor.
Healthy families, like healthy biological systems, move in and out of
chaos in daily life, following the *self-similar patterns* of strange attractors, never exactly the same, but patterned enough to be recognizable as
part of a dynamic system. Chaotic patterns have an enhanced capacity
to adapt to new circumstances and their needs. Healthy families and individuals under challenge respond to turbulence by breaking out of the
mold and *self-organizing* into a new adaptive pattern, while constrained
families repeat old habits that are not effective. Families and individuals show *fractal scaling* in development: The patterns of interaction of
the parents show up in sibling interactions and in the personality pat-

terns of the child. The individual's transference to the therapist is a *fractal* of the internal object relationship set, which is a fractal of the family's patterns of relating.

DOES CHAOS THEORY HAVE MORE TO SAY ABOUT THE FORMATION OF A COUPLE OR FAMILY?

When two individuals form a couple, the patterns of their personalities based on their histories behave as strange attractors, each of which interacts with the other and exerts a tuning force on it until the systems combine to form a new strange attractor, namely the pattern of the joint marital personality. When that couple has a child, the strange attractors of the two parents' personalities and of their relationship pattern exert tuning forces that create basins of attraction that interact with the inherent personality patterns of the child, pulling the child's self toward this or that system of organization. When we compare each parent's strange attractor pattern, the joint marital personality, the developing personality of the child, and the overall family interaction patterns, we notice that they show fractal similarity to one another.

HOW DOES THE CHILD BECOME A NEW OBJECT FOR THE PARENTS?

The baby that a couple shares is a living embodiment of their interpenetration, and gives life to their partnership. The child arises from, and is a representative of, the sexual coupling of the parents. In addition, the child is a person in his or her own right, therefore a new object of affection, interest, and hate for the couple. At the same time, the child is also a *reminder* of the parents' original objects, their own parents; for aspects of them are imagined in the child through the parents' projective identification. Experience with the child is installed as a complex new/old internal object that restructures the parents' selves and their couple relationship. Just as the sea and the land shape each other at the edge of chaos, parent and child sculpt each other's interactions and personality.

HOW DOES CHAOS THEORY EXPLAIN THE PROCESS OF CHANGE IN THERAPY?

All this leads to the question of how we can promote change when individuals and families seek help. Family and individual dynamics are strong basins of attraction for repeated behaviors. They represent self-same, limit-cycle attractor patterns that are difficult to change. When these dynamics have become disorganized, for instance by the chaos of having an ill member, falling in love, living in an unfamiliar culture, or exploring the unconscious in therapy, they are most open to change.

Therapists function as new strange attractors, often with a powerful tuning force. By introducing *perturbations* into psychological operating systems, we disturb the relatively fixed, limit-cycle systems in which families and individuals are stuck. We use the tuning force of our own internal object relations organization, honed by training, therapy, and supervision, to create a new basin of attraction, and join with patients to structure a new strange attractor system with better capacities for adaptation. Because of fractal scaling and sensitive dependence on initial conditions, relatively small changes can have major effects. An exact interpretation of the transference in a single therapy session can, like the butterfly effect, produce a thunderstorm's worth of change in the person's state of mind and way of interacting with the world. A change in one family member can affect the whole family. And when the family's overall pattern changes, this exerts a new tuning force on each member of the family once again. Such change does not happen every time; it does not need to happen every time. It need happen only periodically to help a person or family make fundamental change.

CAN YOU GIVE A CLINICAL EXAMPLE CONNECTED TO CHAOS THEORY AND OBJECT RELATIONS THEORY?

A combined concurrent individual, family, and couple therapy example dealing with the parents' sexual difficulty, its impact on their children's development, and their progress in therapy was described in *Founda-*

tions of Object Relations Family Therapy and *Object Relations Couple Therapy*. Here David Scharff presents another of this family's therapy sessions with him from the vantage point of both object relations theory and chaos theory (and we return to this family in chapter 21).

Lars and Velia Simpson, parents in their late thirties, and their children, Eric, Alex, and Jeanette, had been in weekly family therapy for eighteen months. Velia was still in intensive individual therapy with a colleague. The couple had been in sex therapy weekly for fifteen months to deal with her sexual aversion and his premature ejaculation. The sex therapy had been going well but slowly, complicated by their histories of sexual abuse: Velia had been fondled by her brother and physically abused by her father; Lars had been sodomized at the age of ten by his father as the father's way of explaining sex. Lars, a pilot, was withdrawn. Velia was depressed and angry. Her dark moods and angry outbursts made Lars despair. Eric was destructive, Alex soiled his pants, and Jeanette clung to her mother in a sexualized embrace. The session that I have chosen followed my two-week vacation.

As this session begins, Velia, the mother, looks depressed and has a severe headache, and the father, Lars, is quiet. On the floor, seven-year-old Alex builds with blocks. The ten-year-old, Eric, has two fighter planes in a dogfight. Jeanette, age five, makes a paper airplane and builds a fence around it with blocks. "Here's his hiding place, Momma," Jeanette calls out. I think silently that the fenced-off airplane refers both to my absence and to father's hiding from the family emotionally.

The parents watch as they talk about a disappointing setback during the past two weeks, referring to their sex therapy. I am thinking of Jeanette's comment about the airplane's hiding place and imagining Eric's play of two airplanes chasing each other without catching up as an aggressive unconsummated primal scene. I ask the parents, "Do you think your backsliding as an intimate couple had to do with feeling abandoned in my absence?"

Velia answers, "I can say 'yes' for myself. I don't know about Lars."

Lars shakes his head and says, "I really wouldn't know."

I say, "Well, it's likely that without my support over the last two weeks, you have felt shaky, but Lars, you can't connect that to my being away, because you have trouble making links."

I have in mind Bion's concept of attacks on linking as a reflection of traumatic disconnection. I attribute Lars's difficulty to the attack on the integrity of his mental functioning because of sexual abuse by his own father.

Jeanette and Alex are now playing with a toy helicopter and a small doll in a bathtub. Jeanette's doll calls to Alex's helicopter, "Goodbye! See you tomorrow." One of Eric's planes is shot down by the other and Eric throws it to the floor.

I think of the children's play as a reaction to my absence. The family's feeling of rejection has acted like a strange attractor to organize the events of their week and this session is a fractal of the week. I say, "Lars, you would have missed me if you could have thought about it. That's what the children are showing in Eric's angry chase, and Jeanette and Alex's missing helicopter."

"I wouldn't know," Lars repeats, shaking his head in disbelief.

Suddenly a puppet pig snorts loudly from behind the play table, demanding attention.

"I'm hungry!" says Eric for the pig.

Jeanette and Alex take puppets, too. "We're having a picnic. We're eating carrots," says Jeanette, as her pink rabbit and Alex's cow chew on my pencils. They put a furry, purple monster puppet on my hand. In a voracious, teasing, and even loving way, the children's puppets bite my monster's nose, saying, "Honk! Honk!"

I say to Velia and Lars, "Some people are mad at me for leaving them hungry."

"Yes," says Velia, smiling from underneath her headache. "They aren't the only people who might want to bite your nose." She makes a pinching gesture as though she were honking my puppet's nose too.

Feeling her anger as though it were my actual nose she was pinching, I say half defensively, "Maybe if you could talk about that, you wouldn't have such a headache."

"Maybe so," she agrees, widening her smile.

Lars now impishly says to Velia, "You go over and honk his nose, too."

Before I know it, I find myself saying, "No! Why don't you just talk about it?" Sheepishly, I realize that Lars's teasing has got to me.

Jeanette strides away from me, her heels clicking on the floor, then strides back.

She says, "Hello! I've been away for a trip." Her pink rabbit starts chewing on my purple monster's nose again.

"What's happening?" I ask.

"I'm honking someone's nose," she says. "He's been mean to us, so we're being mean to him!"

I recognize that the tuning force of betrayal of trust is organizing this session. I now have language for reaching Lars: "The whole family has been missing me and is mad at me about being away. It's true for you, too, Lars," I say. "But you can't link my being away with your trouble functioning with Velia. Your trouble linking things goes back to when you asked your father to help, and he hurt you instead. Now you can't trust me to support you."

Lars says, "My first impression is: You don't even think about it!"

I seize on the grammar of his speech, a fractal of his difficulty thinking. I know he consciously means "a person doesn't think about it," but I say, "What you have just said, Lars, is, 'You don't even think about it,' meaning that *I* don't think about what I mean to you."

"I meant that *I* don't think about it," he protests.

I say, "That's not what you said. You *said*, 'You don't even think about it.'"

Velia joins in, teasingly making the link better than I can. "Nyah, nyah. You got caught in a Freudian slip!" Lars playfully slaps her knee, acknowledging her point.

As I now elaborate on Lars's difficulty knowing he missed me, a piece of play confirms the family's transference anger. Eric uses a toy ambulance to knock down the building that Jeanette and Alex are building. Lars says, "Eric, stop trying to distract us."

I say, "Eric, I know you've been upset today. Those airplanes are fighting. Now the ambulance knocks down that building. And ambulances are connected to doctors."

"I see it," says Velia. "The ambulance-slash-doctor knocked down the building." As she says this, she slices the air with her hand to indicate the grammatical slash in ambulance/doctor.

Thinking of "slash" as the wound a knife makes, I say, "I liked the part about the 'ambulance-slash-doctor.'"

Velia laughs. "I see, 'Slash the doctor!' Yes. I see."

Lars lets out a laugh. As the session ends, Jeanette laments, "I don't want to go!"

Applying Object Relations Theory to the Session

We can understand this session first by applying object relations theory. The therapist supplies the holding and containment to build a safe place for reflection and mental processing. We see the first reference to a problem in holding when Jeanette shows her mother the therapist's hiding place. His absence has threatened their safety and inhibited their continued growth. Then, while the children play out issues of separation and anger, the parents spell out the lapse in their own sexual connection and their failure to maintain links between objects and between mental processes during separation. For a while, the therapist blocks projective identifications of anger and disappointment, momentarily unable to process them emotionally himself, superficially acknowledging their anger but not taking it in.

Then the children play the game of the hungry pigs that reveals the projective identification of the anger that they have taken in, contained, and now express in detoxified form. As they attack the therapist, the underlying emotions organize the family as a group to make a link that expresses anger now softened with humor and love. When they do so, the therapist is able to take it in and think about it, to help them make their own links once again. When Lars tells Eric to stop attacking his siblings, and Velia tells the family the meaning of Eric's disruption of the play, we see signs of progress in the family's capacity for containment, holding, and reflection.

The Session from the Vantage Point of Chaos Theory

The session is an *iteration of the family's operating principles*. The family members aggressively try to connect with the therapist as an object of dependency, and they attack the therapist for abandoning them by leaving on vacation. As they iterate their equation, the therapist enters a confusional state, cannot accurately track the children's play, and then seizes on this old pattern of dependency to explain the attacks on themselves, and to orient himself. The family has used old patterns to tolerate the pain, and the therapist has turned to old interpretations in the struggle to make sense of the chaos. The situation continues to iterate as he grasps for meaning.

The therapist cannot find meaning in Eric's airplane duel or Jeanette's airplane with its hiding place. His thinking falls victim to the attack expressed in Velia's headache and Lars's inability to think. The whirlpool of anger in the family affects them all; it is an *infantile attractor,* an old pattern from childhood, powered by dread, which pulls everything into it.

Then something different happens that signals the *family's sensitive dependence on initial conditions.* As the iterations continue, the flexibility acquired through *therapy constitutes a new tuning force,* changing the previous inflexibility—their *limit-cycle attractor*—to become *a more adaptive strange attractor.* They move into chaos, and then new strange attractors form out of the *basin of attraction offered by the therapist.* In the next iteration in the session, the children's play offers yet another new attractor in the language of childhood. The puppets attack the therapist with humor, and then explain the reasons: hunger and the effects of his cruel hiding and deprivation. This tuning force repatterns Velia's anger into humor, and allows her, in turn, to ally with the therapist in helping Lars join together the fragments of his dispersed mind.

Therapy relies on *fractal scaling* and *the butterfly effect.* A small change in one part of the system and at one order of magnitude can affect the larger dynamic system at larger orders of scale. Let's look for fractals by comparing the individual and the family group. Patterns that dominate the family have a fractal similarity to those in the personalities of the individuals, although each individual expresses different parts of the pattern (through parceling out of group projective identifications). Lars carries the fragmentation of meaning; Alex carries the effects of mental and physical assault on the body, expressed in his enuresis and encopresis; Velia and Eric carry the anger; and Jeanette carries an aspect of sexualization as an attempt to heal the fractured bonds with overly excited links.

As the session iterates, we glimpse first one strange attractor, then another, as various individuals speak up or put their play in the foreground, and then sink into the background chaos. One individual joins with another to make a dyad (another order of scale) to give a new pattern; then three people join together; and then the whole family joins the children's playful lead in directing object hunger and anger at the therapist, and iterates themes until they can finally be understood in new ways. The different orders of scale—individual, dyad, triads, whole family group, and family plus therapist—show fractal similarity. Inside each individual are internal object relations, which are fractals of the internal object relations of the previous generation. They emerge in current versions of feeling assaulted and neglected in each therapeutic moment. The healing potential of therapy extends to the generations of children and families that stretch forward from this point on, a fractal of the future.

HOW CAN WE USE CHAOS THEORY TO UNDERSTAND THE POTENTIAL OF THERAPY?

Small effects in therapy cause perturbations that break up old patterns for families who live on the edge of chaos. We help them move from the destructive basins of attraction in which they live, dominated by limit-cycle attractors, so that they can let go. We encourage them to enter the new state of useful chaos that our strange attractor patterns provoke, and then to reorganize into better patterns under the influence of our therapeutic tuning force and basins of attraction. Because families are exquisitely sensitive to small changes in initial conditions, exposure to the new strange attractors of the therapist's way of thinking iterates their equations in new ways. In this way, we dare to hope that sessions of an hour a week can make a major difference 24/7. Sometimes even a single therapeutic contact can release adaptive patterns. But ongoing therapy is more effective: Longer exposure to our tuning force gives greater likelihood of change.

Sensitive dependence on initial conditions, perturbations to individual and family systems, the influence of new strange attractors, tuning force and basins of attraction, reorganization at the edge of chaos, and the butterfly effect at multiple levels of fractal scaling combine to reorganize family and individual structure. Family members always influence one another in a cycle of powerful interconnections. The therapist becomes another strange attractor that changes the operating formula among the family's primary objects as they circle and interact, influence and are influenced. As we flap the wings of therapeutic action, we may change the winds of influence on every level of scale.

12

THE THERAPEUTIC RELATIONSHIP
AND THE GEOGRAPHY OF
THE TRANSFERENCE

HOW DOES OBJECT RELATIONS THEORY
HELP IN CLINICAL PRACTICE?

Our mentor, the late Jock Sutherland, liked to say that object relations is not so much a theory as a way of working. Object relations theory puts the relationship between the therapist and the patient at the center of the way of working. While the therapist and patient join together in the task of examining the patient's internal world and its effect on the patient's relationships, at the same time the patient and therapist are in a relationship themselves. This therapeutic relationship forms the laboratory in which the therapist learns most centrally about the patient's difficult ways of relating. As the therapist processes the experience of this current relationship, he or she is able to inform the patient about this experience. In this way, patient and therapist have a current shared relationship that both can study and learn from.

The patient (or the group of patients when we see a family, couple, or therapy group) establishes a current relationship with the therapist that reflects the internal object relations set that is brought to all relationships. In therapy, we take it as our task to experience these current expressions of object relationships in the interpersonal field. As therapists we experience them within ourselves in terms of fantasies or feelings that are somewhat foreign to us and that arise within us specifically in response to the patient before us. This way of working is characterized by the use of what Sigmund Freud termed *transference* and *counter-transference*.

WHAT CONSTITUTES THE TECHNIQUE OF OBJECT RELATIONS THEORY?

There is no series of separate techniques to be applied systematically, like communications theory interventions or behavioral techniques. The technique of object relations therapy comprises a stance, a relationship, and a set of attitudes. These set the frame of the therapy and hold it steady to allow the emergence of an in-depth, committed therapeutic relationship. This relationship offers a transference-countertransference microcosm in which to display, experience, and modify the patient's internal object relations difficulties over the span of the treatment. There is not a right or wrong way of working so much as a set of conditions to be met in order to enable a relationship to grow and deepen.

WHAT IS TRANSFERENCE?

In object relations terms, *transference* is the manifestation of the patient's projective identification in the clinical setting. Sigmund Freud described the way that a patient aims the drives at the therapist as a new edition of the original target. At first, Freud thought that the transference got in the way of therapy by muddying the waters, but he quickly came to see that transference was the engine of the therapy. Transference gives the therapist a living example of the way the patient copes with forbidden thoughts and feelings. In object relations theory, we do not see transference as the displacement of primitive impulses, as Freud suggested. We see transference as the expression of internal object relationships experienced externally in the therapeutic relationship through projective identification.

HOW ABOUT COUNTERTRANSFERENCE?

Freud originally used the term *countertransference* to refer to those feelings and attitudes stirred up in the therapist owing to the interference of the therapist's unresolved difficulties. Freud did not develop his idea of countertransference as fully as he did that of transference. We've already remarked that he began by thinking of transference as an impediment and later came to see it as the principal vehicle of analysis. Countertransference can be seen the same way. Freud originally described countertransference as an impediment to work, but modern object relations therapists have come to see it as the vehicle for therapeutic interaction and the basis of understanding and interpretation. The set of feelings and attitudes stirred up in the therapist forms a model of what is evoked in the people with whom the patient is in relationship. Providing that therapists have been well trained and have had personal therapy so that their own personal issues do not interfere, they are then in the position to use their internal experience with their patients to make sense of the patients' ways of relating. Therefore, we expect object relations therapists to monitor their internal states of feeling and the ideas, associations, and fantasies that occur to them during treatment in order to make sense of the relationship with the patient. While we do not advise therapists to report these experiences in raw and unmetabolized form to their patients, we do expect therapists to examine them thoughtfully as the best set of clues as to the patients' problems in relating in depth and then to use the countertransference to inform ensuing interpretations of the transference.

CAN YOU EXPLAIN THE TERM
GEOGRAPHY OF THE TRANSFERENCE?

We use the term *geography of the transference* to describe our map of the patient's stance in relation to us and the total situation of treatment. Mapping the geography is a useful exercise for training therapists to extract and track the transference elements of a session. Knowing how to use the map is like having a car with a global positioning system. In therapy we may go along for a long time without having to make ourselves consciously aware of the transference-countertransference position, because we have an intuitive sense of where we are. But when we are feeling uncertain or simply lost, a map that marks the geographical features of the journey is helpful.

WHAT SHOULD WE BE LOOKING FOR?

We look out for the elements of the geography as we might check the lines of longitude and latitude on a map by asking ourselves, "What, When, Where, and How does transference appear?"

What kind of transference is it—primarily contextual or focused? The contextual transference is directed at the therapist's psychological holding of the patient and provision of safety for her. The focused transference is a projection of a discrete part of the patient's libidinal or antilibidinal self, exciting or rejecting object into the therapist. See figure 12.1.

How is this transference feeling expressed—in words, in the atmosphere of the therapy, or in the body? How is the feeling detected—in the patient's transference or in the therapist's countertransference?

Where is the intense feeling located—inside the patient, inside the therapist, or in the space between them?

When did, does, or will this feeling occur—now (the present), back then (the past), or "if-and-when" something happens (the future)?

Table 12.1 shows where the patient's concerns are currently located and their meaning for the transference. We can locate the transference in terms of time (past, present, and future), space (here in therapy or there in life outside therapy), and containment (in the therapist, in the patient, or in the space between).

Here:
1. *The here-and-now*: the patient's feelings directed intently at the therapist.
2. *The here-and-back-then*: the patient's memories brought alive in therapy.
3. *The here-and-if-and-when*: the patient's fantasies of the future of the therapeutic relationship.

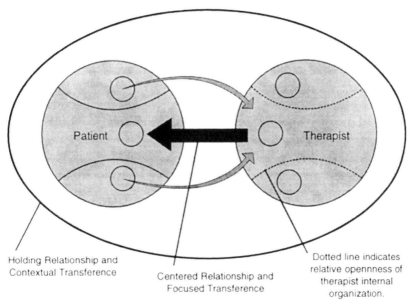

Figure 12.1. Focused and Contextual Transference in Individual Therapy. Within the envelope of the holding relationship (to which the patient has a contextual transference) patient and therapist examine the patient's inner object relationships and their effect on external relationships, and in so doing, the internal object relationships are projected onto the therapist (which is the focused transference) and modified in interaction with the therapist's less rigid splitting and repression of internal object relations. (See also chapter 16.) The relationship itself is the agent of change. Reprinted from *Object Relations Individual Therapy.* Courtesy of Jason Aronson. Copyright David E. Scharff © 1998.

There:

1. *The there-and-back-then*: memories of childhood, the early history of a marriage, life in the community and the wider society.
2. *The there-and-now*: the patient's current life outside therapy: family life, social life, work, and society.
3. *The there-and-if-and-when*: the patient's fantasies about the life in the future.

CAN YOU GIVE AN EXAMPLE OF PLACING THE TRANSFERENCE IN TIME AND SPACE?

Let's say a man who appears to get along well with his female therapist tells her about being upset because his wife is too controlling (the

Table 12.1. Transference in Terms of Time and Space

SPACE:	Here	There	
	In therapy	In family In society	
TIME:	Past:	Here-and-back-then	There-and-back-then
	Present:	Here-and-now	There-and-now
	Future	Here-and-if-and-when	There-and-if-and-when

there-and-now). The therapist wonders if the man's transference to his domineering mother (the there-and-then) is coloring his perceptions of his wife or evoking controlling behavior to fit the demands of an internal object relationship. Let's say the man feels the therapist is telling him what to think. The therapist now senses the man's transference to her as a controlling object (the here-and-now) and realizes that in talking about his wife he was referring to a denied transference to the therapist. Alternatively, the man may feel grateful that the therapist could make the connection to his experience with his mother (a positive contextual transference in the here-and-now), the opposite of how he feels about his troublesome mother of the past or his wife of the present (a negative direct object transference in the there-and-then and the here-and-then). If the man then goes on to contemplate divorcing his wife, the therapist might wonder if he is referring only to the here-and-then, or if he is covertly drawing attention to a shift toward a negative feeling of wanting to terminate treatment (a negative contextual transference in the here-and-now). Or is he fantasizing that in the future, the treatment relationship will sustain him should he decide to leave his wife (positive transference in the if-and-when dimension)?

CAN YOU GIVE AN EXAMPLE OF LOCATING THE TRANSFERENCE IN THE PATIENT OR IN THE THERAPIST?

If a depressed patient says that she feels fed up about being depressed like her father, her self has identified with her internal object. The object's transference to her self and her self's transference to her object are both expressed inside her. If the woman seems upbeat despite the de-

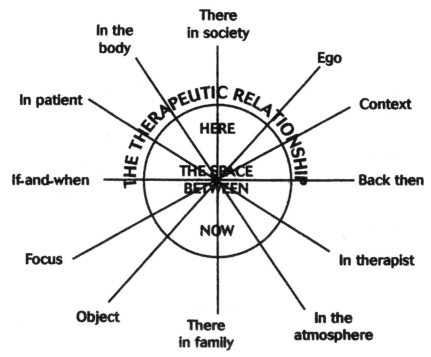

Figure 12.2. The Multidimensional Compass of the Total Transference and Counter-transference. Reprinted from *Object Relations Individual Therapy.* Copyright Jill Savege Scharff © 1998.

pressed things she is saying, but there is a depressed atmosphere in the therapy, the transference is contained in the space between therapist and patient and in the here-and-now. If the therapist feels a knot in her stomach, the there-and-then material is also present in the here-and-now, contained in the body of the therapist and not in the woman.

CAN YOU REPRESENT TRANSFERENCE GEOGRAPHY VISUALLY?

Some of us don't like to read maps but find a compass more useful. When we sense unfamiliar territory, that's a good time to pull out the compass and orient ourselves. Figure 12.2 uses a compass format to summarize the elements we want to observe.

NOTES

For clinical illustration, see chapter 16.
Transference (Freud 1905a).
Countertransference (Freud 1910a).
Countertransference and projective identification (J. Scharff 1992).
Geography of the transference (J. Scharff and D. Scharff 1998).
The therapeutic relationship (Jacobs 1991).

RELATION TO OTHER THEORETICAL SYSTEMS AND CLINICAL APPROACHES

HOW DOES BRITISH OBJECT RELATIONS THEORY RELATE TO OTHER THEORIES?

British object relations theory is one of the psychoanalytic theories of the personality.

HOW IS IT THE SAME AS AND DIFFERENT FROM FREUD'S CLASSICAL PSYCHOANALYTIC THEORY?

It is the same in that it rests on the concept of a dynamic unconscious that Sigmund Freud's theory provided, but it is different in that it has departed from the instinctual basis of that theory. Freud held that human beings are motivated by unconscious instinctual sexual and aggressive drives that aim for discharge and seek gratification by an available object (namely, the mother) so that the personality can return to a comfortable state of being in which homeostasis is restored. He thought that we seek objects principally to gratify impulses. In contrast, British object relations theory holds that the human infant is motivated by the need to be in relationship with the mother and her partner, separately and as a couple, and with important family members. Object relations theorists see the drives as deriving their meaning and energy in the context of relationships. They do notice the phenomena of sexual and aggressive impulse discharge outside of the context of relationships, but instead of regarding these as instinctual, they see them as the products of relationship breakdown, rather than as the building blocks of relationships.

Despite this fundamental difference in theory, Freudian theory and British object relations theory in practice share a number of techniques, including working with the unconscious, following the affect, valuing insight, dealing with transference, working with dreams and fantasy material, and communicating most effectively through interpretation. British object relations theory, however, puts more emphasis on analysis of the countertransference as the vehicle for understanding the patient's personality difficulties.

IS OBJECT RELATIONS THEORY LIKE KOHUT'S SELF PSYCHOLOGY THEORY?

Self psychology is a theory of the self put forth by Heinz Kohut. Object relations theory and self psychology theory are interested in the development of the self and how it is affected by the quality of the object. Both theories recognize that our capacity to understand the object is much advanced over our capacity to understand the self. Since the self is a private thing experienced only inside oneself, it is much harder to observe that self in action than it is to observe the action of the internal object relationships that are being expressed in the interpersonal realm. Both theories value introspection and empathy, but self psychology emphasizes the concept of empathic understanding based on the therapist's attunement to and identification with the patient's self, while object relations theory uses countertransference both to parts of the patient's self and to the various objects contained within it. Object relations theory uses the concept of projective identification to conceptualize the therapeutic re-creation of the internal object relationships in the transference.

In object relations theory, internal objects are in relation to parts of the self, bound together by affects, resulting in internal object relationships that are in dynamic relation. In self psychology, the self contains self-objects. The self-object is a psychic structure in which the internal object is used to support the cohesion of the self and to regulate the self's sense of well-being and self-esteem. Kohut's theory has usefully extended our understanding of the use of internal and external objects in clinical conditions due to problems of the self, namely splitting of the self in borderline states and narcissistic personality disorders. It has informed the therapist's sensitivity as to how to become the necessary object for such a patient. Similarly, Harry Guntrip, an object relations theorist, has contributed to understanding the splitting of the self that happens when the libidinal ego has deeply regressed to the point of withdrawal, resulting in a sense of loss of the self. Like Kohut, he recommended the provision of a therapeutic relationship sensitively attuned to this level of self-functioning. Both theories agree that the security of the self lies at the center of psychological health, but object relations theory regards the self-object, that is, the one-way use of an object as a support for the self, not as a healthy structure but as a breakdown in the mutuality of self and object in a relationship in which each should be of use to the other. Self psychology has not explored the reciprocity between self and object, and therefore we have found it less applicable than object relations theory to couple and family therapy, although Marion Solomon and Mel Lansky have used it in treatment of the borderline and narcissistic marriage.

Kohut's exploration of the development of the self and the way that a person needs his or her objects as self-objects in order to form a coherent, reliable, and mature self is a great contribution to the understanding of the development of the self and to the therapist's role in clinical work focused on problems of the self. His ideas supplement Guntrip's work on deep schizoid problems focusing on loss of the self. In summary, the work of Kohut and his school focuses exclusively on the use of the self-object by one person's self.

In object relations theory, we are interested in reciprocity: That is, wherever there is a self relating to an object, there is also an object relating to the self. When one person relates to another, the process is mutual, and resulting interactional and interpersonal processes affect the development of both persons involved. Reciprocity between self and object occurs simultaneously in the interpersonal and intrapsychic realms. When the self psychologists consider all problems to relate to the coherence and resilience of the self using the self-object, they consider only one-half of this mutual and resonating process. So self psychology has been appreciated for understanding the problem of narcissism, whereas object relations theory has been criticized for assuming relatedness.

DOESN'T TOO MUCH EMPHASIS ON PROJECTIVE IDENTIFICATION OVERLOOK PROBLEMS OF NARCISSISM?

We can be so engaged in problems of how the self deals with its objects that we can overlook problems of how the self relates to itself as its primary object. In narcissism there is an insistence that the other person be there to service and admire oneself. At the same time, there is a conviction or despair that the other person will not be willing or able to do so. So the person has to find this within the self. Then the self's inner world predominates over the interests of the other person. The intrapsychic dimension is not in free communication with the interpersonal field.

We see narcissism as a state of blocked projective identification. The narcissistic person is unable to use the healthy end of the projective identification continuum to develop empathy for others and has little capacity for introspection based on having understood the self in relation to others and their experience. In narcissistic self-relating, the self cannot take in a suitable object and introjectively identify with it.

Too much emphasis on projective identification also overlooks the process of introjective identification, an equally important psychic mechanism that has been largely ignored. Introjective identification refers to the taking in of experience with others and using it to build psychic structure. The process of introjective identification operates along a continuum from healthy selective identification to pathological excessive, unintegrated introjection. Since introjective identification is happening inside the self, it is harder for us to see it occurring than projective identification, which can be noted in terms of its effects on objects outside the self. In narcissism, the self is stuck without the normal cycle of mutually influential projective and introjective identificatory processes shaping the personality, interacting with the outer world, adapting, accommodating to others, and developing a modified reality within the self.

HOW IS BRITISH OBJECT RELATIONS THEORY DIFFERENT FROM THE AMERICAN OBJECT RELATIONS THEORY OF KERNBERG, MAHLER, JACOBSON, AND MASTERSON?

In addition to a formidable grasp of Freudian psychoanalytic theory including American ego psychology, Otto Kernberg knew the work of Melanie Klein, Ronald Fairbairn, and Wilfred Bion especially thoroughly. He used Edith Jacobson's work as the springboard from which he blended American ego psychology with British object relations theory. Donald Rinsley based his object relations approach on Fairbairn. The developmental research of Margaret Mahler on the phases of separation and individuation of the infant from the mother contributed to understanding the development of object relations in early childhood. Taken together, these theoretical contributions have been the mainstream of American object relations, notably applied by James Masterson to the treatment of character disorders, especially borderline personality syndromes.

British object relations theorists have not been interested in accommodating their theory to theories of drive and the development of the ego. They believe that most problems in human development and psychology concern the relationship between the self and its internal and external objects. Problems of ego functioning and adaptation, which captured American interest, are simply not focused upon. The intense interest in the use of transference and countertransference that characterizes British object relations therapy has not been echoed in the American clinical approach until recently.

British object relations theory views projective identification as a process with both normal and pathological aspects occurring along a continuum from health to paranoia, whereas in Kernberg's object relations theory, projective identification is almost always a psychotic or borderline phenomenon. Getting down to the technical nitty-gritty, in Kernberg's theory splitting is viewed as a more primitive mechanism of defense than is repression, which is regarded as typical of higher-level neurotic conditions. In British object relations theory splitting and repression are regarded as mechanisms that occur simultaneously in the formation of psychic structure; there cannot be one without the other.

In British object relations theory, there is less emphasis on diagnostic category. Splitting and repression are processes common to us all and are not divided up along diagnostic lines.

WAS LOEWALD AN OBJECT RELATIONS THEORIST?

No, Hans Loewald was a Freudian revisionist, but he has some features in common with the American object relations theorists. For instance, he didn't believe in the primacy of the instincts, and regarded sexuality and aggression as variables instead. He thought that the drives developed in interaction with the mother and he redefined Freud's concept of libido as a drive for affiliation and reunion with lost objects. His interest in the unity of consciousness and unconsciousness in the self is reminiscent of the object relations position.

WHERE DO GROTSTEIN, OGDEN, AND MITCHELL FIT?

They are American analysts who have been influenced by British object relations theory. James Grotstein is committed to a dual track theory of feeling and thinking/knowing derived from his integration of Fairbairn, Klein, and Bion. Like us, he is interested in the relevance of chaos theory for psychoanalysis. Thomas Ogden translated Klein's concept of projective identification, Frances Tustin's insights on autism, and Jacques Lacan's ideas about language for the American reader. To the continual movement between depressive and paranoid-schizoid positions, Ogden added the autistic-contiguous position (see figure 7.1 in chapter 7). He cautions against throwing away the concept of the drives because he is convinced of the instinctual basis for the search for objects and the organization of meaning. His most useful clinical contribution is the term *the analytic third* to describe the creation of a new entity contributed to by patient and analyst.

Influenced by Harry Slack Sullivan's interpersonal theory and Fairbairn's object relations theory, Stephen Mitchell's is a relational/conflict model of the personality being centered in, interacting with, and influenced by the human environment—character, constitution, and nurture, early experience and current relationships being equally important.

HOW DOES GROUP THEORY INFLUENCE OBJECT RELATIONS THEORY?

Group theory is quite crucial to the object relations approach. It amplifies the interpersonal expression of intrapsychic object relationships and it gives us the ability to apply object relations theory to the conjoint therapies (family, couple, and group therapy). The original group studies from which we draw are those of S. H. Foulkes and Wilfred Bion.

Bion held that a group has a conscious level of task organization in which the group cooperates with the leader's instructions to get the job done. The group also has an unconscious level of functioning, organized not by the task or the leader, but by subgroups that form according to assumptions about how to get shared needs met by the group, if not by the leader. Bion noted that various individuals in a group are attracted to each other to form these subgroups. He used the term *valency* for the individual's propensity for instantaneous combination with others in subgroupings. Bion described three main categories of subgroup formations organized around basic assumptions that sometimes support the task but more commonly interfere with it. See table 13.1.

In basic-assumption dependency, the group is dominated by a subgroup that expresses needs to be cared for and directed by the leader. In basic-assumption fight/flight, the subgroup is angry at the leader for not making everything perfect and wants to fight his authority, flee from the task set by the leader, or select a new leader or task. In basic-assumption

Table 13.1.   Bion's Basic Assumptions of Group Life

- Dependency
- Fight/flight
- Pairing to create a new leader

pairing, in frustration that individuals cannot have preferred pairing relationships with the leader, the group produces two individuals who pair
instead. The fantasy is that theirs will be a creative pairing to produce a
new leader who will save the group.

Our experience with family groups confirms the validity of Bion's basic assumptions and leads us to add a more basic assumption to Bion's
list. See table 13.2.

We find this assumption of fission/fusion operating in the threatened
family that regresses to a state of primitive merging (fusion) or splinter-
ing of the membership (fission). In fusion, merging substitutes for understanding and conflict resolution, whereas in fission, conflict attacks
linking and murders understanding. Like a group of people in group
therapy, the family that is stuck in dealing with its developmental task
can learn in family therapy to detect the basic-assumption interference
and attend to its unconscious needs and fears, so that the family can return to its current developmental work.

Bion himself made no explicit integration of his group work with his
individual theory-building about in-depth unconscious communication.
Putting together his individual concept of containment with his group
theory of valency and basic-assumption functioning, we can see that individuals are in unconscious communication with others based on their
shared object relations. The individual develops psychic structure from
experiences in important primary groups—the family, the peer group,
and the work group. The individual continues to find groups in which to
live and work and grow throughout the life cycle.

Foulkes pointed out that each member of a group acts like a node in a
grid. He said that the individual incorporates the group, and at the same
time the group reflects aspects of the individual. Integrating and applying Foulkes's and Bion's ideas to group behavior, we can describe the expression of individuals' internal object relations. The group, like the in-

**Table 13.2.   Bion's Basic
Assumptions Expanded**

- Dependency
- Fight/flight
- Pairing to create a new leader
- Fission/fusion

dividual, has a system of conscious and unconscious parts in dynamic relation. The individual is a system that includes an internal group.

DOES SOCIOLOGY HAVE AN INFLUENCE ON OBJECT RELATIONS THEORY?

From his background in sociology and psychoanalysis, Earl Hopper drew attention to the impact of the social unconscious on perception, development, and transference in psychoanalytic treatment, and he expanded Bion's theory of unconscious group life. Hopper noted that regressed groups that become incohesive oscillate between *massification* (individuals clumped together like a lump of soft clay) and *aggregation* (individuals totally separate like marbles in a pouch). He called it the *fourth basic assumption.*

CAN YOU GIVE AN EXAMPLE OF THE FOURTH BASIC ASSUMPTION IN GROUP LIFE?

Let's take a family as an example of group life. The parents came for help because their sixteen-year-old daughter, who was attractive, well spoken, and gifted in computer science like her father, was nevertheless failing in high school and had no friends. Their thirteen-year-old daughter, already in a full-day treatment school, was a moderately severely autistic girl who paced constantly, made odd gestures with her hands, hooted frequently, and had no words. The mother worked full-time and the father worked at home, ostensibly because he could capitalize more effectively on his bursts of creative genius, but also to feel near his family. The parents were distant from the members of their families of origin, except for the mother's father on whom they depended financially, but they were extremely close to each other in the nuclear family.

When the thirteen-year-old was to come for an individual session, the whole family accompanied her. In family sessions, all of its members were so intent on reducing the disruption and confusion she brought with her behavior that it was hard for us to get a conversation going. In clinging together, the family showed massification, an adaptation to the confusion and constant threat of incohesion in the family. In being isolated at school, the sixteen-year-old expressed the family's tendency to aggregation against which they defended by massification.

HOW CAN OBJECT RELATIONS THERAPY BE INTEGRATED WITH A SYSTEMS APPROACH TO COUPLES AND FAMILIES?

Again, group theory is the key. The individual grows not only in relation to a mother, as so many theories emphasize, but grows within a family group. The individual takes in the experience with this family group to build an internal group of object relationships in a dynamic system. Thus the individual personality can be seen as comprising an internal system that then creates interaction with other internal systems in significant others. In this way object relations theory provides a bridge between individual, couple, and family that enables us to cross from one treatment modality to another.

HOW CAN THE SYSTEMIC FAMILY THERAPIST INTEGRATE THE NONDIRECTIVE OBJECT RELATIONS APPROACH?

The object relations approach requires you to try not to do too much. This could be a major difficulty if you are committed to an extremely interventionist model. If family therapists are interested in learning more from the family as to how to proceed, perhaps they will find it useful to back off and wait for the direction to emerge from within the here-and-now experience.

Leading family therapists describe a change in the family therapy field toward giving up the stance of knowing for certain what it is that the family requires for therapeutic process to occur, in favor of seeing the family not just as a source of information about its difficulty but also as a collaborative therapeutic resource. The object relations approach, based on a collaboration for growth in the matrix of the therapeutic relationship, can be quite useful in systems family therapy. We encourage the systems family therapist to develop the capacity to sit back and learn from the ongoing experience rather than having to know things ahead of time and impose things on the family system.

ISN'T THE HERE-AND-NOW EMPHASIS THE SAME AS IN EXPERIENTIAL THERAPY?

Like experiential therapy, object relations theory and therapy values the here-and-now. The difference is that in object relations therapy the here-and-now is connected to its roots in the past. Previous experience is re-created in the here-and-now. In object relations therapy, that connection has to be made. The unconscious influence of previous experience can be made conscious, so that a person can have control over current behaviors and ways of relating.

DO YOU AGREE THAT OBJECT RELATIONS THERAPY IS A FEMINIST APPROACH?

Object relations theory does not speak to issues central to the feminist position, such as poverty, powerlessness, physical abuse, sexual stereotyping, reproductive choice, the glass ceiling on earning, and so on. Object relations therapy does not regard itself as a political process, and the object relations therapist has no agenda more radical than analyzing the blocks to individual freedom. Nevertheless, feminist writer and therapist Deborah Lupnitz regards object relations family therapy as the psychoanalytic method closest to sharing feminist values, because our approach is nonauthoritarian and because we care about women's experience. Object relations theory and therapy fully values men, women, and children, and promises a fair and mutually facilitative approach that appeals to the feminist family therapist. Our approach does not qualify as feminist. On the other hand, it is not sexist. We value a humanistic stance equidistant between the sexes, committed equally to male and female development.

Feminist psychologists such as Nancy Chodorow, Carol Gilligan, and Jean Baker Miller criticized Sigmund Freud's and Erik Erikson's male-centered view of development as a progression from fusion to autonomy.

They said that those male theorists had failed to account for female development. Unlike men who value individual agency, women derive self-esteem from their responsiveness to the needs of others and their abilities to maintain relationships. From these observations, feminist psychologists conclude that the female self develops in a state of continued dynamic interaction with the mother and significant others. This finding is compatible with the tenets of object relations theory.

According to object relations theory, the self—whether male or female—develops in a relational matrix. There, the self ruthlessly uses the object for its relational needs. The resulting relationship provides the stuff of its being. As the infant matures, the self becomes capable of experiencing concern for the ruthlessly used object and repairing any harm done. The capacity for tending to the other and to the relationship between self and other characterizes the maturing self, whether the infant is male or female.

HOW IS A NONDIRECTIVE METHOD LIKE OBJECT RELATIONS THERAPY COMPATIBLE WITH BEHAVIORAL THERAPY AND SEX THERAPY?

We have written extensively about the integration of an object relations therapeutic approach with that of sex therapy grounded in a behavioral format. Object relations therapy can be integrated with other behavioral formats beyond that of sex therapy, but neither of us has had this experience. In sex therapy, the behavioral framework is set up and followed. When impasses occur in response to the behavioral strategy, the patient or couple is then asked to work associatively in the ordinary psychodynamic way. Psychodynamic understanding of the object relations history and its relational expression in the marriage is applied to the difficulties in behavioral progression. In practice, sex therapy involves not only a behavioral format of the type originated by William Masters and Virginia Johnson, but also a good deal of education about sexuality. Even this is compatible with a nondirective approach. When education is not sufficient for the couple to keep progressing, analysis of the unconscious factors must occur before learning is possible.

We remain nondirective at the unconscious level even when the format calls for a directive or educational approach at the conscious level. That is to say, we attend to the couple or family's reaction to our directive interventions. We continue to watch the flow of associations to guide us to underlying unconscious themes. We use our countertransference experience as the clue to the transference being expressed through difficulties in working with us. We then interpret the transference interference to the couple. In this way, we use analytic technique within a behavioral or psychoeducational format.

NOTES

This chapter reviews similarities and differences between object relations and other theories, from the psychoanalytic to the behavioral:

Self psychology (Kohut 1971, 1977).
The withdrawn self (Guntrip 1969).
The narcissistic marriage (Lansky 1981, Solomon 1989).
Object relations theory (Kernberg 1976, 1980).
Splitting and repression (Kernberg 1987).
Self and object representation (Jacobson 1965).
Separation-individuation and object relations (Mahler 1968).
Fairbairn's theory and American object relations theory (Masterson 1981).
The individual and the group (Foulkes 1948).
Unconscious assumption groups and valency (Bion 1959).
Feminist family therapy reacting to object relations family therapy (Luepnitz 1988).
Feminist psychological view (Chodorow 1978, Gilligan 1982, Miller 1991).
Behavioral sex therapy (Masters and Johnson 1970, Kaplan 1974).
Incohesion and the fourth basic assumption (Hopper 2003).

II

OBJECT RELATIONS THEORY
IN PRACTICE

14

PRINCIPLES OF ASSESSMENT

Assessment is a complicated, evaluative process that precedes the making of any therapy contract. During the assessment process, patient and consulting therapist review the person's difficulties, develop a tentative object relations formulation, and decide whether therapy is needed or wanted. If treatment is in order, the consulting therapist considers what therapy format to recommend, which modality, which combination of serial or concurrent modalities, and which family members wish to be treated. Individual, couple, or family assessment may require only one interview, but more commonly it spans two to four. The assessment process offers the therapist a chance to get to know the patient and/or family and it gives them a chance to get to know the therapist. The question of fit between patient or patient group and therapist should be considered. Sometimes the individual or family will prefer referral for therapy to a colleague with whom a better fit can be expected. The therapist has not made any commitment to the patient at this point and is free to be quite objective in making observations and recommendations. Assessment also operates as a minitrial of therapy that gives the patient a sample of therapeutic process on which to base the decision about future needs for therapy.

WHAT ARE THE FEATURES OF
THE ASSESSMENT PROCESS?

The assessment process covers eight major areas. See table 14.1.

Provision of Therapeutic Space

First we set the *frame* of treatment. We agree on the appointment date and time and the length of the consultation session or sessions. Over the period of the assessment, we demonstrate our commitment to being available predictably and consistently and our openness to discussing any points of disagreement in dealing with the frame and any problems in relating to us. Within this frame, we provide a comfortable space that we call the *therapeutic holding environment.*

Our main effort goes not into discovering a whole lot of information about the patient but, rather, simply creating an environment that the patient can move into comfortably so that the patient can share private information with the therapist. We listen without judgment and without pursuing a systematic line of inquiry. We follow the patient's train of thought and notice those thoughts or memories that connect to feelings. We follow the affect to its sources in the object relations history. By our interest in hearing all about the patient, our relaxed attitude to whatever may emerge, and our willingness to experience pain and then make sense of it, we offer *containment for anxiety.* The patient and therapist join in assessing the patient's psychodynamics, motivation, and therapeutic capabilities.

Assessment of Developmental Phase and Level

From the way that the patient relates to us, in the anxious situation of crossing the boundary from life into the consulting room, we can see op-

Table 14.1.   The Eight Major Tasks of Assessment

1. Provision of therapeutic space
2. Assessment of developmental phase and level
3. Demonstration of defensive function
4. Exploration of unconscious assumptions and underlying anxiety
5. Working with dreams and fantasies
6. Use of transference and countertransference
7. Testing of response to interpretation and assessment format
8. Making a formulation, recommendation and treatment plan

erating the predominant developmental phase echoed in the form of the repressed object relationships and coloring the patient's personality. For instance, a person who has unresolved issues at the oral level of development may be somewhat clinging or may use words as weapons or as seductive objects with which to hook the therapist. Someone who has unresolved issues at the anal phase tries to control what the therapist may or may not say. We may note the showing off and physical display of the patient with issues at the phallic-oedipal level of development.

Stages of Psychosexual Development

Oral, anal, phallic, and oedipal psychosexual stages of development were described by Sigmund Freud. He said that they arose according to a predetermined sequence as the drives change their character and shift the erogenous zone of their expression.

Ronald Fairbairn preferred to relate the psychosexual stages to techniques of relating. For instance, a woman at the oral level relates in a heavily dependent way even when in conflict about such dependency, whereas one operating at an anal level is more interested in control of the object and access to the object. The man with oedipal-level conflict will trust his therapist and be able to manage separations from therapy, but may fear the therapist's retaliation if he competes successfully.

An object relational assessment of phases of development focuses on the patient's capacities for relating. We assess the use of *transitional techniques* for seeking the good and avoiding the bad in handling relationships according to table 4.1 in chapter 4. We look for whether the self locates the good and bad objects inside or outside the self and whether it seeks or avoids them. We look for evidence of function in the paranoid-schizoid and depressive positions, which we described in chapter 7. The vigilance of the paranoid-schizoid approach is appropriate in the opening moments of assessment before the therapist has earned trust. The concern of the depressive position is revealed in the attitudes expressed about important figures in the patient's life and, by giving a full account, showing concern for the therapist's need to hear the story and understand it. We check out attachment style, based on the history of relationships, the way the story is told, and the expectations about us that the patient has. A person with autonomous/secure attachment expects us to be reliable and consistent. That person tells a coherent story. People with in-secure attachment may obscure details, gloss over facts, interrupt the narrative flow with pauses, hesitations, and slips, and wonder if we will be there for them. We note whether the insecurity leads the person to dismiss us (avoidant/dismissive), cling to us (resistant/preoccupied) or do both at once (anxious/ambivalent), or in a state of grave insecurity, induce in us a state of confusion or disconnection (disorganized/unresolved).

Demonstration of Defensive Functioning: Projective Identification

As we work, even in the course of one interview, we will notice some repetitive patterns whereby the patient, couple, or family acts toward therapist or family member in a characteristic way to defend against the anxiety of being in a therapeutic situation. We point out the pattern when we first notice it and again when we see it repeated. We try to re-late the behavior to the object relations history. We look for ways in which the patient is projecting into the therapist and identifying parts of the self or the objects in the person of the therapist. Then we show the patient that these projective identifications are happening as an attempt to communicate with the other person and as a way of defending against anxiety in the relationship. We find that the interpersonal behavior be-tween patient and therapist, or between members of a family, or be-tween family and therapist, reflects the internal object relations set.

Exploration of Unconscious Patterns, Internal Object Relations, and Underlying Anxiety

To look for evidence of repressed object relationships, we listen to the clinical material, follow the affect, and observe and experience the pa-tient or patient group in relation to ourselves. In the individual session, we review the patient's current and former relationships. If these are not addressed spontaneously, we will remark on their absence and ask for elaboration. We point out recurring patterns that are reported as occur-ring with significant others and that are directly observable in relation to ourselves, and we show that these serve a defensive purpose. We then speculate as to what anxiety is being defended against. In therapy with couples and families, we note the interactions among family members and the way that the family as a group deals with us. These interactions tend to occur in a pattern that defends against shared underlying anxiety and takes form as shared unconscious assumptions about the requirements of family life.

Working With Dreams and Fantasies

We might not expect a spontaneous sharing of dreams and fantasies in assessment, but we certainly always let patients know that this is part of our area of examination. Dream and fantasy material may give access to deeper issues than can be fully addressed during the assessment process. Nevertheless, some work with dreams lets us begin to assess the unconscious fantasies and internal object constellations, which are not directly observable and yet determine conscious behavior, and it gives the patient an opportunity to see what can be done with psychodynamic technique. This use of dreams and fantasies does not stand alone but is interpolated with all the other material to arrive at a first approximation of unconscious organization. This assessment work gives the patient a chance to evaluate the usefulness of therapy.

Use of Transference and Countertransference

We remain alert at all times to the effect that the patient or family is having upon us. We monitor our feelings and, from within our own experience, try to make sense of the patient's effect on us and on others in important relationships. We might even make a trial countertransference-based interpretation of the transference during the assessment process. (See also chapter 16.)

Testing Response to Interpretation and to the Assessment Format

When we have made some supportive remark, linking comment, or interpretation, we watch to see how the patient responds to what we have said. We may have to make further interpretations to help patients get beyond their resistance to the area of interpretation. Other patients will respond quite favorably and use the interpretive work to get to a deeper level. In either case we are interested in how patients work in the interpretive mode, so as to determine whether object relations therapy is going to be suitable and productive.

We are also interested in how the person responds to the frame of the assessment process. Some patients will reveal tendencies to cancel a session, come late or early, renegotiate times, forget to pay fees, object to billing policies, or otherwise attempt to change the conditions that we have established for the assessment process. We work interpretively with these attempts to bend the frame. We understand that their aim is to undo the importance of the assessment intervention and reduce its power. Patients respond to the frame in this way in order to protect themselves from their understandable anxiety about what will be revealed if the assessment process is allowed to proceed in the precise and efficient way originally planned.

Making a Formulation, Recommendation, and Treatment Plan

From our experience with the patient and information given to us, we make a tentative formulation of the object relations. We decide whether this person's object relations set requires treatment. If it does, we then recommend the appropriate level of therapy and the format that is applicable. We might recommend individual psychotherapy, individual psychoanalysis, couple therapy, family therapy, group therapy, group analysis, or any of these in an effective combination. We negotiate this with the patient and when an agreed-upon plan is arrived at, we are then ready to move to a therapeutic contract.

CAN YOU ILLUSTRATE WORK WITH DEFENSE, ANXIETY, COUNTERTRANSFERENCE, AND INTERPRETATION TO DEMONSTRATE THE OBJECT RELATIONS SET OF A COUPLE DURING ASSESSMENT?

This illustration comes from a consultation that we did together. It was a two-session assessment for couple therapy with Michelle and Lenny, referred by Lenny's individual therapist. Aspects of this assessment have been described by David Scharff in *Refinding the Object and Reclaiming the Self* and by Jill Scharff in *Clinical Handbook of Couple Therapy*. Michelle and Lenny had been together for four years, but Michelle, an outgoing social activist, had been unable to marry quiet, conservative Lenny because he seemed so passive. A nice, attractive man from an upper-class family more advantaged than her own, successful in business, and loyal to her, he had many appealing qualities. He treated her well, he adored her no matter how she treated him, no matter how fat she allowed herself to get, but she hated his steadfastness and was full of contempt for his passivity. No way could he meet her expectations. She wanted a man like her amazingly energetic, confident, and admirable brother, whereas the most Lenny offered her was security and devotion. He loved her as much as she hated him. He was steady as a rock, always there, never changing: She was bubbling with energy, rushing along, full of ideas and vivacity. So why was she still with Lenny?

"Because I can't seem to dump the guy. He's a great boyfriend, classiest guy I've ever known," Michelle admitted. "But he is not the kind of man I'm attracted to. With him I'd be trapped in a boring marriage, always lighting a fire under his toosh!"

Lenny was not put off by her contempt for him. "I offer her security," he said proudly. "I am a rock, and she's a river running over it. I'll always be there for her. I love everything about her," he affirmed. "The way she speaks, the way she feels. I don't mind her being in the forefront: good protection! She's the world to me."

Provision of Therapeutic Space

And so they went on, their hectic bantering creating a hilarious routine that made the therapists feel uncomfortably amused, fascinated, and appalled. Even though we were uncomfortable, we had to bear these feelings in order to create an accepting environment where the couple could behave in their usual way and we could be affected by their interaction.

Developmental Phase and Level

Michelle and Lenny were concerned with issues of holding on and letting go. They are at the developmental phase of formation or dissolution of the ambivalently viewed premarital couple and their developmental mode of relating is at the anal level. Through her overeating, Michelle cannot let go of this unsatisfactory relationship to risk new opportunities, and she holds on to food stores, in case of feelings of deprivation should she let go of Lenny. Lenny sees himself as a rock.

Demonstration of Defensive Function: Projective Identification

We showed how Lenny adored Michelle as his mother had adored him. In her, he found a projected, lost part of his ego, while he was identified with his own object. At the same time, Michelle felt that Lenny's passivity was pushing her to be a mother to him, and she adamantly refused to go along with that. It would have re-created for her the envied relationship between her own mother and her brother who had everything. Their projective identificatory system was fashioned from unconscious communication of their repressed internal object relations seeking expression, confirmation, and modification, but having to be avoided.

Exploration of Unconscious Patterns, Internal Object Relations, and Underlying Anxiety

In this case, we demonstrated the defensive pattern of their way of relating and their underlying anxiety by studying the effect on the countertransference experienced in cotherapy between the cotherapists.

Use of Transference and Countertransference

I (Jill) made a determined effort to engage with the couple actively and seriously, while my cotherapist (David), who is normally rather energetic, almost fell asleep. Both of these responses reflected our wish to avoid the pain of being with them: mine was closer to the defensive structure of their relationship; David's response was closer to the underlying anxiety. His examination of his countertransference response led to our talking about the underlying sadness in the couple's relationship. Manic defenses had been projected into and identified with by

Michelle and me, while the passivity and depression and been projected into and identified with by Lenny and David. The couple's defenses had been split into manic and depressive components, projected into each other. These had now been projected into the cotherapy relationship, and distributed between the cotherapists along gender lines rather than according to the therapists' usual valencies for accepting projections. The therapists were able to discuss their experience in the session and interpreted the defensive projective identificatory system as a defense against the void the couple would face if their destructive bantering were to stop.

Testing the Response to Interpretation

Immediately the couple responded to our interpretation with a change in the level of affect.

"It's like the jazz bands playing at a funeral," Lenny confirmed, seriously.

Before returning to their defensive position later in the session, the couple was able to explore the void just a little. Lenny's void came from the lack of an active father when he was growing up. Michelle's came from her perception of herself as a girl who did not feel as secure with her mother as her brother did. So she wanted a man like her brother to complete herself, and he wanted a powerful, active woman to replace the adoring, protective mother and sisters he had depended on. Lenny had what he wanted, except that Michelle rejected his projective identification of her, whereas she did not have what she thought she wanted, but instead had someone, enviable like her brother and despicably lacking like herself, with whom to relive her frustration about what she lacked.

Work with Dreams and Fantasy

This couple did not bring in any dreams. Whereas in individual therapy, a prospective patient already expects the therapist to be interested in dreams, in couple therapy, we have to let the couple know of our interest. We did have access to plenty of unconscious material, including

Michelle's fantasy of an ideal man based on the model of her brother. Giving up that incestuous attachment would require work in future therapy.

Further Work on Developmental Phase and Level

"Lenny is so average," Michelle complained in their second session. "Average is boring. Whereas I'm special. So why do I hate myself? My mother did that to me. I used to dread being feminine. Now I wouldn't change it for the world. But I was such a tomboy. My brother has that specialness, but he has all the confidence to go with it. A complete winner! And I really envy him because of it. Because I'm missing that little part. There's a part of me that constantly finds holes in herself."

To an analyst, these words speak of penis envy from the phallic stage of development. Usually we address this issue in the broader terms of envy of the man's world. But in this case, both aspects of Michelle's envy were close to consciousness.

"Whatever it is that he has—the confidence that makes him a complete mensch—I'm missing," she added.

"You feel this envy for Lenny, too, as his mother's great little kid," I suggested to Michelle.

But it was Lenny who answered.

"Yes," said Lenny. "In my family, I'm the confident male. In her family, it's her brother. But he's self-confident, cocky. He knows he's good. I'd love to be him, myself."

"Lenny doesn't have that confidence," Michelle continued. "When he's called upon to be a mensch, he can be in certain cases, but not where it counts to me."

"What about where it counts in bed?" I retorted, recalling her feelings about the penis and what it meant to her.

For once Michelle was nonplussed. "You talk about that, dear," she said, yielding the floor to Lenny.

Now we learned that in bed Lenny was the confident sexual partner who had shown great sensitivity to Michelle's vaginismus. He helped her to tolerate intercourse and find sexual release with him. He found her beautiful whether she was fat or thin. For Michelle, who hated her body, Lenny's adoration was both gratifying and contemptible.

"Sex is a pain to me, but I'm as comfortable with Lenny as I can be," Michelle said with resignation. "You know, for a girl who had penis envy as a child, I hate them now. So there's something obviously wrong with me."

"One thing about Lenny you appreciate is that he doesn't force himself on you powerfully in intercourse," I said.

Michelle said, "Right. He's very good to me."

I said, "But as a child, you saw the penis as a source of power."

"I don't remember anything about the penis itself," Michelle corrected me.

I had taken my cue from her use of the words "penis envy." But Michelle had generalized her envy.

"I mean the boy's world," I amended. "The things boys had that you didn't. What I'm saying is that now that you've taken possession of your adult femininity and enjoy a woman's world, it's sad for you that you can't take pleasure from the penis, because you still see it as a source of envied and threatening power."

Michelle said, "I see it as an intrusion! I hate it. I've come a little distance, but I used to see it as a man sticking it to a woman."

I said, "Now you don't *see* it that way, but you still *feel* it like that."

Michelle said, "Not as much as I did before. I used to see it as another way of a man's control, which I hate. But it's never, ever been like that with Lenny."

Making a Dynamic Formulation

Applying Freudian theory, we can say that as a child, Michelle had thought that a boy like her brother did not feel the ache that she felt for her rejecting mother. She imagined that he did not feel empty as she did because he had the penis that she was missing, while her vagina felt like an empty hole. In her adulthood, the penis continued to be threatening because it could enter that painful hole. That childhood hatred for the penis, she now felt toward the man in her adult sexual relationship. The better Lenny did with her sexually, the more she had to attack him enviously. Lenny, though sexually competent, had some inhibition against being assertive generally and sexually, and used Michelle as a phallic front for himself so that he could avoid castration anxiety. Taking care of her sore vaginal opening reminded him that his penis was not causing damage and therefore would not be damaged in retaliation.

In object relations terms, each was using Michelle as a manic defense against emptiness and sadness. Each was using Lenny as a depository for the schizoid defense against emptiness. The pain of the void was projected into Michelle's vagina for which she had a psychophysiological valency, and their shared longing for healing of the void was focused on attention to her sexual dysfunction. In therapy they would need to take back these projective identifications of each other and develop a holding capacity for bearing their shared anxieties.

Response to Assessment Format: Making a Recommendation and Treatment Plan

The couple's response to the assessment format reflected their ambivalence about staying together. In their first interview, they worked well with the therapists and seemed to benefit from the insight they got. But they did not want to return. Then they called for a second appointment, after which they again wanted no more contact. When we discussed the possibility of couple therapy, we were not surprised that Michelle seemed reluctant: to her it implied a couple commitment that she did not want emphasized. We recommended that Michelle and Lenny each continue their individual therapies, and that Michelle increase her individual sessions.

CAN YOU SHOW HOW A DREAM IS USEFUL IN INDIVIDUAL ASSESSMENT?

A dream may introduce a topic that the child can't face consciously, or it may serve as an elaboration of the child's conflicted relationships. In the vignette that follows, the child's dream and his associations link his symptom to his family relationships, his internal object relationships, and his transference to the therapist as a frightening teacher.

Mike was an eleven-year-old boy who was frightened to return to school after two years of home schooling. Mike talked easily about his family and his teachers. He said that he got along well with his mother, but that his father preferred his brothers. He said that the teachers at his old school were mean because they didn't give him extra time to move between classes when he was on crutches after surgery for a congenital hip problem. Taking his cue from this, the therapist gave Mike plenty of time to move between his various concerns, letting him talk and draw. When the therapist asked for a dream, Mike told his worst nightmare:

"I had to go to my old school and my mean old teachers were there. They said 'Come in! Don't you want us to teach you?' I said 'No,' but I couldn't get away. Then they said, 'We're really glad to see you. We're gonna get you, because we're gonna really give you a lotta homework.' I ran and got out of there."

After telling the dream, Mike compared the burdensome teachers at his old school to the wonderful teacher in another school. The therapist showed him how the two kinds of teacher were like the two kinds of parent that he had described. Mike held a split image of his parents: mother an ideal object to whom he was extremely close; and father the source of the rejecting, frightening internal object that Mike projected onto the teachers. His therapist guessed that Mike was already experiencing him in both these ways unconsciously, but he refrained from premature interpretation because Mike was not yet focused on the therapeutic relationship. Mike explained, "My Dad can't really help it. Both his parents are really mean. At least I have one really good parent, so I'll be able to love my kids and still be firm with them." Mike had split his images of his parents along lines determined by his reactions to their personalities, but his last comment shows that he understands that comfort and discipline should be integrated in dealing with children. This offers hope that Mike's internal objects will be modified in therapy.

HOW IS THE WORK THAT YOU DO IN ASSESSMENT DIFFERENT FROM THERAPY?

It is like therapy, but it is different in that it cannot have quite as free a form as therapeutic sessions that enjoy the luxury of having plenty of time.

In assessment, the therapist is sampling the patient's personality rather than experiencing it in its fullness. Nevertheless, assessment involves therapists in an examination of their responses to the task of connecting with the patient at the surface of the personality, which is often just as meaningful and revealing in its own way as the later in-depth engagement when the transference has developed. Another important distinguishing feature is that there is no commitment between patient and therapist. So, if the patient in assessment cancels an appointment, we do not charge for the missed time. During assessment, time is sold on an item for service basis rather than for long-term commitment. The significance of the move from assessment to therapy is emphasized by the shift in policy.

Some therapists are more active during the assessment phase than they would be later in therapy. For instance, a therapist may feel that a patient is working well in one area of exploration. This tells the therapist that the person can work in this area, while others are untested. The therapist may tactfully interrupt to point out that other areas are being ignored or may simply inquire about them to complete the picture. For instance, a patient may be talking usefully about family relationships, but avoid the topic of sexual adjustment. In therapy, sexual issues would emerge in due course, but in the assessment phase, it could well be important to ask directly about sexual relating. We do, however, limit the amount of direct questioning, because it interferes with the unconscious flow. The same considerations regarding questioning apply to confrontation or interpretation. The therapist, during the assessment phase, may decide to confront or interpret in order to see how the patient accepts or works with it, while in therapy there is more emphasis on waiting for the right moment to give an interpretation. Nevertheless we try to follow the patient's associative flow in the assessment process, much as we do in therapy, acknowledging, however, that there will be times when we need to interrupt and broaden our focus in order to get a comprehensive assessment.

WHAT IS THE ROLE OF
HISTORY-TAKING IN ASSESSMENT?

We do not advise taking a formal history because we find this generates answers to our questions rather than allowing the patient to generate questions for therapy. We prefer to ask questions about history at moments when that history is alive in the room, for example, at a moment of affect when the patient is talking about a current relationship. We suspect that the current relationship carries a charge from an earlier relationship. We find that this is an advantageous moment to introduce the question of history.

DO YOU USE GENOGRAMS?

Some psychoanalytic marital therapists, such as Christopher Dare, do use genograms. We, however, do not use genograms. As with formal histories, we find that genograms generate information out of context. A person who has a lot of experience taking genograms may make good use of this way of getting the wider picture, but we have found it better to work with affect and transference to generate the information about transgenerational transmission of problematic areas of thought, feeling and behavior.

On the other hand, during an assessment and usually in the first interview, we generally ask about the relationship to parents and the family of origin, if the information has not emerged spontaneously. Here we are not looking for a comprehensive history but simply for a description of parents as individuals and as a couple and a sense of how they related to their child. During the course of therapy, we would ask about the relationship of an event in current life to experience with parents, specifically after working on its reverberation in the transference, when meaningful internal object information will be linked to healing.

DO YOU ANSWER DIRECT QUESTIONS FROM
THE PATIENT DURING THE ASSESSMENT PROCESS?

Questions relating to the management of the therapy should always be answered. For instance, "Will you accept my insurance? What is your fee and billing practice? When do you take your vacations?" At the same time one bears in mind any unconscious significance that these issues might have for the patient. Another question that must routinely

be answered pertains to the therapist's professional training and qualifications. While personal questions about marital status, children, reli-
gious or political affiliation will not be answered, questions about previous clinical experience and professional background and training call
for an open response. Patients have a right to know the qualifications
of the therapists to whom they will be making a commitment. Any request for consultation from a colleague should be honored and facilitated. Patients have a right to a second opinion, particularly in the con-
sultative phase and when therapy seems stuck. And they also have a
right to shop around to get the therapist best suited to their needs. We
may regret the added stress on us that we face when a patient may
choose to reject us and work with someone else. Nevertheless, it is in
the best interest of the patient and the ensuing therapy that we cooperate with this process.

While all these questions and issues receive a forthright answer, at the
same time the therapist wants to bear in mind their reflection of the patient's unconscious issues. Maintaining the balance of considering and
perhaps interpreting the unconscious issues while addressing the practical matters openly is, of course, a delicate matter.

HOW DO YOU MAKE A DIAGNOSIS FOR
THIRD-PARTY PAYERS?

The requirements of the insurance companies and other interested
third parties have to be met, when that is the patient's wish. We cooperate fully in meeting these economic requirements and at the same
time discuss them openly with the patient. If a diagnosis must be written down, we discuss the choice and its implications with the patient.

When we make an object relations assessment of the patient, we come
up with a psychoanalytic formulation that we do not share with the third
party payer. To some extent we put on a different hat in order to arrive
at the diagnosis that fits the DSM IV requirements. Working with the patient to review the symptomatology, we choose a relevant diagnosis that
will justify the patient's treatment needs and warrant reimbursement.

Like all therapists, we regret the invasion of privacy that managed care
and insurance reimbursement introduces into the therapeutic process.

We share patients' concern, in this age of computer theft, that their material will not be kept confidential from employers and future employers. So, we discuss with patients the risks, we show them what we are thinking of writing on the insurance form, and arrive at a suitable adjustment to the realities.

HOW DO YOU HANDLE PEER REVIEW?

Many of these same issues apply to peer review, which may occur at the point of assessment or later on. Here, every effort must be taken to ensure confidentiality and privacy for the patient. Sometimes, a longer narrative report of the psychodynamics and personal issues is requested. Such information must be separated from the patient's actual identity and submitted in an appropriately anonymous way. All of this must be discussed with the patient for protection of the patient's privacy and for the legal protection of the therapist.

In these days of managed care and the national collection of insurance data, mental health professionals need to be particularly circumspect. We find that the safest course is to give the smallest amount of detail that will permit the patient to qualify for reimbursement and to discuss this fully with the patient. We advise the patient that, after years of discussion in committee, there are laws to protect individual privacy, but we do not feel at all reassured. We warn patients about the risks of applying for reimbursement and then we work together to minimize the intrusion into their privacy.

WHAT DO YOU MEAN BY ESTABLISHING A FRAME FOR THE ASSESSMENT PROCESS?

At the end of the assessment process, we establish a treatment plan. Within this plan, there is a format in which the treatment will take place. By format, we refer to the plan for, let's say, twice-weekly individual therapy, once-a-week couple therapy, or an agreed-on combination of therapies. Once the plan is set, we stick to it, and we do not switch to a different plan unless it is clearly indicated and thoroughly discussed. We establish a fee, how the fee will be paid, a time by which the fee will be paid, and a series of meeting times that will be regularly kept. We start and end the appointment on time. In this way we demonstrate the clarity of the boundaries of the therapeutic space.

It is important to establish a clear frame at the outset so that both patient and therapist understand the initial conditions for establishing therapy. Then we are in a position to examine deviations from the frame. This does not mean that a plan may not be changed later on. But it will be changed by discussion and design rather than by "accidental" infringements brought about by the patient's unconscious acting out. Similarly, of course, we expect that the therapist will not infringe on the frame either. When the therapist fails to hold the frame, she undermines its usefulness as a fruitful stage of examination and makes it hard to encourage the patient to examine and learn from infringements on the frame.

NOTES

The task of assessment is to create an environment for personalized exploration that takes account of the short time frame and limited focus and yet is sufficiently open-ended to give a fair sample of the work of any future therapy:

Psychosexual stages (Freud 1905).
Analytic family therapist's use of the genogram (Dare 1986).
Confidentiality (Bollas and Sundelson 1995).
This chapter is mainly a clinical introduction to principles that are addressed and referenced in the next chapter.

⑮

TECHNIQUE I:
SETTING THE FRAME, IMPARTIALITY,
PSYCHOLOGICAL SPACE, AND
THE USE OF THE THERAPIST'S SELF

OVERVIEWS OF TECHNIQUE

In Technique I (chapter 15) we focus on the opening phase. We pay attention to creating a good holding environment in which psychological work can happen. We deal with resistance to acknowledging problems and with anxiety about the process of therapy. We listen and follow the words and the feelings. We notice repeating patterns of behavior, and speculate as to how these behaviors defend against specific anxiety, including the anxiety of being affected by us and being liked or rejected by us. We put negative feelings and fears about us into words to detoxify the threat that we pose and to build a trusting relationship.

In the midphase, described in Technique II (chapter 16), we work more openly with our feeling responses to the individual, family, or couple. We become wise to their ways of dealing with us. From our own feelings we detect their transference to us and we show them how it reflects earlier experience with people in their families of origin. We recreate the problem in the therapeutic relationship and explore it from every angle and in every version.

In Technique III (chapter 17) we describe continuing this exploration in greater depth by using our own reactions and by gaining access to dreams, fantasies, and, in the case of working with children, play. Working through in this way continues until termination is possible. Then we have a termination period in which we recap and revise the entire process of therapy.

WHAT ARE THE MAJOR ASPECTS OF TECHNIQUE?

We can summarize the elements of technique and put them in order of importance as therapy progresses (see table 15.1). In the opening phase, we are most concerned with *setting the frame* to allow therapy to begin on a sound footing. By listening attentively to whatever the patient brings to us but without judging or prejudging the issues, we *maintain a neutral position of involved impartiality*, and create *a psychological space with good holding and containment*, just as we do in assessment. As therapy extends over time this space becomes one in which it is safe for *transference and countertransference* to be expressed and experienced in the countertransference. This is where the *use of the therapist's self* comes in. We fine-tune our awareness of our reactions and use them to understand how the patient has perceived others, related to them, and affected them.

It takes personal analysis or therapy, supervision, and clinical experience to prepare our therapeutic self as a therapeutic instrument that is sensitive, receptive, and responsive. We use the instrument primarily for detecting and modifying the transference. We recognize that we are in the grip of transference when a powerful emotion or behavior is

Table 15.1.   Elements of Technique of Object
Relations Therapy

Setting the frame
Maintaining a position of neutral, involved impartiality
Creating a psychological space for work
Using the therapist's self
Using transference and countertransference
Working with dream and fantasy
Interpreting defense, anxiety, and inner object relations
Working through
Termination

evoked in us by projective and introjective identification, and as a result we are induced to take on a particular role relationship with the patient (our countertransference). Together we have created an interpersonal rendition of the patient's internal object relationship right there in the session for us to examine (the transference/countertransference dialectic).

We hope to be given access to *dream and fantasy* life, which takes us closer to understanding the unconscious. With history, current information, and personal experience in the here-and-now, we recognize repeating patterns of defensive *resistance* to recovery of conflict and upsetting memories, and then develop hypotheses about the nature of the underlying anxiety that calls for these defenses. We figure out whether anxiety is connected to external impingements or internal conflict at the level of the object relationships. We set our sights on gathering the transference because this is the fulcrum for change (for elaboration see chapter 12). Over time working at the surface and the depth, in the past and in the present, in the potential space between patient and therapist, in the transference and in the countertransference, we go through many repetitions of recognition, experience, and interpretation. This *working through* at many levels and locations stabilizes change. Then the patient is ready to begin the work of *termination*.

Now let us go back to the beginning and devote the rest of this chapter to establishing the treatment space.

ESTABLISHING THE FRAME OF TREATMENT

Robert Langs described the need for a frame, consisting of psychological boundaries and agreed conditions under which therapy will take place. John Zinner applied his ideas of the frame to describe the use of the flexible frame in family therapy. At the administrative level, the frame consists of the meeting times, the length of the meetings, the usual way of working, who will attend, fees, cancellation policy, and regularity of attendance. Once this is done, patient and therapist have made a commitment to an openly agreed-upon, acceptable framework in which to proceed. Nevertheless, the frame is not to be rigid. It remains flexible to suit changing needs and goals and can be modified by mutual agreement of patient and therapist.

Patients will often try to modify the frame without agreement by the therapist. The frame of the therapy itself becomes the stage for reenactments of the patient's inner object world, as repressed object relationships seek expression in relationship to the therapist. It is, therefore, important that the frame not be bent by patient or therapist and that attacks on the shape of the therapeutic frame be understood as enactments. This is different from the modification of the frame, that is, the frame kept flexible by mutual agreement as the therapist and patient think through changing needs as they are revealed during the course of the therapy.

WHAT IS RESISTANCE?

During therapy patients often express excuses as to why it is impossible to attend sessions, why they come late, and why they should not discuss certain topics. These behaviors are manifestations of resistance. *Resistance* is the term for the patient's effort to repress painful feelings and fantasies and keep them in the unconscious. An analysis of why patients need to defend themselves in these individually significant ways is known as *defense analysis*. Understanding fantasies of shame, embarrassment, or guilt should enable patients to feel more comfortable in revealing the repressed material. Working toward de-repression requires tact and firmness at the same time.

Harry Guntrip described a number of major sources of resistance. He said that resistance occurs when the adult part of the patient feels ashamed when experiencing the child part of the self in relation to the therapist. The main source of resistance to therapy is the tenacity with which we hold on to our libidinal attachments to our parents, no matter how troubled our actual relationships with them may have been. At first, patients long for their therapists to rescue them from their parents. Then they become afraid that they will meet their parents again in the person of the therapist. Lastly, when change seems possible, they fear that the therapist will rob them of their internal parents and expose them to the underlying void.

HOW IS THERAPY ESTABLISHED?

In the beginning phase of therapy, the therapist wants to listen to and learn from and about the patient. Rather than a barrage of questions, the therapist's enquiring attitude encourages the patient to reveal the problems for which therapy is sought and the nature of the patient's life, relationships, and inner conflicts. The therapist attends to conscious and unconscious material. We remain neutral as to what we find out. We are empathic, but not sympathetic, to the patient's basic needs. In this phase, as in other phases, we follow the patient's lead while noting our own internal responses, without necessarily doing or saying anything about them.

The therapist does take the lead, however, in the way of working. This means asking some questions about affective connections between current conflicts and past conflicts, and understanding the importance of current relationships and their connection to the object relations history.

HOW DO YOU CREATE A PSYCHOLOGICAL SPACE?

In the ways we have described, we use the safety of the therapeutic environment to create a psychological space inside us and between our selves and the patient. This space that communicates between self and other is comparable to Winnicott's "potential space." Into this space, aspects of the patient's internal and external worlds are brought for examination. Therapist and patient experience and observe their impact on each other and on the relationship between them. They play in the gap between patient and therapist to create new ways of perceiving and relating.

WHAT DO YOU MEAN BY THE TERM
INVOLVED IMPARTIALITY?

We apply Helm Stierlin's term *involved impartiality* to refer to our therapeutic attitude: We maintain a position, neutral as to symptomatology, goals, direction of the therapeutic process, and outcome. We remain equidistant between the conscious and unconscious parts of the patient's personality and equidistant in our temporary identification between self and object and between the various generations represented in the functioning of the internal object relationships affecting the transference. With previous experience and therapy, we prepare ourselves as the ground for object relating in which patients can discover themselves and grow. In other words, we make ourselves available for use as just the kind of object that the patient requires us to be in order to find him- or herself.

HOW DO YOU TAKE AN OBJECT RELATIONS HISTORY?

Some therapists stress an exhaustive history as an important part of an initial evaluation. In object relations therapy we, too, are interested in those aspects of a patient's past that illuminate the current conflict. Rather than trying to get an exhaustive developmental or relational history, however, we are more interested in asking an open-ended question, such as "What was it like for you?" For instance, when a couple comes with a marital conflict, we might ask what it was like for them to be growing up with their own parents and how were their parents' marriages experienced by each of them in childhood. Thus the history that we get relates to the internal object relations as they are expressed currently in everyday relationships and self-experience. We limit the ambition of our history-taking because we have found that a more exhaustive history is at such a distance from the patient's current emotional life as not to be particularly useful. We prefer to gather gradually a history of earlier relationships brought to mind at moments of affective intensity or impasse in the course of therapy, rather than getting an early catalog that will probably not be remembered by either the patient or the therapist.

HOW CAN YOU ENLARGE THE AREA OF OBJECT RELATIONS UNDERSTANDING?

In individual therapy, we encourage the patient to tell us more by our attitude of interest and by asking questions or making observations related to what the patient has already told us. As patients give us more pieces of information, we see links between them. Together, we work to understand more. For instance, if a patient has told us about a current conflict and then about a period of conflict during an earlier developmental period, we might ask how those two periods of time are similar or different. We might ask if there have been echoes in earlier adult developmental phases, or in the lives of members of the previous generation, especially the parents. We also suggest affective links between episodes as they occur to us, and then we wait for the patient to confirm or modify our hypotheses. Gradually we get an enlarged picture of the patients' external lives, their internal object relationships, and the links between these.

In couple and family therapy, we enlarge the field of observation by asking for the perspectives of all those present and giving each person a chance to speak. This has the same standing as asking individual patients to describe aspects of their lives from several points of view. Observations of all the participants in the room develop this shared family or marital view.

WHAT ABOUT USING THE HERE-AND-NOW VERSUS THE THERE-AND-THEN?

We especially value what we have called the *core affective exchange*. This occurs between patient and therapist, or in the conjoint therapies, among family members or between family and therapist, at an emotionally intense moment. This means that internal object relationships are alive in the here-and-now of the room, brought into the session in a full and immediate way. Experiencing these exchanges in the here-and-now gives us a more powerful way of understanding the individual, and couple or family relationships, than when experiences are reported as having occurred at some other time and place.

WHAT IS NEGATIVE CAPABILITY?

We also develop a capacity to be uncertain and not know exactly what is going on while we explore unknown, unformed, and anxious areas. This capacity has been called *negative capability*, a phrase that derives from John Keats's description of Shakespeare's poetic capacity for "being in uncertainties, mysteries and doubts without irritable reaching after fact and reason." Wilfred Bion applied this technique to his therapeutic stance. He encouraged therapists to be "without memory or desire" in relation to the patient. Christopher Bollas writes that it is the therapist's task to help the patient give form to the "unthought known," aspects of the self that have not been recognized in thoughts and words. We do not put words on them. We do not want to know any more than the patient does. We interpret the patient's blocks against knowing and thinking, so lost parts of the self can be rediscovered. We do not want our own therapeutic ambition to block the patient's search.

The therapist allows the therapeutic task to emerge from the patient, just as the mother allows her baby to explore. The mother needs to have an ideal of maturation and growth in mind, but she does not impose a form on it that would violate the baby's need to develop a self. This paradox of knowing and not knowing, of form and formlessness, is at the heart of therapy. Therapists can have their own values about growth, development, and maturation, but they prefer not to impose their own images of the improved patient, since this destroys the patient's self-discovery of what Bollas calls "the personal idiom."

At the same time "being without memory or desire" does not mean that the therapist is not to know anything. We do form hypotheses about the patient's conflicts and difficulties. These get tried out by being given as interpretations to the patient, who then works with them, and provides corrections, confirmations, or the conclusion that certain hypotheses do not fit with the patient's organization at all.

CAN YOU PROVIDE AN EXAMPLE FROM THE OPENING PHASE OF INDIVIDUAL THERAPY?

Mrs. Epstein (referred to again in chapter 20) originally consulted me (JSS) about her anxious eleven-year-old daughter, with whom she had a conflicted relationship. The relationship was exhausting and left Mrs. Epstein feeling fatigued, tearful, defeated, and "low as a skunk." It was important to Mrs. Epstein to be a good and loving person, and so it was terrible for her to feel that her daughter did not love her. She overfunctioned to take good care of her child. She was uncomfortably aware of her intense fears of something bad happening to the girl, and she had to engage in many obsessional rituals to prevent her fears from coming true. She could not admit to her underlying rage at her child. She was also unable to ask for therapy for herself.

The Flexible Frame

The frame for our working arrangement was that of a consultation with family interviews and individual interviews for Mrs. Epstein and for her child. This frame was impinged upon when Mrs. Epstein telephoned to ask for additional sessions for herself. I did not arrange these, but asked her to discuss her request in the next family meeting. Her husband, who had been aware of her depression and obsessions, was relieved that Mrs. Epstein wanted to talk to me, and a change in the frame was agreed. The consultation would be extended over a few more weeks, with two sessions a week for Mrs. Epstein, while her child completed psychometric and educational testing with a colleague, prior to the final interpretive session in which I would make my recommendations to them.

Object Relations History

In her individual extended assessment sessions, Mrs. Epstein linked her worry about her child to her own traumatic loss of her mother at the age of twelve. She had adored her mother and was devastated by her sudden death in a car crash. During the assessment phase, Mrs. Epstein also idealized me. Much later in subsequent treatment, she began to experience me as a remote and uncaring object, in a re-edition of her experience with a sad, withdrawn mother and a neglectful father.

Working with Defense and Anxiety about Destructiveness

Destructive wishes against her child (who stood both for her own bad self that might have caused her mother's death and for the mother who abandoned her) were being defended against by fear. After we had worked on this defense against destructive urges, Mrs. Epstein could discover and admit to her own impulses to harm her daughter. Mrs. Epstein now realized that she was depressed and needed help for herself more urgently than for her child, but she resisted making a commitment to therapy.

Working with Resistance

My first task was to create a safe environment in which Mrs. Epstein felt that her needs would be taken into account, as well as those of others in her family. She needed time to assess my commitment to her before she dared to open up to me, even though analysis was the form of treatment that she herself thought was her last hope. Reassured by my neutral attitude that I would neither judge her nor reject her for her neediness and badness and that I would not drop dead in response to what she told me about her nasty self, Mrs. Epstein became able to confront her resistance. She said that she was afraid to lie down because she might experience a strong urge to go to sleep. Associations to a dream made it clear that she wished for and feared a deep sleep in which she could join her mother in peaceful union. After analyzing this fantasy, Mrs. Epstein told me that she now felt able to lie on the couch and make a commitment to treatment, but only if I could be her analyst.

Impartiality

Some years before, a transfer from a trusted therapist to an analyst had been disastrous for her, and she could not face that again. Since the child had not catapulted herself into a transference relationship with me, I agreed with Mr. and Mrs. Epstein that it would be best to refer the child to a colleague for individual therapy while Mrs. Epstein would have analysis with me. It could be argued that I did not remain equally partial to all family members in this case, because I chose to work with the mother, not the presenting patient. But I think that I made my recommendation from a position of involved impartiality to the needs of the whole family. This facilitated the emergence of the mother's individual needs, and she was ultimately more able to be helpful to her daughter.

Use of the Here-and-Now, Transference-Countertransference, and Negative Capability

Mrs. Epstein had been talking about her wonderful mother, about whom she had the fondest feelings. According to her memory, they had never been angry at each other. Her mother was a vital, engaging woman who had never been sick until the day she died. A month after Mrs. Epstein began analysis, I caught a severe cold. Mrs. Epstein became silent every time I coughed. I could not understand why I felt so ill from just a cold. Perhaps the cold virus was particularly virulent, but more likely the infection was moving into my chest because I felt compelled to suppress my cough. Although I dutifully attended to the patient's material, I could not listen freely and respond cognitively or emotionally, because I was anxiously inhibiting any changes in my breathing that might trigger another cough, lest I aggravate her dread of my fate.

What was this doing to my state of negative capability? I was certainly not without memory or desire. I kept remembering Mrs. Epstein's frozen reaction to my coughing. I was full of the desire to stop coughing and to have the patient go away and leave me alone. My state of negative capability was being impinged on by my own concerns. On the other hand, meaning was about to emerge from this experience.

I felt quite sick. I needed to be able to cough and get rid of this infection and its interference with my state of freely suspended attention and negative capability; so I took the next day off to recover. Mrs. Epstein was unnerved. She could not contain her anxiety. She yelled at her children, then spent a sleepless night worrying about whether they would die. I recognized this as an early transference manifestation. Mrs. Epstein had experienced me as her mother suddenly being absent. Her rage at me was not expressed directly, but was displaced onto her child, as was her rage at her mother. Sobbing guiltily, Mrs. Epstein told me that she thought that she had caused my illness by her failure: If she had been a more loving person, this illness would not have happened to me. From the here-and-now of therapeutic relationship experienced by her in the transference as fear of loss of me and guilt at causing my illness and experienced by me in the countertransference as a worsening of my physical condition, we moved to a preliminary reconstruction of Mrs. Epstein's guilt about her mother's death. We would return to this many times in the course of therapy, each time understanding more about her fantasy of having killed her mother.

DO YOU USE THE ANALYTIC CONCEPT OF ABSTINENCE?

We follow Sigmund Freud's advice to abstain from seeking gratification from the patient. This means that we do not entertain personal, social, or sexual relationships with patients, because we are dedicated to putting aside our own interest in receiving pleasure from the patient in order to clear ourselves for use as the necessary object in fantasy. It also means that we do not gratify the patient's wishes, but rather seek to understand them. For instance, in intensive therapy we generally do not respond with a direct answer to questions or give advice, so that we do not undermine our task of uncovering and exploration. On the other hand, abstinence does not require being rude and rejecting to patients. For us, abstinence refers to our intention to remain in the work mode of the central ego, available for use as whatever object we are required to be in fantasy, but in reality not introducing ourselves as either exciting or rejecting objects. In practice, this means that we behave naturally, but professionally, supporting the expression of whatever wishes the patient struggles with, but not gratifying them. Through abstinence, we ensure that we do not smother, undo, make up for, or obliterate painful desires.

DO YOU MEAN THAT YOU NEVER
GIVE SUPPORT AND ADVICE?

There is some room in object relations therapy for support and advice, but they do not form the heart of our method. It is not that support and advice are against the rules: They are simply not the workhorses of object relations therapy. In supportive psychotherapy or in parent guidance, giving advice has a greater role than in a more ambitious therapy, in which exploring unknown territory and interpreting what is learned will be more important. There is nothing more truly supportive than an accurate, correctly timed interpretation.

NOTES

After listing the major aspects of technique of object relations therapy, we describe and illustrate how to create a firm, safe, but flexible therapeutic space in which to work psychologically with defense, resistance, and anxiety toward object relations understanding. Most important is the use of the therapist's self, in particular the ability for involved impartiality and negative capability:

The frame of treatment (Langs 1976, Zinner 1985).
Resistance as a defense (Guntrip 1969).
Potential space (Winnicott 1951).
Core affective exchange (Scharff and Scharff 1987).
Involved impartiality (Stierlin 1977).
Keats's term "negative capability" (Murray 1955).
Without memory and desire (Bion 1970).
The unthought known, personal idiom (Bollas 1987, 1989b).
Abstinence (Freud 1915b).

16

TECHNIQUE II: WORKING WITH TRANSFERENCE, COUNTERTRANSFERENCE, AND INTERPRETATION

Developing negative capability and maintaining abstinence and neutrality enable us to respond to the patient's transference. In studying our reactions to the unconscious material in individual, couple, or family therapy we find that countertransference experiences that are evoked by patients' transferences tend to cluster into two groups. We have called these the contextual and the focused countertransferences. The *contextual countertransference* refers to the therapist's reaction to the patient's *contextual transference*. The *focused countertransference* refers to the therapist's reaction to the patient's *focused transference*.

Contextual transference is the patient's reaction to the therapeutic space that we have provided, corresponding to the care offered by the "environment mother." The patient reveals this transference in attitudes about the frame of treatment in conscious feelings and behavior toward the therapist as the provider of the therapeutic environment.

The *focused transference* refers to feelings that the patient displaces onto the therapist as an object for intimate relating, corresponding to the "object mother" in relation to the infant self. This early relationship can be re-created in the transference in two ways that were pointed out by Heinrich Racker from his study of the therapist's countertransference to them. He noted that the countertransference arose from a state of concordant or complementary identification. Where the therapist is identified with a projected part of the object, we call this a *complementary identification*. Conversely, sometimes the patient identifies with the object mother and experiences the therapist as a part of the self in relation to that object. Where the therapist is identified with a part of the patient's ego, we call this a *concordant identification*.

Most of what has been written about transference in psychodynamic therapy refers to the focused transference. In this aspect of transference, the therapist becomes a discrete object fashioned according to the requirements of the patient's internal object relationships, or a part of the patient's ego in relation to a discrete object. This aspect of transference develops only after quite a long time has elapsed in therapy, and especially in psychoanalysis.

The earlier and therefore more common form of transference is the contextual transference. In a positive contextual transference, the patient expects the therapist to be benign and facilitating. In a negative contextual transference, the patient expects that the therapist will interfere or be destructive. In response to a positive contextual transference, the therapist feels trusted and potentially helpful. When there is a negative, rejecting contextual transference, the therapist is apt to feel abused, ignored, or mistrusted. In response to an excited form of a negative contextual transference, the therapist may feel excited, aroused and endangered, seduced, suffocated, or drained. The transference is diagnosed from review of its effect on the therapist.

CAN YOU PROVIDE AN EXAMPLE OF FOCUSED AND CONTEXTUAL TRANSFERENCE AND CONCORDANT AND COMPLEMENTARY COUNTERTRANSFERENCE IN INDIVIDUAL THERAPY?

Ms. Harvey (also reported in *Object Relations Family Therapy*, chapter 11), a single, thirty-two-year-old graphics artist, in the midphase of individual psychoanalytic psychotherapy, began her therapy session with a challenge to me (DES):

"Say something! Don't you know this is no way to do this with me? You're so stubborn."

When I tried to ask her a question about her feelings, she yelled at me, "No, that's not it. You just interrupted me again. You never ask at the right time."

I said that I felt silenced, and, although I knew that Ms. Harvey could not always answer such questions, I asked what this reminded her of from her early life.

She said testily, "You know goddamned well it's my mother. So, what else?"

"But you've told me before that you didn't yell like this as a child."

"No, I never yelled," she agreed. "I couldn't even speak! But *she* yelled at me, and I just felt worse and worse."

So, Ms. Harvey was acting like her mother and treating me the way she had felt treated as a child. Our task was to understand the reason she had to act this way now.

In this example, the patient complains about the contextual transference, but in fact she works openly and trustingly within it, an improvement since the early part of her treatment, when she was too fearful of the therapeutic relationship to allow this kind of material to emerge. At that time, her *contextual transference* to the contextual holding provided by the analyst was pervaded by distrust derived from her early experience, but interpretive work and experience of a reliable therapeutic holding environment permitted the development of a sufficiently secure contextual transference. With that in place, she could now convey the substance of her core relationship in the *focused transference*, by projecting into the therapist a part of herself while she acted like the persecuting internal part-object of her mother.

A few weeks later, Ms. Harvey began with her recurrent refrain, "I'm too tired to talk today. I've been up all night on a project deadline and if you want me to do anything here, you are going to have to ask me the questions. You know I don't agree with the way you try to get me to talk."

I felt annoyed, with a "here-we-go-again feeling." But I wanted to be helpful and decided to ask if anything occurred to her about the situation of being questioned.

"That's not the right question, you dolt!" she retorted. "I've told you and told you, that if you want me to tell you anything, you have to ask me specific things." She continued to rail against me in similar vein.

Eventually Ms. Harvey told me about a situation at work where her boss had asked people in detail about their projects. Ms. Harvey had felt dumb, and speechless. She was so mad at him for "quizzing her" that she wanted to be able to yell questions back at him and grill him.

I realized that I had been feeling grilled and harassed in the first part of the hour, and that Ms. Harvey was far angrier than she had been earlier in the analysis. This helped me to realize that I was being treated as the patient felt treated, and I now realized that I often felt "abused" by her in this way. I tended to get pulled into a fight with Ms. Harvey, a way of working that left me feeling contentious and dissatisfied with myself. After a few moments, I would grow silent, only to be dragged back into the ring by Ms. Harvey's demanding, "Where are you? I need for you to ask me a question. What do you think about what I have just said?"

Working with my feeling badgered and dissatisfied, I asked, "When I don't answer your question the right way, who do I remind you of?"

This time Ms. Harvey responded, "The person you're acting like is *me*! And I'm acting like everybody else: my sister, mother, teachers I've hated as a teenager, my ex-husband. I would never fight. When they asked me questions, and I got confused, I would get silent. I would tell myself that the thing to do was to not get in a fight. But I wanted to yell!"

"My mother used to sit me in a chair and try to teach me to read. And she'd yell at me if I got words wrong. She'd say, 'You're not performing up to your potential. You'll never amount to anything if you keep going like this.' And she'd be screaming at me. I was five years old, for Christ's sake! I'd get so quiet, and she would shout, "Don't sit there! You better talk or else!' And I'd want to yell at *her*, just so she'd know how it felt, what she was doing to me."

I now felt relieved. I no longer felt taken over by a strange and unlikeable part of myself, badgered into a contentious silence. I felt more relaxed, more like myself again.

Ms. Harvey had taken back a painful part of her own internal experience.

In the same hour, Ms. Harvey now went on to tell me about her new relationship with a man with whom she felt more trusting and loving than before. It was so different from her marriage. She was able to relate her attack on me to her feeling that I did not have confidence in this new relationship. She noted that she was now ready to admit that if I had been suspicious that her previous relationships with lovers were not mature, I would have been right, but that previously she did not trust me enough to admit it. In fact, she would insist that they were mature even while knowing that if I saw her with these men, I would have been dubious right away.

"I never could have told you that before," she admitted. "You know, I can only yell at you like I have been, because I trust you. And I've never trusted anyone enough to yell at them, no matter how angry or upset I felt. And then I can also tell you about this new relationship. I do appreciate it that you've forced me to keep going tonight although I was tired. You've been a prod to me, keeping me going."

The word "prod" resonated for me. I realized that that was a function I felt made to perform, with the implication of punishing, teasing, or goading the patient in a pseudophallic way.

I was projectively identified with the patient's ego, while she was identified with her persecuting maternal object. My asking her about the origins of this role relationship was like the "prodding" that the patient experienced with her mother. After this work by the patient, I felt relieved of the projective identification, or *focused transference* from her persecuting object, which had partly taken me over. When she trusted me in the *contextual transference* enough to tell me about her new relationship, I felt restored to being a benign object for her. From this more secure position, she confirmed her previous lack of trust in the contextual transference earlier in the analysis.

To understand the contextual transference, I had to tolerate feeling attacked and badly treated. Ms. Harvey repeatedly attacked my ability to contain the work. But, as she made clear in this hour, her ability to attack me now represented a newfound capacity for a trusting contextual transference, an ability that she had given up early in her life, or perhaps never had at all. My overall capacity to contain her anxious assaults eventually gave the patient faith in being held safely in my mind. This vignette demonstrates conviction in the strengthened container that allows the focused transference and counter-transference to grow and fosters the work on understanding them.

Later in treatment, within a confident contextual transference, the focused transference became more intense. In contrast to the earlier example in which I was identified with part of her self and she was identified with her own persecuting object, this time the transference was to me as her object, while Ms. Harvey was now identified with her self. Ms. Harvey became extremely vulnerable to experiencing me as an abandoning object when my vacations approached.

A few weeks before the summer, Ms. Harvey became suicidal. She immediately found another new relationship, recovered her hold on life and assured me that because of her new man, everything was fine. When I suggested that the relationship, and the speed of its formation, might have defensive functions to ward off her fear of depending on me when I was soon to be away, she became furious. She scratched her head in disbelief and dismay, and said in twenty different ways that I seemed not to be able to understand anything at all.

"Shut up! It doesn't matter whether you understand or not," she concluded.

When she left at the end of the hour, she straightened her hair, and said "I'm sorry for being such a bitch. I know I have to do it, but I'm sorry you have to put up with it!"

The next day, she came in and said, "It's not easy to say this. As soon as I got to my car I knew you were right. I think I have been mad at you for going on vacation. You are like my father deserting me, and I can't stand to have you leave when I need you so much. And I can't stand to say it to you. I mean I can now, but it's still not easy."

The *focused transference* is contained and modified in therapy by the therapist's willingness to be experienced as projected parts of the patient's ego and objects while at the same time being his own less harsh self. The patient moves from a *projective identification*, in which the therapist is felt to be the patient's antilibidinal object, to an *introjective identification* with that modified projective identification after it has been detoxified by its journey through the therapist-container. In addition, the patient grows through introjective identification of the therapist's containing function and better-metabolized internal object relations.

CAN A FOCUSED TRANSFERENCE BE SUBSTITUTED FOR A CONTEXTUAL TRANSFERENCE?

Some patients impose a premature focused transference on the therapeutic situation. Frequently in the diagnostic category of borderline or hysteric, these patients will attempt to recruit their therapists as immediate replicas of critical or excited figures from their life. Fearing that the therapist will not be able to hold firm as a facilitating environmental figure, the patient substitutes an erotic, aggressive, or other distorted object in place of the neutral therapist in order to compensate for the missing environmental object of the patient's internal world. Interpretation of this phenomenon is required early in such a therapy in order to address the patient's fear that therapy will not provide a safe holding environment.

HOW IMPORTANT ARE TRANSFERENCE AND COUNTERTRANSFERENCE?

Transference and countertransference are central to the technique of object relations therapy. They provide a workable, current version of the patient's object relations as lived out in the relationship with the therapist. This forms the laboratory in the here-and-now where the internal object relations can be felt and lived out and thereby understood— rather than simply talked about intellectually.

IS TRANSFERENCE THE SAME AS PROJECTIVE IDENTIFICATION?

The answer is No and Yes. In Sigmund Freud's terms, no: Transference refers to the displacement of impulses onto the person of the therapist as their new target. In object relations terms, yes: Transference is the same as projective identification. The therapist is identified with a part of the object, or a part of the self that has been projected into him, and the internal object relationship is then re-created between the patient and the therapist where it can be reworked.

WHAT IS THE ROLE OF INTERPRETATION IN OBJECT RELATIONS THERAPY?

From James Strachey, an early Freudian who knew object relations theory, to Harold Stewart, a contemporary analyst in the British Independent group, analysts have used the word *interpretation* to refer to a continuum of therapist interventions from complex formulations to simple comments, on the way to building shared understanding. The therapist gathers observations—including the patient's own observations—feeds them back to see if the patient agrees with them, and links or clarifies things that have been diffusely presented but not clearly understood by the patient. The patient is given the chance to object to or modify what the therapist has said, partly to respect the patient's need for defense and partly to have the patient fine-tune the interpretation. With experience and in supervision, we learn when to take a patient's correction of an interpretation at face value and when to take it as a disavowal. We generally find that an overly energetic denial such as Ms. Harvey's "Shut up!" is more likely to be denial than a thoughtfully suggested modification. We take the patient's reactions fully into account in continuing to modify our own understanding.

Interpretation begins with linking and clarifying and proceeds all the way to understanding how whatever happened long ago in the patient's life influences current difficulties in relationships. The most effective interpretation begins with the current reenactment in the transference and countertransference and proceeds to the reconstruction of repressed internal object relationships.

NOTES

Relevant work includes:

The focused transference and countertransference, the contextual transference and countertransference (D. Scharff and J. Scharff 1987).
Complementary and concordant transference identification (Racker 1968).
Transference (Freud 1905a).
Interpretation (Strachey 1934, Stewart 1990).

TECHNIQUE III: THE USE OF DREAMS, FANTASY, AND PLAY

HOW IS THE DREAM USED IN OBJECT RELATIONS THERAPY?

Sigmund Freud said that dreams were the royal road to the unconscious. Dreams enable the patient to get to a level far beyond conscious understanding. When the patient brings a dream, we listen and wait for associations to the dream in the standard psychoanalytic way. We do not ask questions or look for answers to puzzles in the content of the dream, but we simply record the patient's thoughts that occur in relation to the dream. The therapist, who knows the patient well, may also have thoughts in relation to the dream, which may facilitate the patient's coming forth with more material and understanding. The form of the dream reveals the patient's internal object relations. Whether in psychoanalysis or less intensive psychotherapy, the dream is most effectively interpreted as it reflects the transference.

In family, couple, or group therapy, dreams provide a communication in the interpersonal field. Here the dream is first understood by the dreamer, who gives his or her own thoughts and understanding of the dream. Then the dream is opened up to associations from all others in the therapeutic setting—spouse, family members, or group members. Their thoughts and associations form part of the field of understanding, not only of the individual dreamer but also of the dream's implications for the entire therapeutic group. The individual's dream is regarded as a communication about the transference from the couple, family, or group.

In Freudian theory, the dream results from the intricate combination of the mind's residue of the day's events with internal fantasy and expresses the fulfillment of an infantile wish. In Fairbairn's object relations theory, the dream reveals intrapsychic structure.

In chapter 4 we described Ronald Fairbairn's six-part model of the endopsychic situation: a central ego and its ideal object, characterized by reasonable internal harmony; the rejecting object and the internal saboteur (which he later called the antilibidinal ego), characterized by anger, persecutory anxiety, and frustration; and the exciting object and the libidinal ego, characterized by longing and the anxiety of excessively aroused neediness. The internal structures of the ego are capable of generating meaning and action, and they are in constant dynamic relationship with each other. Fairbairn thought that dreams were to be understood not as wishes, but as *statements of internal psychic structure*. He demonstrated the relationship between the elements of the psyche as illustrated in the dreams.

HOW DOES THE DREAM REFLECT THE BEGINNING THERAPEUTIC ALLIANCE, THE CONTEXTUAL TRANSFERENCE, INTRAPSYCHIC STRUCTURE, AND COUNTERTRANSFERENCE?

Adam, an unemployed twenty-six-year-old engineer, recently remarried, sought treatment with me (DES) when I was a fledgling analyst. This example is elaborated in *Reclaiming the Object and Refinding the Self*. Adam needed help for his dependency on women, his fears of sexual inadequacy, and his inability to get a job. In the middle of his first analytic session Adam reported a dream from the night before.

He said, "In my dream, the Los Angeles Dodgers asked me to play right field because they were a player short. What would the pitchers think of me? How should I bat against them? I tried to keep from dreaming what I would do when at the plate. I said to myself, 'Why not wait until you're up at bat?' I worried that I'd drop the ball in right field."

Adam went on to tell me about the resentment he felt toward his father. He said that his father's impatient criticism during baseball instruction from the age of four was the reason that Adam had worried about performing sexually. Then he thought of Thomas Mann's *The Magic Mountain*, in which the doctor-patient relationship is homosexually consuming and does not cure the patient.

The Dream and the Beginning Therapeutic Alliance

The dream conveyed Adam's fears that beginning psychoanalysis would be like learning baseball with his father. It suggested that he wanted me to teach him something, but saw me as threatening and disapproving, like his father, or seductive.

"He would watch at practice or Little League games and I'd just feel I never played well enough," Adam said. "I remember dropping the ball once in right field to lose a game and I couldn't face him. I was so mad at him for wanting me to do well."

"You were mad at him for wanting you to do well when you felt you couldn't measure up," I said. "You're afraid of that recurring here. I'm like the pitchers: You're worried what I'll think of you, but you are also playing against me, as I throw balls that you have to hit."

"I think you'll be trying to get me out," he corrected me, "or that you'll be a much better player than I am. After all, this is your sport. You're the one who is supposed to know how to play."

As an inexperienced analyst too eager to let him know that I understood, I quickly responded, "So you're trying not to worry about it, while you wait to see if you can hit the ball. But you're also worried that when I hit the ball to you, you'll drop the ball."

"Yeah, then there's nothing you could do to help me," he said flatly.

"Then it would be like the relationship between the doctor and patient in *The Magic Mountain*," I acknowledged. "Consuming but it won't cure."

The Dream as Comment on the Contextual Transference

I felt threatened by the allusion to the homosexual relationship between the doctor and patient, and the question of whether I would be exploitative. I decided to comment on Adam's anxiety about starting treatment, ostensibly for the correct technical reason of securing the treatment. I did not work with the countertransference idea that popped into my head as a question: "What sort of balls will I throw at him?" Deciding that it was too soon to comment on his homosexual fears or wishes, I filed them away for future consideration.

The dream also revealed his resistance to therapy. Even though he wanted to please both me and himself as a transference from his relationship with his father, he also wanted to compete with me and he feared failing. He also feared my failing. He moved rapidly toward this premature focused transference to me as the opposing pitcher and hitter because he was afraid that I would not be like a benign, well-meaning coach who would support his efforts to grow and compete.

The Dream as a Display of Intrapsychic Structure

Adam's dream also revealed his intrapsychic structure. Here was a boyish part of himself—his libidinal object relationship—locked in an intense, self-defeating struggle with the rejecting object relationship, based apparently on his relationship to his father. The possibility of playing and being praised was as elusive as the tantalizing exciting object. The inevitability of being blamed stemmed from the rejecting object. The internal saboteur made him drop the ball. The "one player short" for whom he was substituting refers to the inadequacy of his central ego functioning, as demonstrated in his symptomatology. Being a good team player embodies the ideal object that he does not have. Perhaps the "one player short" also refers to a feeling of deprivation in relation to his feeding mother, a feeling that his father may have shared, hence his extraordinary pressure on his son to gratify him. For whatever reason, which we might expect to discover later in treatment, Adam had not come to terms with oedipal defeat gracefully, and so had been unable to compete successfully and aggressively in the world of work. In his intimate life he was not confident of his sexual functioning, and could not love a woman without recruiting her as a source of support.

Countertransference in Work with Dreams

Adam's dream not only told us about him, but plumbed the depths of my valency to respond to his self and object projective identifications. In my countertransference to the dream, I felt consciously more identified with Adam (his *self-projective* identification) than with his physician-father. Would my efforts be any better than the all-consuming relationship that did not cure? Would I drop the ball? What would my analytic teachers think of me? On the other hand, like his father (his *object* projective identification), I desperately wanted Adam to do well, so that I could do well and make it to the major leagues as a fully certified analyst. That was why I had shelved the homosexual reference: I could not face how dependent I felt on Adam for my training. My countertransference reflected the homosexual longing of the doctor in *The Magic Mountain* and at the same time the patient's fears of empty promises about an incurable disease.

As well as revealing intrapsychic structure, dreams convey interpersonal meaning even within the intrapsychic focus of individual therapy or psychoanalysis. The telling of a dream in psychoanalysis or individual therapy is an interpersonal communication. Dreams join in the conversation of the therapy and express the issues between therapist and patient, sometimes expressing the resistance of the dreamer, sometimes portraying the transference, other times heralding a shift in psychic structure.

HOW DO WE USE FANTASIES IN OBJECT RELATIONS THERAPY?

Fantasies are dealt with like dreams. We hear the fantasy, observe the associated affect, and wait for the flow of associations. A fantasy may seem to be a private expression of the intrapsychic realm but it also has its expression in current object relationships.

Working with Fantasy and Inner Object Relations in the Midphase of Couple Therapy

Dr. Arthur and Mrs. Rhonda Clark (more fully described in *Object Relations Couple Therapy*, chapter 6) had been working with me (JSS) for a year. We had worked on Arthur's passivity, his inability to earn Rhonda's admiration of him as a successful, ambitious, caring man, and his need to denigrate her by comparison to the nurses at the office. We worked on her tirades and outrageous behavior that alienated him, his office staff, and his family, and that left her feeling contemptible. Their sex life had improved because he was less demanding and she less likely to balk and cause a fight. Their tenacious defensive system, in which she was assigned the blame and was the repository for the rage, greed, ambition, and badness in the couple, had not yet yielded to interpretation, although Rhonda was no longer on such a short fuse. I could see improvement in the diminution in the volume and frequency of her reactions and in the degree of his contempt, but the basic pattern stayed in place until Arthur felt safe enough to tell Rhonda and me the full extent of his sadistic and murderous fantasies in which he raped and axed various women who had abandoned him. Catharsis played a part in securing some relief for him, but the major therapeutic effect came from work done in the countertransference on the way he was treating the two actual women in the room with him, his wife and me, as he told his fantasies about other women.

As he concluded, Arthur said that he was terrified that people would think that he would act out his fantasies, which he had never done and would not do. Turning to me, he said, "You would understand that fear."

I felt extremely uncomfortable. If I acknowledged that I was familiar with such a fear, I felt I would be siding with him in assuming that his wife was ignorant.

Excluded and put down, Rhonda retorted, "You said *she* would understand as if *I* wouldn't."

"She's a psychiatrist. She's heard all this before. She'll know I don't have any urges to do this in real sex," he replied.

Rhonda had a good point to make: "How does she know you're not going to act those out? How do I know? Do *you* know? Because you seem really scared."

I said, "There is no evidence that Arthur will act out the fantasies in their murderous form. But there is evidence that he's scared they'll get out of hand. We also have evidence right here that you do sadistic things to each other in this relationship, not physically, but emotionally. 'Put-downs' you call them."

"Like what just happened here!" exclaimed Rhonda. "Sure, she's trained, but I can understand it, too."

"Not that I'm going to go out and do it," he reminded her.

"Right," she rejoined. "It's how you're going to feel it. Arthur, I feel so relieved that it's not just been me. All these years I've been taking the shit for fucking up the marriage. Do you know, I feel so relieved. Finally, after all these years he's taking responsibility. Finally."

"But I told you about my sadistic fantasies," he said.

"You never did," Rhonda objected. "I'm not saying you never talked about fantasies before, but you never went into your real self, never in this detail. You've always said that I'm this, I'm that. It's always been me. Now I see in our marriage that your fantasies are totally in the way. Now *rape* I could maybe see as exciting, but why do you have to picture *murders*? That is scary."

I said, "To some extent the threatening part of the fantasy is arousing to both of you. But by the end of it, Arthur, you are terrified of losing control, and Rhonda, you are frightened for your life." They were nodding, thoughtfully. I went on, "We're not talking put down, here. We're talking put *out*. These are compelling and forceful fantasies."

"This has been a big interference to you and to us," Rhonda replied. "This is like what you would call a breakthrough for us."

I felt inclined to agree with Rhonda's evaluation. The longer Arthur kept the fantasy to himself, the more it seemed to be the real him, terrified of being found out, hidden inside yet demanding to be heard. Furthermore the way it got heard was through projection into Rhonda who identified with it. In her rages and attacks on Arthur she gave expression to that attacking, chopping up part of him, for which she had a valency. Meanwhile, he contained for her the greater calamity of the wish for death, a wish and fear that stemmed from early loss of an envied and hated older brother.

Working Through the Interpersonal Expression of Fantasies Late in the Midphase

Following the revelation, the Clarks had a session in which Rhonda talked of her continued sense of gratitude that her husband had shared his fantasies with her. Although she felt unusually tentative about responding to him sexually, she felt close to him and committed to working things out. For the first time, she felt an equal level of commitment from him. Summer was approaching and she was taking the children to visit her family in Maine for a month, as usual. Until now, Rhonda had viewed her annual summer trip as a chance to get away from Arthur's criticizing her and demanding sex of her. For the first time, she felt sad that they would have to spend the summer apart.

The sharing of the fantasy had been a healing experience. The couple could now move beyond a level of functioning characteristic of the paranoid-schizoid position toward the depressive position in which there is concern for the object whose loss can be appreciated.

In a session following their vacation, Rhonda reported that she had got so much from the last session that it kept her thinking and working for four weeks. Even when Arthur expressed no affection during his phone call to her in Maine, when he did not even say he missed her, she felt hurt but not outraged as before. She realized that in some way he just wasn't there.

I suggested that Arthur had been unaware of feeling angry that Rhonda had left him alone for a few weeks and had dealt with it by killing her off.

"I was kind of pissed off at her being in Maine, getting to lie around on the family boat," Arthur admitted.

"He just cut me dead," Rhonda confirmed.

I said, "Well, there's the fantasy of killing operating again."

"Right," Rhonda replied. "But I didn't take it personally. It's just him. These last two weeks, I've been able to have grown-up feelings. Even though he belittles me, I don't live in a world of little feelings any more. That's a big change for me."

Arthur's revelation of his murderous fantasies released Rhonda's capacity for growth and revealed that the silent operation of the unconscious projective identification expressed in the fantasy had been cutting her down and killing off her adult capacities.

The Individual's Use of Cultural Fantasy

We are not limited to using only unconscious fantasies that are the product of the patient's imagination alone. We also work with cultural fantasies, such as the themes of movies or books referred to by the patient. The associations of the patient (or of the family) are used to understand the meaning of this conscious fantasy that connects to unconscious fantasies. The personal emphasis or distortion of elements of a story or movie whose plot is known provides information about the patient's internal object relations and the way in which those operate. For instance, in response to the movie *The Prince of Tides*, in which a woman psychiatrist encourages her patient's brother to remember and reveal repressed and suppressed family history, in the course of which she falls in love with him, four patients responded quite differently and idiosyncratically. One patient was most affected by the trauma of the man's remembered rape scene and through it recovered her own anguish over being raped years before. The second patient to mention the movie focused on the healing aspect of the affair between the man and the psychiatrist in order to repress her retaliatory aggression against her promiscuous husband. The third patient, a woman who was unconsciously defending against homoerotic feelings for her female therapist, was most upset by the psychiatrist's enactment of her erotic countertransference. The fourth patient, a man who had resented his mother's seductive attachment to his brother, focused on the psychiatrist's denial that her lover, who was her patient's brother, was really in treatment with her, too, and therefore should have been protected from his wish to seduce her by her adherence to a clear code of ethics.

DO YOU USE PLAY IN
OBJECT RELATIONS FAMILY THERAPY?

Children learn in the context of relationships. They build their psychic structure out of their experiences. When they play they rework what has been happening to them and they rehearse for future roles. They shout and run about, which helps them deal with anxiety. They have fun, and at the same time they display their internal object relationships. Some children show their family experiences and their feelings about them in a literal way as they move the doll family figures in the dollhouse. Others work at a more symbolic level on various aspects of their internal object relationships: They express the associated affects through their choices of color; they reveal the conflicts between parts of the self when they play with the furry puppets and the hard blocks; and they indicate their internal structure as they build with cards, blocks, or dominoes. From the way they care for the toys, we can infer the kind of holding environment in which they have been raised. From their choice of toys we can determine the developmental level at which they operate emotionally—for instance, feeding and baking games, holding on and letting go of a ball, hiding and seeking, and games of separation and reunion, competition, and oedipal romance. The play also communicates the transference to us. Sometimes this is directly obvious. For instance when a toy character points a gun at his therapist's head, he knows the child wants him dead.

Sometimes we receive information about the transference in our countertransference to the play. For instance a boy drops paint into a basin of water and swishes it around so that it splashes, all the while talking about his mother who was too busy. His woman therapist comments that as his production is about to spill over the carpet, the boy wants her to know how full of feelings he is about his mother. Then he drowns a clay spider in the water, again an expression of rage at his mother. But let's say that the spider is one the therapist has made for him in an earlier session. In this play, the boy conveys his wish to drown out the therapist's idea and sink her wish to help him with his feelings.

Working with Fantasy Expressed in Play

Children may share their fantasies verbally but more commonly express them in the form of play. Through play, the child can speak for issues that the grown-ups may be more defended against.

The Warrens (more fully described by me (JSS) as the W. family in *Foundations of Object Relations Family Therapy*, chapter 24) consulted us for help in managing the clinging behavior of their toddler. In a diagnostic session, Mr. and Mrs. W. talked with us while their daughters Terri, age four, and Brooke, age sixteen months, played beside them.

The children's play expressed fantasies about separation from the pre-oedipal mother and inclusion or exclusion from the primal scene of the parents in intercourse.

Mr. W. complained that his wife did not keep the house immaculate. She felt overwhelmed by his expectations and by having to run the household and manage two young children without help. She spoke of missing her mother who lived far away and whom she used to call on for support and advice. As she spoke Brooke sat on her mother's lap, sucking her pacifier, a visual image of her mother's longing.

Typical of a four-year-old, Terri made a low, enclosed building on the floor with animals in and around it. Two sheep were inside and Oscar the Grouch was coming outside.

The play spoke to us of a fantasy of leaving the mother-child dyad. The one who left might be grouchy. But did the sheep couple represent the mother-infant couple from whom Terri was excluded, or that Brooke must now separate from, or the parental couple from whose bedroom both girls were excluded?

As the parents spoke more heatedly about their differences, Brooke left her mother's lap and messed up Terri's game. Terri punched her and Brooke returned to her mother's lap. The parents had to interrupt their discussion to deal with the fight.

David Scharff suggested that the girls had fought to divert the parents from their fight. But Mrs. W. corrected him, saying that the girls interrupted any time that the parents talked together. Mrs. W. went on to describe Terri's insistence on being heard and on interrupting her parents' conversations.

"So, Terri wants to bust up Mother's and Father's being together, as well as Mother and Brooke's closeness," I (JSS) said.

Terri and Brooke responded to this interpretation in play. Both girls now played without conflict. Terri had Oscar the Grouch peek out at some cows who he hoped might want to play with him. "He's wondering what they are doing," she explained.

Brooke put dolls in cars and said "Bye-Bye" to them.

Terri's play suggested to us her feeling of exclusion from the parents' excitement, her hope of inclusion, her oedipal curiosity, and her desire to watch them. Brooke's play indicated that she was getting on with her task of practicing separation. Each girl had responded to anxiety about the parents' relationship in ways colored by their age-appropriate concerns.

Terri continued to play with the animals, and said that the horse outside the barn was lonely, but the two sheep were not because they had each other. Mrs. W. spoke feelingly of her attachment to her mother, with whom she would go out shopping every weekend, leaving her father at home to make a perfect job of his home and garden. Later, Brooke got in the doll bed herself and lay still as a corpse. Then Mrs. W. told of how her father had died one weekend in his garden when she was nineteen years old.

We had been led by the children's play to understand the unconscious fantasy that when two people are close it will hurt a third. Brooke's playing dead and Mrs. W.'s narrative went together to introduce the theme of death. Oedipal concerns about rivalry and exclusion could not be solved because of worries about killing. In fantasy, loss of the third party pushed the person back to the earlier dyad for safety. When Mrs. W. felt this way, it was hard for her to let her child separate, and it was troubling to be close to her husband over her children's objections. It was also hard for her to keep a neat house, because her father's compulsion to do so was seen as having killed him.

Children reveal their unconscious fantasies in their play, much as adults do in reporting fantasies or dreams. In couple and family therapy, the individual shares his fantasy verbally or through play and the family cooperates to associate to it. What we find is that a fantasy may have been unconscious until now, but, nevertheless, has found expression in symptomatology and has gained living form in the nature of the relationships within the family. In object relations therapy, we aim to make unconscious fantasy conscious to interrupt its destructive effect on family relationships now and to modify the internalization of internal objects based upon them.

CAN YOU ILLUSTRATE THE USE OF A DREAM IN THE MIDPHASE?

Henry, a bright man suffering from depression, poor self-esteem, and feelings of distance and loneliness in his marriage, enjoyed and valued his twice weekly therapy with me (DES). So he found it odd when he had the following dream:

"I dreamt that I was in your waiting room and you were being mean and nasty to me. Then I came in here into your office and you were your usual pleasant and professional self."

Henry went on to say that I had never been mean like that and neither had his parents or anyone else. When I (DES) said that the phrase "mean and nasty" sounded like a child's words, Henry remembered how ruthlessly his brother teased their younger sister, who still showed the scars, how he himself would never tease her, how afraid he had been of being hazed in high school, and how well he hid his upset when he was teased. Hiding his upset left him feeling lonely. He noted that, although his mother totally approved of him, she could be brutally scornful of people who had poor taste, inferior intellect, or were slaves to fashion, and that his father did not challenge her, but withdrew.

I said that Henry hid his fear of being tormented by withdrawing like his father, and then felt lonely like he believed his father felt. The need to distance himself from his fears left him feeling distant from his wife.

Henry said that no one had ever listened to him until he found his way to therapy, and he liked being listened to. On the other hand, he kept feeling that therapy was an indulgence when he wasn't really sick. He told me that his mother had grown up in New York where psychoanalysis was in fashion among her friends, and she never lost an opportunity to denigrate psychoanalytic treatment and her silly, needy friends for wasting their time with it. I now said that Henry carried his mother's critical voice inside, and his guilty enjoyment of the attention to his needs for understanding called down the scorn of that internal voice.

In the office, my actual presence was consistent and reassuring, but my absence was upsetting. While waiting eagerly for his session in the dream, Henry's confidence in the therapeutic relationship was invaded by the scornful part of his mother and by the ruthlessly teasing part of his brother—internal persecutory objects that led him to feel inferior and to anticipate being tormented by me. Coming eight months into the therapy, this dream ushered in the theme of insecurity in relation to waiting for the caregiver, warned me of his disavowed transference to me as a persecutory object, and heralded the emergence of his own deeply repressed mean and nasty parts, of which he was ashamed, and which he therefore located in me instead.

CAN YOU SHOW HOW A DREAM IS ANALYSED IN COUPLE THERAPY?

We listen to the individual's dream as a product of the couple and their therapeutic relationship. We hear the dream and accept the dreamer's associations as we would in individual therapy. We wait for, or ask for, the partner's associations, not to interpret the individual's dream, but to use it to arrive at shared insight about the couple and how they feel about the therapist. Here we show how dreams give access to sexual and emotional difficulty and the nature of the transference.

Shared Fear of Intimacy after Infidelity

Robert and Diane, in their midforties, seemed to have everything, but they were on the brink of divorce. Diane had been uninterested in sex with Robert, and Robert had periodic difficulty with his erection when with her. Diane doubted Robert's love; he doubted her love and his potency. In therapy they were encouraged to reveal the secrets of their affairs to each other. The emptiness of their marriage was emphasized by the passion in their affairs. They were still working through their reactions as they worked on building trust.

Robert's Two Short Dreams

The first dream: "A big guy wanted to beat me up. I told another man I would give him $2,500 to defend me, and he did."

The second dream: "I was in the bathroom of a motel where people go with lovers. I was in the bathroom with Diane and an Indian man. We were naked and measuring our penises. I had a strong erection, but his was stronger, and I thought he had a better angle."

Robert associated to a woman whose husband had forgiven her for having an affair with an Indian man. Perhaps he could forgive Diane for her affair, too.

Diane associated to Robert: Robert being touched by a lover, imagining her touching her lover, and his feeling inferior. Robert began to cry because Diane had made him feel humiliated and angry. I heard a transference communication here. They paid me money to help them, and perhaps they felt beaten up in the process. I asked if they were feeling bad because I was penetrating the emotional depths of their marriage at a more effective angle than they were used to. They did feel that, but they also felt helped, as they are helped by each other's revelations and confrontations.

Diane's Dream

"I was swimming with other people in a gorgeous pool below a waterfall, wearing a white bikini that looked great. It was time to go home. A guy got out of the water with me. As we walked up a hill, over some rough spots, he placed his hand on my shoulder. I said he was abusing me, and he reacted like, 'You're a stupid woman to think I did something wrong!' We got in the car. Another guy sat next to me. It was crowded and his legs touching mine felt awful. Now the white bikini seemed more like underwear and I felt naked and exposed, but not vulgar."

Diane said that she felt uncomfortable wearing underwear in the company of these men, and this reminded her of the discomfort of her affairs. Robert said that the two guys stood for her two affairs, and that the dream showed him that she felt exposed, vulnerable, and out of control.

I said, "The sexual woman alive in the affairs and in the pool feels uncomfortable in underwear with the men in the dream just as Diane feels reluctant to bare herself at home with Robert and to expose her feelings in therapy."

Diane said, "The car is therapy, which feels too close for comfort. You touch me uncomfortably when you remind me of unpleasant things."

Discussion

Diane's dream begins in the gorgeous pool, an image that reflects their idyllic lifestyle. The men in her dream echo the rival men of Robert's dreams. Robert's dreams depict his hurt that Diane is sharing herself with someone else, and his need for a strong man to support him against a persecuting inner rival that shrivels his penis and leaves him feeling inferior. The dreams show transferences to me as the Indian man (a reference to my summer skin color) who might help the couple reach forgiveness but who might humiliate Robert with the success of it and as the paid bodyguard who first assaults and then defends them (asking for revelation and supporting reparation). Their mixed feelings about me echo their ambivalence toward each other. Robert's dream shows how the couple's shared contextual transference expresses their problem and thereby becomes a vehicle for its resolution (Scharff & Scharff 1991). Together, their dreams lead us to an understanding of the interplay of jealousy, rivalry, and envy.

NOTES

Dreams, conscious and unconscious fantasies, and children's play all offer a route to the unconscious:

Dreams (Freud 1900).
Endopsychic structure revealed in dreams (Fairbairn 1944).
Use of fantasy in couple therapy (D. Scharff and J. Scharff 1991).
Use of play in family therapy (J. Scharff 1989a, D. Scharff and J. Scharff 1987).

18

BRIEF THERAPY

SINCE OBJECT RELATIONS THERAPY IS IN-DEPTH, HOW CAN IT BE APPLIED TO BRIEF THERAPY?

Object relations applies equally to brief therapy, long-term individual therapy, and even to a single session. It is useful for crises in well-functioning individuals and families, and when circumstances limit how much the patient is able or willing to do.

HOW IS BRIEF THERAPY DIFFERENT?

Brief therapy and single session consultation require us to hold a tighter focus than we do in long-term work where we have the freedom to pursue multiple avenues. The main idea in brief work is to maintain a consistent dual focus on symptomatic and dynamic issues. We work initially with the symptoms, and then explore dynamic issues that might shed light on the meaning of the symptom, using inquiry, clarification, and interpretation to move between the two areas. We cannot try to do too much in brief therapy, so we do not expect to get a complete picture of the patient or family's object relations or to reach the same breadth and depth of understanding that we hope for in long-term therapy. Nevertheless, by using the approaching deadline of the end of the brief therapy to sharpen the focus, we create a high pressure system with a considerable tuning force for pulling the personality toward change. The small changes realistically achievable in brief therapy continue to effect greater change after termination and may actually create enough turbulence to drive the patient back into longer-term or serial brief therapies.

HOW DO YOU USE THE TRANSFERENCE IN BRIEF THERAPY?

In brief therapy there is no time to gather the transference into the basin of attraction that long-term therapy provides. Nevertheless, transference and countertransference manifestations are always present. We use them in brief therapy to track the course of the therapy, monitor the patient's sense of security, and assess the ability to work. If negative transference interferes, we link it to the presenting symptom, so as both to deal with the resistance to treatment and to interpret underlying anxieties. However, if the transference is positive and the work goes smoothly, we may keep our transference understanding to ourselves.

CAN YOU GIVE AN EXAMPLE OF BRIEF INDIVIDUAL THERAPY THAT SHOWS THE DUAL FOCUS ON SYMPTOMS AND DYNAMICS?

Raj was a thirty-year-old man who had been fired from his job as a junior administrator in a civil rights nonprofit institution. He sought consultation with me (DES) because he was worried that the issues that cost him his job might keep him from a productive career. He and his wife would be moving for her new job in another city, and so he could make a commitment to therapy for only twelve weeks.

In the first session, Raj outlined the story of his firing. He said that the woman who was the agency director objected strenuously and stubbornly when Raj allowed one of his employees extra leave for a family problem. He found her position grossly unfair and lost his temper in outrage, and was promptly fired. I learned that a complicating factor in his feelings about her concerned her sexual relationship with a married man who was the chief administrator in Raj's department and who was neglecting his family responsibilities because of it.

Over the next sessions, Raj told me about his family life. His mother died when he was eight months old. Then, taking baby Raj and Raj's older brother and sister with him, his father left India to take a job as a college professor in the United States. As the children living in America became oppositional teenagers, Raj's father threw them out of the house. For several years, Raj lived with foster families and with his older sister. His father sent for an Indian woman to marry. She was only five years older than Raj, and quite beautiful.

I told Raj that his rage at the injustice shown by his boss had formed around his father's treatment of him, and his experience of discomfort around the agency director and her senior administrator triggered his rage about his father and new young wife. Raj acknowledged the impact of this correspondence and said that he was now worried that he would continue to run into situations resembling this dynamic throughout his life and would be unable to refrain from expressing his anger and getting fired.

In the next session, Raj said that he now knew he must tell me something that he had not told anyone before. When he was sixteen, the family of a girl he knew agreed to take him in. He adored that family, and they loved him. He began to sneak into the girl's room at night to fondle her. When the family found out, he was asked to leave. He was deeply ashamed of this, and felt that they could never forgive him. Yet, they kept in touch and invited him to the girl's wedding last year.

When I asked more about this foster family, Raj told me that the foster parents had not been getting along well, and divorced soon after he left. Now he felt to blame for bringing harm to them as well as to their child. I said that his shame and guilt were conveyed in his reluctance to tell me this secret, and they were expressed in his unconscious conviction that he was responsible for their divorce. Picking up the strain in the foster family, he felt guilty for that and for his part in wishing to break up his father's family with his new young wife. His attempt at reparation emerged as a sexual longing for the girl in the foster family.

Raj's outrage at the woman boss for ignoring the family needs of the employee and threatening to break up the administrator's family derived from his guilt at the idea that he had wrecked his own place in a family with his father, and then destroyed the foster family he loved. Subsequent sessions allowed time to explore the ramifications of this link between symptomatic anxiety and dynamic focus, to explore his anxiety about the new career he planned, and to have a short period of termination. His mother's death when he was eight months old created a loss and vulnerability that set the stage for the development of outrage, guilt at contributing to family loss, and self-defeating protest. These would have required long-term therapy for more adequate explanation. I used the brief therapy format to show Raj what was possible and to point the way to more thorough long-term treatment in his new location.

CAN YOU GIVE AN EXAMPLE OF A BRIEF FAMILY THERAPY?

The Smith family came for crisis intervention after the father had almost died of anaphylactic shock from eating shellfish. After this traumatic event, their six-year-old son Mark clung to his parents, having nightmares and sobbing uncontrollably, and he was unable to go to school. Mark had been terrified when he saw his father gasping for breath and his mother searching hopelessly for epinephrine and frantically calling for help. Mark had to leave them behind while he ran alone down the half-mile drive to meet the emergency team and direct them to their house in the woods.

   In four sessions with the family, we went through the details of the traumatic event. As they argued about the narrative, it became evident that the parents were in conflict and that it predated the trauma. With my encouragement they acknowledged they had problems in getting along. Mark talked about how worried he had been that they would get a divorce and leave him. The parents each admitted to being afraid that the other would leave in despair. With these fears made explicit, Mark's nightmares ceased and he stopped clinging. He returned to school and resumed doing well. In this brief family therapy, the child's presenting symptom was linked to the single shock of the near death of a parent and the cumulative strain of a problematic marriage. This intervention in which the parents accepted responsibility for their problems and let the child share his fears about them was enough to free the child from the grip of the projective identificatory system of the family and proceed with developing normally. Ongoing couple therapy would be required if the parents decided to work on improving their relationship.

NOTES

Brief therapy can be effective if the therapist uses the impact of the impending deadline and focuses both on symptoms and underlying dynamics.

Brief therapy (Stadter 1996, J. Scharff and D. Scharff 1998).

TECHNIQUE AND THEORY REVIEW WITH CLINICAL ILLUSTRATION

CAN YOU REVIEW THE PRINCIPLES OF THEORY AND TECHNIQUE THROUGH A CLINICAL EXAMPLE FROM FAMILY THERAPY, FOCUSING ESPECIALLY ON COUNTERTRANSFERENCE AND INTERPRETATION?

(This clinical example is drawn from a case presented by David in chapters 4, 10, and 12 of *Object Relations Family Therapy,* and is also referred to in this book in chapter 21.)

My (DES) countertransference to the Jansens was well seasoned, after seeing them for almost two years. Mr. and Mrs. Jansen originally came to see me because Tom, then nine years old, had broken into an electrical store and destroyed quite a lot of equipment. They explained that although he was a good kid basically, he was regularly the butt of teasing at school. Incidentally, they added, what really got to them most was the endless fighting with his two older brothers in which Tom bullied them, even though he was two years younger.

Right away, I was struck with the denial in their presentation. Like many parents, they wanted it both ways. In their fantasy, they had a boy who was a good kid; nothing was wrong really. But in reality, they had a troubled boy who needed fixing. So they wanted me to fix him without making them face his need to be fixed.

While I evaluated the situation, I absorbed the difficulty. Part of it lay between the parents. Mr. Jansen was the more controlling parent. His wife had been in psychotherapy for some time, and had faced the family difficulty rather openly, but Mr. Jansen alternated between being proud of Tom's aggressiveness and close to despair. His brittleness left me feeling that it would be easy to say the wrong thing to this man, whom I quickly sensed could be so hurt that he would withdraw from the scene.

The couple's own differences added up to a marital problem, but they told me little about it. Mrs. Jansen was willing, and told me in an individual session that they had sexual problems and that they fought often, much of it about Tom, sometimes over the other boys. But she was quick to confirm that her husband was thin-skinned about this, and she felt they would not be able to deal with the marital conflict, at least not for a while.

Right in the beginning, I was left with a substantial countertransference to the parents' restrictions that kept me from operating the way I wanted to and from saying the things I felt should be said.

The feelings that David developed in response to the encounter with this family are the ordinary lot of therapists. While the growth of these feelings could be understood as a reasonable and unremarkable response to dealing with difficult or controlling people, our experience has taught us that it is more usefully regarded as a noteworthy marker to be used in charting therapists' paths while orienting themselves and beginning the process of taking in families' difficulties. It is through this emotional charting of such encounters that we absorb the families' inner experience.

I (DES) understood the family's difficulty with trust and the controlling behavior of Mr. Jansen to represent a shared family difficulty: The parents had not been able to offer Tom all that he needed to steer a satisfactory course, and they were afraid that I would not be able to either. Mr. Jansen had an expectation or transference that anyone in authority was likely to harm him and the family, and this was his way of trying to manage that possibility. But he was not alone in this feeling. When Mrs. Jansen expressed a more open position, she did so without conviction, and with a fear of her own, that if I pursued things too directly with her husband, he would rebel and refuse to get Tom and the family the help she thought they needed. In sum, they shared a feeling that most outsiders could do them harm, and that there was considerable question if any could be helpful. And they tenderly guarded their own fears that something was wrong, lest they expose their fear that they had caused harm to someone they loved.

In getting this message across to me, in filling me with their own doubts and leaving me hamstrung, they had imparted more to me than a warning. They had shared the anxious worries so that I, like them, became full of feeling that the world of working with them was a tentative place, that it was hard to know where to walk without stepping on a land mine. And I felt I began to know what life was like for them, from the inside.

The case of the Jansen family shows how countertransference can be a vehicle for understanding a family in depth through temporarily sharing its reality. During engagement with families, parts of therapists' own internal worlds are stirred in an internal resonance that illuminates the meaning of the family's struggles to the therapists. The process starts from the beginning, from the way a family enters the therapist's office. This interplay is part of every session. Our way of working with families is built on the experience that if we are willing to join families by making sense of our internal encounter with them, we will then be able to understand them in depth. We can then offer a level of understanding that has the power to transform the families and the relationships of family members to each other.

In the initial family session, Tom erupted at his two brothers and then ran out of the room to the car. Mr. and Mrs. Jansen were unable to persuade him to return. When I met with the parents the following week, Mr. Jansen would not allow Tom's brothers to be seen in family therapy. He said, "One of our sons has gone to the dogs; we aren't going to let him contaminate the ones who are okay."

Tom was not the only balky member of the family. Mr. Jansen would not agree to participate in family meetings either. He agreed readily to individual therapy for Tom, and he agreed to come for monthly parent guidance meetings with his wife as long as we focused on Tom. Mr. Jansen said, "I want you to understand that this is not to be therapy for us!"

It was the only contract the parents would allow, so I accepted it, with the hope that things would go well enough that they would trust me more over time, and we might eventually expand the work to include family therapy and perhaps couple therapy. After about six months, Tom's behavior improved at home and at school. A "trial family session" went without severe disruption and Mr. Jansen agreed to expose all the children to family therapy.

My countertransference had by now become weathered by the work with this family. I was used to the couple's dance of vulnerability in which their shared fear was that I would harm one or the other by discrediting their parenting. I had become more sensitive to the fear of being victimized that they shared—a fear lived out in Tom's being picked on at school. When I felt bullied by them in the sessions, I had come to know that we were not far from their fears that *I* would bully *them*, a derivative of the fear that each member of the family would turn bully to the others.

And things had gotten better. Tom was no longer the scapegoat for marital difficulties. We had been able to discuss his penchant for picking up the strain in his parents' marriage and in the family and his self-destructive attempts to solve their problems by making himself an object of concern by his delinquent behavior. We had discovered that at the point he had broken into the electrical shop, his mother was threatened with a serious illness, and the marriage had been in crisis. The family had learned a great deal about taking back their projective and introjective identifications.

A short review of these concepts may be helpful before we apply them to understanding this family. The term *projective identification* was coined by Melanie Klein to denote the unconscious process of projecting parts of the self outside the self and into others, dealing with the others as though they were then characterized by those parts of the self. The parts that are projected out may be hated parts of the self or object—let's say, a sense of badness or weakness—or they may be treasured parts that feel too endangered inside the self to survive. *Introjective identification* is the complementary process, in which a person takes in the projections of the other to solve an internal problem, and then acts in identification with those parts.

Klein's concepts of projective and introjective identification are even more useful when put together with Ronald Fairbairn's theory. Fairbairn held that it is the fundamental human need for a relationship that motivates psychological growth and development throughout life. He suggested that infants and children organize their psychological structure by taking in experience with their mothers and fathers, in the form of *internal objects* that then form the basic building blocks of psychic structure.

"Internal object" is really a technical term. It does not imply that personal relationships are to be understood in mechanized ways. Rather the word "object" stems from Freud's use. He thought that in central relationships, one person was the "object" of the sexual and aggressive drives of the other. A better term than "internal object relations" might well be "internalized personal relations," but the use of the word "object" has persisted because it continues an important tradition of clinical theory begun by Klein and Fairbairn.

These internal objects are closely related to parts of the self, and the relationship between a part of the self and an internal object forms the structure of an internal object relationship. In projective identification, the intolerably painful parts of these internal, unconscious relationships are split off and put outside the self and into another person. For the process to be complete, the other person must be partly taken over by them without quite knowing it. That is, there must also be a complementary introjective identification in another person for the transactional part of projective identification to be complete. In this way, projective and introjective identification become the vehicles for unconscious communication. In all intimate relationships, projective identification is a mutual process, which is the normal basis for unconscious understanding and empathy. When it is skewed, it is also the basis for shared unconscious misunderstanding and for unconsciously collusive pathology.

In the Jansen family, Mr. Jansen projected his unconscious sense of weakness into his wife and Tom. Mrs. Jansen projected strength and even stubbornness into her husband, and went along with that part of herself that she found in him. And Tom projected his inner goodness and strength into others, taking in through introjective identification the sense of weakness and badness for the family, unconsciously hoping to leave the rest of his family better off in the process.

I had accumulated this sense of them and their improvement. Tom and his parents entered my office about a year after the beginning of the weekly family sessions. The two older boys had attended regularly. There was usually a lot of brotherly bickering. The work had enlarged the three boys' awareness of many of the family issues. After the previous session, the two older boys had left for a month at camp. In the next section of this report, I will detail my own responses in order to illustrate their progress and my use of countertransference during a single session.

Tom sat in a red swivel chair, in which he rotated during much of the session, to Mr. Jansen's annoyance. Mrs. Jansen said they had not fought this week in any way, in contrast to last week when they had fought on the way to the session. Tom had used this in the session against his father. Mr. Jansen said that all of them, even Tom, were missing the older boys.

"Sure I am," said Tom. "They're my brothers."

"But you used to fight so much!" said Mrs. Jansen.

"Well, we love each other. That's just the way brothers are," said Tom. "But I also like having the house to myself."

So far, I felt this was an interesting byplay, and I noted that Tom did indeed seem fonder of his absent brothers than he would have admitted to being a year earlier. Already, I had a countertransference sense of uneasiness about the way the parents were getting him to show off his progress, but I appreciated it partly too, as if it were a credit to my helpfulness to them. I had the thought, "They're showing off as if giving me a report card on Tom's improvement."

My thought was confirmed a moment later, when Mr. Jansen said that they had gotten Tom's school report card. As he said this, Tom began to get silly and blow in the air, making noises and turning in his chair. Both parents got angry at this, telling him to stop, but he did not stop for some time. This was the kind of thing that made them mad at home.

Finally, Mr. Jansen said, "Tom, no ice cream if you don't stop!"

"That's blackmail!" yelled Tom.

"Sure it is," said Father, "and I mean it!"

Tom continued the behavior, while also beginning to pout. He was daring his father, who said again,

"Tom! I mean it. No ice cream!"

Mr. Jansen said this in such a manner that I felt it was a dance between them, in which Tom would give in just in time to get his ice cream. I felt both frustrated for Mr. Jansen that Tom would not stop, and annoyed with him for setting Tom up in the first place. I had confused and contradictory feelings about the "report" on school progress and on Tom's growth. It seemed to me that Mr. Jansen had gotten away with showing off Tom's increased ability to express love for his brothers. Why did he have to rub it in about school? And I thought that there must be some embarrassment on Tom's part about doing well at school.

Though I could not quite formulate it in the hour, afterwards I realized that Mr. Jansen was doing just the kind of showing off and flaunting that probably got Tom in trouble at school. Tom was doing the clowning, which probably accompanied his own wish to show off his brilliance. Since he had been improving, he now knew better than to do it, but he was being provoked by his father.

At this point in the hour, I was feeling unsure of what was happening, and vaguely uncomfortable both with Mr. Jansen and with Tom. My discomfort was partly with Tom's clowning, which did not seem to be due to his discomfort. All I could feel was that he was showing off. And I was uncomfortable with Mr. Jansen's persistent use of threats, which felt to me to be retaliatory and empty instead of constituting effective limit setting. I now recalled that I had been feeling annoyed with Mr. Jansen for the times he had urged Tom to slug kids when they teased him. I would start out feeling sure that was not a good solution, but Mr. Jansen and Tom managed to present these situations in which Tom was picked on in such a way that I could no longer quite tell what I thought. I knew that my own history of peer relations in latency and early adolescence made this an area in which I am a bit vulnerable, which means that I have to think through a solution each time, rather than relying on innate sense as I might in other areas. So I had ended up slightly confused and thinking, "Well, perhaps it is the thing to do after all."

Here is a potentially valuable opportunity for the therapist. David finds the family in a moment of affective intensity and at the same time experiences in himself some confusion. This indicates that he is in touch with object relationships that are active in the session. Not that it is uncommon for a therapist to be uncertain, or to need to wait for a while to know where things will settle out, but this confusion was different: it represented David's losing his way inside himself. Moments like these are especially valuable, and we urge beginning therapists to tolerate them. This capacity to not know is captured in the term negative capability, borrowed from the poet John Keats (as we said in chapter 15). In one of his letters, Keats described Shakespeare's poetic quality of allowing meaning to emerge from inside an experience, rather than needing to impose ideas on experience with unreasonable speed, before the richness of an experience has blossomed. This tolerance of "not knowing" and of confusion allows meaning to emerge from within the therapist, and adds a dimension of richness to the encounter which can only be achieved by new discovery from the inside. This type of countertransference experience sheds light on a core affective experience in the therapy session and leads to a deeper level of understanding.

In the hour, I only knew that my discomfort was a time-tested sign that there was also conflict and confusion in the patients, and that this was the time to intervene by exploring their confusion. I noticed that Mrs. Jansen was sitting by and letting this go on, as she often did. At that moment, I thought of her as leaving things to Mr. Jansen but slightly smirking as she did so.

As I thought of these things, Mr. Jansen was going on to tell about the achievement in the report card, which was excellent after Tom's shaky start at the beginning of the year.

As the tension eased, I felt ready to use my therapeutic discomfort to advantage before the moment passed.

I interrupted Mr. Jansen, hoping to help the family stay with the themes of blackmailing and difficult behavior. I wanted to enlarge their capacity for observation, and to help them include an understanding of the history of old experience that led up to this moment. I began with a question that might link the events in the therapy hour with Tom's difficulties elsewhere. I said, "Is this exchange in here between Dad and Tom anything like the being picked on at school, something Tom really doesn't like Dad or Mom to discuss, but which together you may be recreating in the session?"

Mr. Jansen was thrown off stride by my question, because it interrupted him as he was charging ahead over Tom's objection. I could see by the way I had confused him in the process that my own discomfort had led me to intervene less smoothly than I would have wished. Mr. Jansen, however, was not too thrown off to respond, so we got by this moment.

He said, "I 'blackmail' him because I don't know what else to do. How do you stop him?" he asked. "But I can see that it might relate to school." He paused, looking down. Then he looked at Tom again, and said, "Tom, did you know that I used to get in a lot of fights when I was a kid. And I used to lose!" And as he said this, Mr. Jansen's tone relaxed and he seemed to change from being in a head-on collision with Tom, to being in a loving, fatherly position.

I could hardly believe the tone of Mr. Jansen's sharing. It was spontaneous and earnest, a new way of presenting himself. I felt relief, and a pang of hope that this new opening might signal a breakthrough.

Tom said, "No! I didn't know that. Did you?" He then stopped playing with the cards he had been fiddling with after he had given up swiveling in the chair, and he looked straight at his father.

My feeling for Mr. Jansen was shifting. This was a moment in which I realized, again more in retrospect than I could consciously get a grip on in the hour, how much I had felt bullied by Mr. Jansen right from the beginning when he took such an outrageous stance about the potential of therapy for "contamination of his good sons," and had used that as a front to avoid investigating or sharing his part in Tom's troubles. Although I felt sympathetic on one level with Mrs. Jansen's tolerance of his bullying, my going along with her in not pressuring him to contribute had meant that I had felt vicariously bullied too. But this episode, with its small evidence of willingness to share, suddenly let me feel that I liked Mr. Jansen more than before. And since I knew how hard it was for him to let down his guard, I felt respect for him with his newfound courage.

One of the basic techniques of object relations family therapy is to ask the family to share old experiences that seem to be like a current problem or impasse. These moments offer more than history. They actually describe the way old relationships determine current history because they are carried alive inside the individual family members. These old internal object relationships exist inside all individual family members and have a great influence on current relationships. David intended to ask Mr. Jansen about such an old experience in the next few moments, but Mr. Jansen beat him to the punch—a good sign that family and therapist were working well together.

Led by my internal experience, I asked Mr. Jansen to say more. This time he elaborated, slightly sheepishly, but willingly:

"I was athletic, which helped. But the older kids would come by and it would always be me they picked on. I couldn't beat them up. It wasn't quite like with Tom. It wasn't the kids my own age doing it, but I did get beat up—often!"

I was thinking, slightly angrily still, that I understood something about how he got them to do this so regularly—that is, I was assuming he must have been provocative. As he made the brief statement about the older boys picking on him, I had a brief scene pass through my head in which I saw him taunting some older boys and saw them ganging up on him. In having this fantasy, I was identified partly with him and partly with the older boys, and partly I saw it from the perspective of my childhood self. I had some sympathy for him, and some for his attackers.

As I was pondering this, Mrs. Jansen said, "I wonder if you didn't do something to provoke them?"

I followed her by saying I had been thinking that Mr. Jansen often seemed to be hoping Tom would fight as a solution to being teased. Since we had been thinking together about how Tom might be provoking the other kids, I wondered if this might fit with his encouraging Tom to cause trouble, even though he was worried about it.

Mrs. Jansen smiled, and said, "Oh, my husband can be provocative himself, you know. He does it with me, for a start."

This moment in the hour began another important direction, critical to the therapeutic task. Mrs. Jansen had taken the lead in linking the total situation, and the work so far in the hour, to their marriage. It is important to understand links between the projective identifications, like the one Mr. Jansen had to Tom, but most especially links to any similar dynamic in the marriage.

In an object relations approach to the family, the dynamics of the family at large are understood to be built on the foundation of the marital relationship. The mutual projective identifications between the parents set the tone for the overall pattern of the family. When a link can be made in therapy between a parent-child object relationship and the parents' relationship, the family's understanding is greatly enhanced. At this point, the family was not only willing to attempt this work, but was initiating it—a sign of therapeutic progress. The greater the working alliance between therapist and family, the sooner the family will be ready for termination.

"Can you give me an example of how he is provocative with you?" I asked.

Mrs. Jansen thought for a moment, and said, "There was the time you were supposed to pick me up and we got our signals crossed."

Mr. Jansen filled in the story: His wife had come home in a blue fury after having to walk home because he had not picked her up and she had no money with her. He knew she was mad when she walked in the door.

"Yes," she said, "but instead of even saying you were sorry I had to walk, you accused me of stupidity in not knowing which corner was which, and you said it served me right. I know I was too mad to begin with, but that's not the point right now. You used it to provoke me." And she smiled, quite fondly to let him know she was not attacking him, and finished, "And you know it, honey!"

"It's true," he said. "I do that to her, and I kind of enjoy it. I shouldn't, but it's true that I do."

I noted that they had managed this piece of the work themselves. I had a hats-off-to-them feeling. I realized that I was feeling proud of them for holding together to do this work.

Having gotten the fact of provocation within the family onto the table, I felt we could try to link it to Tom. So I turned to him and asked if he knew about this part of his father's life.

"Well, I know he can tease Mommy and me," he said. "But, I never knew about the fights with the older kids. That's pretty interesting Dad!"

I now felt emotionally included in a family whose members were not bullying each other and provocatively keeping me outside the group. I felt we were working together in a new way, so that I could try to make a new kind of interpretation that might not, at this moment, meet the usual family unconscious resistance.

I said, "I wonder, Mr. Jansen, if you think you might want Tom to pick off a few of the tormentors for you, a sort of vicarious victory over the kids who used to beat on you?"

"I never thought of that," he said. "Perhaps so."

Because of my understanding and surviving his bullying, and because of his wife's support, Mr. Jansen was able to accept this interpretation.

Mrs. Jansen now put her arm around his shoulder. She did not rub in the way she also feels often picked on and bullied by Mr. Jansen. I thought that because of the gains in this session, in the future we might be able to talk about the way people felt picked on in the family as the original version of Tom's being picked on by his peers at school.

So I said, "The two issues—feeling picked on at home and at school—are related." Speaking with conviction gained from understanding my own feeling of being bullied in this therapeutic session, I added, "Understanding feeling picked on at home ought to help figure out what happens at school."

Tom was interested! At the door he said an unusually cheerful "Good-bye!"

WHAT IS THE ROLE OF INTERPRETATION?

Interpretation, whether spoken by the therapist or by a family member, is a building block in the joint construction of increased understanding. It is not a pronouncement from above, but a shared matter, to be tested, modified, and slowly accepted or discarded in favor of other ways of understanding. In this sense, interpretation is not an end product or something to be valued in itself, but a catalyst for developing shared understanding. In object relations theory, understanding is thought to be crucial in the development of the individual. Mother and baby, lovers, spouses, and family devote themselves to understanding one another's needs. A relationship is not only a matter of getting along or surviving together, but of providing for emotional growth through mutual understanding. Similarly, in object relations therapy, we promote understanding.

HOW IS COUNTERTRANSFERENCE USED?

In object relations therapy, countertransference is used to enhance and guide therapists' understanding, and to inform their interventions. The therapist works by joining with the individual patient's, couple's, or family's experience and allowing it to get inside. Then, working together, the experience is shared and understood. Countertransference represents the therapist's sharing of the experience, one that is in resonance with the internal life of the therapist. When therapists have been able to make sense of the countertransference, they let the patient, couple, or family know of their understanding by giving them feedback. At the simplest level, this feedback consists of making links, or clarifying what the therapists have understood. At the highest level, feedback is given in the form of interpretation, based in the countertransference. Countertransference is the material of the therapist's work. It is the guide that the therapist uses to join the individual or family in restoring it to emotional flexibility and growth. Along the way, it offers the therapist many opportunities for growth as well.

NOTES

Clinical vignettes from long-term combined individual, child, and family therapy illustrate and review concepts that we have already presented. As in therapy, so in teaching we cover the same patterns in slightly different ground.

Projective and introjective identification, object relations (Klein 1946).

Introjection of the object (Freud 1921).

Internal object relationships, object relations, and object relations theory (Fairbairn 1952, 1963).

Keats's term "negative capability" (Murray 1955).

Core affective exchange (D. Scharff and J. Scharff 1987).

Mutual projective identification in a marriage (Zinner 1976).

Intepretation (Strachey 1934, Stewart 1990).

Countertransference (Freud 1910a, Racker 1968, D. Scharff and J. Scharff 1987, 1991, D. Scharff 1992, J. Scharff 1992).

20

WORKING THROUGH
AND TERMINATION

HOW DOES WORKING THROUGH TAKE PLACE?

Working through was Sigmund Freud's term for continued analysis of resistance that persisted and intensified as layers of repression were peeled away. In object relations terms we think of working through as the continuing clarification and resolution of projective identificatory patterns. Projective identifications have to be experienced over and over at progressively higher levels of development. Sometimes when the pattern recurs, we may have an inevitable "here-we-go-again" feeling. Sometimes, we may feel hopeless that the patient will ever maintain gains and get better. We note, however, that the periods in which the patient is operating at the paranoid-schizoid end of the continuum are shorter. Patients can recognize their projective identifications through which they relate to the therapist. Applying the understanding and containing function internalized from experience with their mature therapists, patients can metabolize and detoxify their projective identifications for themselves. Sometimes the work of this phase seems boring, especially to the therapist who enjoys discovery and catharsis. But while the patient learns the maintenance of good self-functioning, the laborious work of standing by is essential. Our boredom is a defense against recognizing that we are about to become redundant. We must take our pleasure, like a good parent, from recognizing the patient's progress, independence, and autonomy.

WHAT ABOUT TERMINATION?

The individual, couple, or family is ready to terminate when they have returned to the appropriate developmental phase of individual or family life. Readiness for termination can be recognized from improvement in the capacities outlined in table 20.1.

We aim for broad goals. We are not interested in terminating as soon as symptom resolution is achieved. The termination will occur when the criteria for termination have been met. Specifically and in the technical sense, we look for signs that the criteria for termination shown in table 20.2 have been met.

CAN YOU SHOW READINESS FOR TERMINATION AFTER WORKING THROUGH IN INDIVIDUAL THERAPY?

Mrs. Epstein (mentioned in chapter 15) had been in a prolonged working through phase in her analysis with me (JSS). She had worked on her projective identification of me in which I was all that was wonderful, while she was nothing. She had discovered how her envy of me (and originally of her mother and her mother's exciting relationship to her husband) had depleted her feeling about herself as a worthwhile person. Her fantasy solution had been that if only she could stay with me for-

Table 20.1.   Readiness for Termination Shown by
Improved Capacity

• To master developmental stress
• To work cooperatively
• To have loving object relationships
• To integrate hate with love, and tolerate ambivalence
• To perceive others accurately
• To have empathy and concern for others
• To differentiate among and meet the needs of the individual

Table 20.2.   Criteria for Termination

- The therapeutic space has been internalized and a reasonably secure holding capacity has been formed.
- Unconscious projective identifications have been recognized, owned, and taken back.
- The capacity to work together with family members or life partners is restored.
- Intimate and sexual relating is now gratifying and satisfying.
- The individual provides good holding for the self, and the couple or family provides a vital holding environment for the individual, couple, or family.
- The capacity to mourn the loss of the therapeutic relationship is sufficient to support a satisfactory termination and to prepare the individual, couple, or family to deal with future developmental losses and to envision their future beyond therapy.

ever, or get from me what I had, or become me, she could feel good about herself. We went over this fantasy over and over again in many different forms until she became able to relate to me as an equal in a collaborative relationship. Previously unable to enjoy what she had, she could now enter her life and give and receive love fully. Previously unemployable, she could now earn a good salary. It was clear that she was close to termination.

But Mrs. Epstein had lost her mother by sudden death in a car crash when she was just twelve years old, shortly after her first menstrual period. She got the idea that growth and autonomy killed the person one had depended on. Since separation meant death to her, termination was to be feared and would require a final piece of working through. After a dreadful experience of deadness and emptiness during her last summer break—which presaged her final separation from analysis—Mrs. Epstein became terrified of terminating in case she would feel dead and empty like that afterwards. She saw that this was her fantasy, based on her earlier loss, and that, unlike that time, she and I could go on living separately after termination. A wonderful dream reassured her of her capacity to have a good good-bye, and she recovered her previous level of functioning within two weeks.

There were some short-lived regressions, but in general, Mrs. Epstein continued to be independent, assertive, competitive, and compassionate toward me. She talked of a feeling of new energy, space, and confidence, with plenty of love to give. She talked of having the good times and the bad times balanced clearly in her mind. She said that she thought that she had retrieved past experience, mended it, and fused past and present into something that would serve the future. She was not worried when I missed a day because of sickness, and she did not get mad at being reminded by a patient arriving too early for his session that someone would be taking her place. Her capacity for self-analysis, for integration of experience, and for recovery from setbacks was consistently in evidence. Her experience of the therapeutic capacity was fully internalized. She no longer needed me and she could at last feel that she had something to give me. Mrs. Epstein was ready to terminate. As she left, she said, "Like the bulbs I've just had planted, what we've done together is in. It's real. I don't have to see it to know it's there. It's not just mine. It's yours, too. But the flowers will be mine."

Mrs. Epstein happened to go the distance in her analysis. Not all patients have such determination and fortitude, or such ambitious goals for their development. We want to be sure that we support patients' or clients' criteria for termination rather than impose our own. Although we have our own views of what constitutes readiness for termination, we do not want our own therapeutic ambitions to define patients' goals.

NOTES

When repression is undone, further resistance against the emergence of conflict needs to be worked through. When conflict is sufficiently expressed, experienced, and understood in terms of patterns of unconscious communication, we can say that the working through is completed. This development ushers in the termination phase.

Working through (Freud 1914, D. Scharff and J. Scharff 1987).
Termination (D. Scharff and J. Scharff 1987).

III

APPLICATION AND INTEGRATION

21

INTEGRATION OF INDIVIDUAL THERAPY WITH COUPLE, FAMILY, GROUP, AND SEX THERAPIES

HOW IS INTEGRATION OF DIFFERENT MODALITIES POSSIBLE?

Integration of individual therapy with couple, family, group, and sex therapies is easy using object relations theory. They share the same theoretical model, in which the group is a unique combination of individuals in a state of unconscious communication, and the individual self contains and relates to a group of internal objects that represent the person's experience with the family of origin. The individual projects parts of the self or object into the significant others—spouse, therapist, family members. This happens in therapy, in long-term friendships, in marriage, in sexuality, and with each successive developmental stage. The projective identifications may form in a stuck cycle or in a new way that allows reworking.

Ronald Fairbairn gave us our view of the individual personality as a system of internal object relations in dynamic relation to each other. It was Henry Dicks's genius to note that when two such personalities united in marriage, this formed a union in which each partner could project unwanted or endangered internal object relationships into the spouse, leading to a state of mutual projective identification. The mutual projective identification system of the marriage enhances the self of each spouse, creates a discernible marital joint personality, and supports their relationship. However, if the spouses are totally dependent on the combination of the two personalities to make them whole, then the projective identification system is actually weakening the self of each of them and blocking growth.

Wilfred Bion applied Kleinian theory to groups. He noted that projective identification occurs between the group and the leader, and among the individuals, to create an unacknowledged series of subgroups. These subgroups come together in order to express certain unconscious assumptions about what the group should be doing, feeling, and experiencing. Individuals get together according to these basic assumptions because of their individual valencies to do so. Similarly, we find that in marriage spouses are chosen because of their valencies to accept particular projective identifications of their spouses. Roger Shapiro and John Zinner were the first to apply projective identification to families. They noted that adolescents were identified as harboring unwanted or longed-for parts of the parents and were then treated as symptomatic and pathological in an effort on the part of the family to isolate and at the same time take care of these disavowed parts. Shapiro and Zinner also described shared unconscious family assumptions, namely, unacknowledged but passively agreed-on views that organize the family and protect its members from facing anxiety that they fear would disrupt or annihilate the family. Zinner applied this concept of mutual projective identification to the marital interaction of the parents in the families that he studied.

We have applied object relations theory to couple and family therapy and to sex therapy. The resulting object relations couple and family therapy is a method that derives from psychoanalytic principles shown in table 21.1.

Table 21.1.   Psychoanalytic Principles in Couple and Family Therapy

- Listening
- Responding to unconscious material
- Developing insight
- Following affect
- Working with dream and fantasy
- Interpreting
- Working in the transference and countertransference toward understanding and growth

The therapeutic relationship offers an environment similar enough for these patterns to emerge, but different enough for identification and reworking, because the therapist brings the capacity for holding, for sharing the couple's experience, for tolerating the anxiety involved, and for providing space for understanding.

HOW DOES OBJECT RELATIONS APPLY TO SEX THERAPY?

In behavioral sex therapy, a couple participates together in private, doing a series of exercises graded from nongenital pleasuring to full genital stimulation, from low arousal to high, leading up to containment of the penis holding still, and finally intercourse. The partners discuss these experiences in their therapy session. What the object relations therapist adds to the situation is an in-depth focus on the source of sexual difficulty, which is seen as deriving from the unconscious communication of the internal object relations of the partners. For instance, a woman who enjoys intimacy with her husband and has healthy breast tissue yet hates to have her breasts touched has converted emotional pain into a physical symptom through which she expresses her fear of being excited and her wishes to be rejecting. Early conflict is contained in splits within her self in which pleasure has been projected into the genitalia, and fear and rejection into the breasts.

CAN YOU SHOW AN EXAMPLE OF COMBINED, CONCURRENT, AND SERIAL FAMILY, INDIVIDUAL, AND SEX THERAPIES?

Lars and Velia Simpson (described more fully in *Object Relations Couple Therapy*, chapters 10 and 11) had been married since late adolescence. They loved each other and were committed to staying together whether they could be helped or not. They were referred to me (DES) for consultation about their sexual difficulties. Velia, who had previously suffered from vaginismus and was still anorgasmic, had a total dislike of sex, and Lars had premature ejaculation. In a couple diagnostic session,

I learned that Velia was from a family where the children looked to each other for affection—sometimes combined with sexual stimulation—in the absence of love and caring from their parents. Lars could remember little from his childhood, except that his parents got divorced after his father's arrest for homosexual solicitation when Lars was seventeen. Lars and Velia were each other's first loves, and the objects to which each escaped from their unsatisfactory families.

In a single diagnostic family session, they reported that, when they fought over their frustration with their sex life, their children tended to get upset and to cause diversionary trouble. Without being inappropriately graphic with children present, they alluded to what they called "difficulty with conjugal relations," and the children did indeed start to fight. In general, their older son Eric tried to be good but seemed to catch his mother's rage anyway. Alex, their middle child, was hyperactive and so afraid to express anger that he was inclined to soil his pants. Jeanette, the youngest, was a cute and unabashedly seductive oedipal child who introduced sexual excitement into the family despite the grown-ups' fear of it.

The parents agreed to my request for an extension of the consultation so that Alex could be evaluated individually. Psychometric testing showed that Alex had attention deficit disorder with hyperactivity. The parents accepted my recommendation of individual therapy for Alex with a psychiatrist who could combine psychotherapy with medication. Velia and Lars were not able to tolerate the idea of sex therapy, but they would have tried family therapy if a therapist could have been found for them. I could not take them on myself at that time, and there was no other family therapist at the clinic. During the consultation, Velia had recognized her underlying depression and accepted referral to a psychiatrist for three times a week individual therapy for herself. Our choice of modality will be determined by the family's preference and capacity for working in a particular setting, as well as by the availability of therapists.

Individual Therapy for Alex

It turned out that Alex was not motivated to be in therapy and could not benefit from it. His hyperactivity at school did benefit from stimulant medication, but his soiling, jealousy, and disruptiveness at home persisted and would require some other form of psychotherapy. I would discover that he was much more able to benefit from family therapy than he had from individual treatment.

Individual Therapy for Velia

Psychoanalytically oriented psychotherapy was combined with antidepressant medication and occasional brief hospitalization when Velia was suicidal. In the transference, she recovered a fantasy of herself as a sexy person who hid so as not to be seen as dirty by her therapist. She learned that she could feel sexy and express these feelings toward him without his responding to her longing. Assured of a safe environment, she found that her most repressed longing was for a trusted parent for whom she could feel longing without enactment of incestuous wishes.

Soon after Alex's individual therapy failed, and while Velia's individual therapy was ongoing, the Simpsons began family therapy with me, now that I had time to see them. In an early session, Velia talked with Lars and me about her fear of physical intimacy and her ensuing rage. The children's play reflected the theme, and displayed the dynamics of the sexual difficulty in the context of the parents' relationship. Alex built a long tunnel out of blocks and called it a firehouse. Jeanette drove a fire truck with an extension ladder through the firehouse and broke it apart. The parents recognized the children's play with the fire truck breaking the firehouse as a symbol of their fear of the destructive potential of intercourse. The children further contributed the idea that a girl who thinks that she should be the driver will always wreck things, and that it would be better to have a boy driving the truck, quite a telling comment on the problem of Lars's trauma-based passivity. As the months went by, we continued to explore the family ramifications of the parents' sexual difficulty. We worked on understanding the parents' projective identifications of their children as aspects of their own abusive parents. But Velia and Lars were still too frightened to confront their sexual difficulties directly.

Sex Therapy for Velia and Lars

Six months later, Lars and Velia began sex therapy with me in addition to weekly family therapy. In response to sex therapy assignments that restricted the fullness of their sexual expression, Velia experienced an enormous amount of agonized, irritable hyperexcitement. Lars was afraid of the masturbation exercises. During the intense focus on physicality and forbidden sexual activity, Velia recovered memories of physical abuse by her father and sexual play with her adolescent brother and relived her longing and revulsion for her brother's penis. Shortly thereafter, Lars, whose forgetting of his childhood was dense, recalled that his father had committed anal intercourse on him, and that he, Lars, had then turned around and done the same to his brother. Each of them had a reason to feel intense shame about their longing for the penis. Having worked this through in relation to their histories and their embarrassing fantasies in their transferences to me, Lars and Velia became able to enjoy controlled sexual arousal and intercourse together.

A reversion to sexual failure occurred during my vacation, and this gave an opportunity to work on their response to me as an abandoning object. In the return of their symptoms, they showed me rather than telling me how I had hurt them. Unable to express their rage at me for being like their parents, who they felt did not care what happened to them, Lars and Velia could not bring their repressed rejecting object relationship to consciousness. It remained unconscious and expressed itself by attacking their exciting object relationship. This internal way of dealing with rage at the object spoiled their capacity for sexual pleasure. Rage was repressing longing. With further work, the Simpsons became able to tell me that they were mad at me and that they had missed me (see chapter 11).

Before therapy, Lars and Velia suppressed their longing for closeness and gave vent to more rage than love. Bringing their sexuality to life through sex therapy for the couple and individual therapy for Velia threatened Lars and Velia with the revival of the bad fathers of their shared longing. In individual therapy, Velia reworked and owned her projective identifications in the transference. Sex therapy enabled Lars and Velia to express wishes to be loved and cared for in the shared transference to the sex therapist as an abandoning and later as a protective, nonincestuous, noninvasive object, after which they could transform each other into nontoxic sexual objects for each other to love and cherish. Family therapy relieved the children of the burden of provoking the parents' toxic projective identifications of them. The children's behavior changed so that they no longer created diversions from their parents' issues or inserted themselves in the war zone between them. With their intimate relationship repaired, Lars and Velia became more available as a parenting couple in whom their children could trust.

Because each form of therapy is built on the same basic theory, individual, couple, sex, and family therapy are theoretically and practically compatible with one another. The recommendation for an individual patient, couple, or family is based on a consideration of the fit of a suitable approach or of a mixture of modalities with the patient's preferences and readiness for therapy. Once we make an initial recommendation for a treatment plan, we want to try that treatment plan until we run into an impediment or further information that might cause us to reconsider it. For instance, we might recommend concurrent individual and family therapy and find that for some period of time this goes along well, with both therapies effective. Then, perhaps, the family work ends and individual therapy continues or vice versa.

WHAT IF THE WHOLE FAMILY DOES NOT ATTEND?

Imagine a session for a family of five where three members do not show up. This leaves the therapist with two "identified patients," who are there as if by accident at the convenience of the others. It is important not to change the therapeutic plan under this kind of pressure, but to use the experience to understand the family's resistance expressed in substituting individuals for a shared family group. The therapist hopes to reestablish the family commitment to therapy. If there is no response to interpretation of the resistance, and the two members continue to attend alone and to identify themselves as in need of help, the therapist might then agree to a change in the treatment format. Before offering to find another individual therapist for the second motivated family member, the therapist will work on acknowledging the loss of the motivated family and helping the remaining members to mourn the loss of the family treatment.

HOW IS IT USEFUL TO MOVE FROM
ONE MODALITY TO ANOTHER?

Movement from one format to another can be a sign of progress. When a family's holding capacity has improved in family therapy and the family is ready to terminate, the decision for one of its members to continue in individual therapy with the family's support is a sign of the family's newfound ability to differentiate among and meet the needs of its individual members. For instance, in a family where the mother had been sexually abused as a child, she did not have the confidence to tell her story outside the family. After family therapy was terminated, with her husband's unexpected encouragement, the woman was able to join a survivors-of-incest group. An individual may complete an analysis, and later, facing unanticipated developmental challenge, may bring his family for family therapy. In the case described in chapter 19, the parents refused family therapy. The nine-year-old boy was seen in individual therapy and the parents in parent guidance sessions. After developing trust in the therapist, the parents accepted the necessity for family meetings, and the individual therapy continued. In *Object Relations Family Therapy,* chapter 12, we described a case in which child analysis was combined productively with couple therapy for the parents. The important point is that switching from one format to another should not be a random response to resistance or transference enactment. Concurrent, combined, and serial therapy formats should be carefully and thoughtfully planned and then adhered to. As always, the frame of treatment is crucially important.

NOTES

Because object relations theory applies equally well to understanding individual, couple, and family dynamics, we find that individual, couple, family, and sex therapy methods can be compatible with one another when each is based in object relations theory. Combined, concurrent, or serial therapies can then be undertaken:

Fairbairn's view of internal object relations (Fairbairn 1963).
Mutual projective identification in marriage (Dicks 1967).

Basic assumption subgroups (Bion 1959).

Projective identification in families, shared unconscious family assumptions (Zinner and Shapiro 1972).

Mutual projective identification in marriage (Zinner 1976).

The integration of individual, couple, family, and sex therapy (D. Scharff and J. Scharff 1987, 1991).

②②

THE APPLICATION OF
OBJECT RELATIONS THEORY
TO VARIOUS SYNDROMES
AND POPULATIONS

DOES OBJECT RELATIONS THEORY
APPLY TO ADDICTIONS COUNSELING?

For an autonomous symptom such as addiction to alcohol or drugs, a nondirective object relations therapy approach alone is not sufficient to deal with the problem. The secondary effects of the addictive habit make the psychodynamic treatment impossible in serious cases. The person requires a supportive and rehabilitative network and a confrontational group system in which the need to stop the addiction can be confronted. However, giving up the addictive symptomology is not the end of the treatment but rather the beginning of therapy. Object relations theory helps the addiction counselor to understand the problem that patient and counselor are facing.

Some patients at the higher end of development will be able to move rather promptly into a psychodynamic treatment and may not require the full course of detoxification, behavioral, and group-based treatment. Those whose substance abuse is mild may give it up without group support and move directly into outpatient object relations therapy. This may happen in cases of substance abuse, but is rarely successful in addiction.

We conceptualize the addictive substance as a representation of the exciting object for which the self longs and hungers. The symptom is a repetitive concretization of the introjective identification of the elusive nourishing object. In its absence, the self has lost the creative capacity to form symbols and find metaphors for describing and metabolizing experience. Instead, the self uses addictive, or in more severe cases, psychotic behaviors to communicate its pain to its external objects while attempting to obliterate its effects upon the self.

DOES OBJECT RELATIONS THERAPY HELP IN THE TREATMENT OF EATING DISORDERS?

Below a certain weight, management of the holding environment may have to include hospitalization to avoid death from starvation or heart attack due to fluid imbalance. Instead of eating as an automatic habit, the self controls food intake to enact its intrapsychic attitude to objects. As in addiction or alcoholism, there is a concretization of object relationships in terms of a substance, in this case food. Object relations therapy can be helpful in the transference work with such patients, who frequently hunger for and reject their therapist's intervention, much as they binge on food or chop it up into tiny pieces that do not add up to a full meal. Applied to the dysfunctional family system in which the anorexic patient has grown up, object relations theory illuminates the way that the starving person contains a familywide anxiety about hunger and the exciting and rejecting aspects of the female body. Before she turned her attention to the use of paradoxical interventions and universal prescriptions, Mara Selvini Palazzoli understood anorexia from an object relations perspective. Kent Ravenscroft has applied object relations family therapy in the treatment of adolescents suffering from bulimia.

IF CLIENTS NEED A PSYCHOEDUCATIONAL APPROACH, HOW CAN OBJECT RELATIONS THEORY BE HELPFUL?

This question is often asked concerning schizophrenic or chronically psychotic and disabled patients, mentally handicapped family members, and difficult-to-educate children such as those with hyperactivity, severe learning and developmental difficulties, and severe behavioral problems.

When the capacity to learn is so impaired that psychological and cognitive growth and academic achievement cannot occur in the ordinary way, then the psychoeducational approach is the treatment of choice. The psychoeducational approach remedies the psychological interference to educational processes, by (1) attuning the educational effort to the psychological needs and (2) treating the psychological disturbance so that the child or adult can make use of education and learning can occur. We think that object relations therapy is applicable to treating the psychological disturbance, but the value of its use has been debated by some experts in the treatment of the learning disabled, neurobiologically impaired, and psychotic populations. Committed to the view that the symptom resides in the index patient, they object to methods that explore the object relations history or the family dynamics, because they think that such an approach blames the parents for the child's condition. But this is an inaccurate perception of object relations therapy. We do not judge, but we do want to help the family change behavior that is affecting symptomatology manifest in one of its members and to modify that member's valency for expressing familywide vulnerability. Reviewing their part in a pattern offers families this opportunity, while not placing the blame on any single family member.

DO YOU USE MEDICATION?

Medication is often required for major mental illnesses, serious breakdown, and psychiatric emergencies, such as suicide and psychosis, not immediately amenable to psychotherapy. Medication is more effective when it is combined with psychotherapy. We are interested in the careful evaluation of the use of medication as a component of an integrated treatment. Nevertheless, we do not rush to medicate, especially in outpatient treatment. We think that problems in living, relational problems, and depression and anxiety associated with conflict are best dealt with by psychotherapy. Many more syndromes and symptoms are treatable by psychotherapy than is often thought. When in doubt, we would prefer to proceed with a course of intensive object relations psychotherapy in order to see if that alone would be enough before prescribing medicine, providing only that the patient's life and well-being are not in imminent danger.

IS OBJECT RELATIONS THERAPY HELPFUL IN MAJOR MENTAL ILLNESS, INCLUDING PSYCHOSIS?

Object relations therapy is fully compatible with treatment of a psychotic patient. Although some early theoreticians thought that psychosis could be fully treated by the object relations approach alone, we now recognize that the biochemical imbalance in most of the major mental illnesses requires pharmacological support. Therapy is still relevant to those elements of character maladjustment, personality issues, secondary effects, and rehabilitation involving psychological growth of the psychotic person. In these cases, we recommend psychotherapy in partnership with relevant medication, with psychoeducation, and with family therapy. The therapy might well have an ego-supportive quality, but would still involve significant aspects of uncovering and reconstruction.

In the hospital treatment of major mental illness, object relations theory is helpful in understanding the dynamics found in hospital wards. Object relations theory applied to group functioning shows us how communities of inpatients will develop subgroups formed in hope of meeting unconscious needs that have been frustrated in the context of the therapeutic relationship with the staff. Mary Main, and Alfred Stanton and Morris Schwartz, have described how patterns of behavior occurring in the therapeutic community reflect each patient's intrapsychic dynamics.

CAN OBJECT RELATIONS FAMILY THERAPY HELP WHEN A FAMILY MEMBER IS PSYCHOTIC?

Object relations family therapy improves the family's ability to help a psychotic member with medication and rehabilitation issues, reduces stress on the family, and changes the dynamics, which decreases vulnerability to psychosis in the index patient and in other family members. The approach is based on research into familywide projective identification systems. These systems had to be understood and given up before the developing child or adolescent could escape from double binds and detach from the family attachment system. During the next two decades, the growing emphasis on the origins of psychosis in disordered genes and neurotransmitters meant that object relations family therapy took a backseat to psychoeducational approaches for supporting families to deal with the disabled family member. Now in Finland, researchers who added psychodynamic family therapy to their treatment program for psychotic patients (the "need-adapted approach") dramatically improved outcome and lowered or eliminated the need for antipsychotic medication. The value of object relations family therapy for psychosis and borderline states is once more appreciated.

HOW DO YOU UNDERSTAND THE DEVELOPMENT OF PSYCHOSOMATIC DISORDERS?

Psychosomatic disorders result from the *hysterical conversion* of problematic internal object relations into bodily problems and illnesses that become the basis for current ways of relating. Sigmund Freud studied patients who suffered from otherwise unexplainable physical symptoms such as paralysis of a limb, a repetitive cough, sinusitis, inability to speak, and fatigue. He found that instead of being conscious of the traumatic experience that they had experienced they buried the memory in these symptoms using dissociation and conversion. Ronald Fairbairn found that hysterical conversion processes were driven by alternating overstimulation and rejection by parents, as well as by unconscious symbolization.

Particularly under circumstances of early deprivation and trauma, which are encoded in the right frontal lobe, the body becomes a principal route for the expression of the highly emotional conflict of early child-parent exchanges. As society has become more open about sexuality and sexual abuse, and more transfixed by images of sexual perfection, hysterical processes now more commonly appear as eating disorders and sexual dysfunction.

Joyce McDougall described the body as a "theater" that replays dramas of early development that are beyond words. Through the transference-countertransference exchange, the therapist receives the message in a physical sensation, an emotional reaction, or a fantasy, and translates the experience into words. Object relations therapy provides a safe space for developing a language for the patient's previously unspoken experience.

DOES PROJECTIVE IDENTIFICATION OCCUR IN SEXUAL ABUSE?

Parents may view a child as a representative either of a part of themselves that was abused by one of their own parents or, alternatively, as a re-creation of that abusive parental object. The child becomes an exciting sexualized object that is adored and hated. In other words, parents may treat their children as parts of the parent's self or obejct. In actual behavior, then, the parent may both comfort and hurt the child. Introjective identification with the part projected into the abused child then re-creates for the parent the trauma of the original abusive situation. In this way, projective and introjective identificatory mechanisms perpetuate the trauma of abuse through the generations.

IS THERE AN OBJECT RELATIONS APPROACH TO AFFAIRS?

We have written about this in our previous books on sexuality and on couple therapy. Affairs occur when aspects of the couple's intimate and sexual life are split off and projected into an alternative relationship. Through this other relationship, the couple unconsciously hopes to find a capacity for creative sexual relating and import it to revitalize the impoverished primary relationship. An affair is an example of splitting and repression occurring in the interpersonal realm rather than in the intrapsychic realm. When the split-off and repressed issues cannot be retrieved, the affair becomes central and the present marriage ceases to be the primary relationship. For the couple therapist, the present marriage remains the primary focus. Elements split out into one or more affairs need to be understood as belonging to the primary marital relationship and reintegrated with the couple's shared marital issues, if the marriage is to be helped.

An affair arises from a deficit in both the holding and centered relationship aspects of the marriage. It represents issues that have been split off and, when the affair is kept secret, repressed outside the boundary of the couple relationship. So, understanding the cause of the affair is the first step toward reintegrating the split in the couple's marriage and the individual's capacity for intimate relating.

TO UNDERSTAND PARAPHILIAS, DO YOU NEED DRIVE-ORIENTED AND COGNITIVE-BEHAVIORAL MODELS?

The term "perversion" has been replaced by "paraphilia," which refers more accurately to the varieties of sexual behavior that run along the sexual continuum. These include rape fantasies, spanking, domination, trampling and other forms of sadomasochism, fetishism, frottage, pedophilia, and any compulsive sexual activity. The mid-twentieth-century psychoanalytic explanation of the perversions (which at that time included homosexuality) was built on a drive model. According to Sigmund Freud and Hans Sachs, perversions represent an isolated piece of childhood sexuality maintained through to adult development. According to this view polymorphous perverse sexuality is normal during early development, but when pathways to mature oedipal development are blocked, the individual's sexuality is fixated in an immature form.

These explanations need broadening into a relational model. In object relations therapy, we think of a paraphilia as an isolated, sexualized aspect of relating that has taken on a concrete, part-object, symbolic form and has been maintained as a compromise in the capacity of the patient to relate to whole objects with genitals. We try to understand the specific compromise that led to the need for this compromise.

Individuals complain of paraphilia when their sexual behavior becomes so addictive as to interfere with their health, safety, work, relationships, and self-esteem. The availability of cybersex has allowed the expression of paraphilic impulses and gratification of the full range of sexual fantasies without personal exposure, and to some extent has reduced the risks. On the other hand it reinforces the paraphilic impulse and leads some users to develop Internet sex addiction.

Couples present for therapy when the partner resents or avoids participation in sexual fantasies that are not shared and when the circumstances for arousal become more important than desire for the lover. In therapy, we work with individual and couple dynamics and object relations histories to understand why an image, voice, or condition is more appealing than a live partner. Object relations therapy may be combined with antidepressant medication for reducing the frequency of compulsive sexual activity, group-based twelve-step programs for sexual addiction, and sex therapy.

OBJECT RELATIONS THEORY HOLDS THAT EXPERIENCE WITH BOTH MOTHER AND FATHER IS IMPORTANT. SO HOW CAN IT BE APPLIED TO WORK WITH A SINGLE-PARENT FAMILY?

In handling the onslaught of developing children, the single parent is inevitably under more stress than a team of two parents, provided that the two parents get along reasonably well with each other and work together. Being a single parent is a handicapping condition. The single parent has to offer both fathering and mothering, and in so doing stands for a parental couple.

Each parent contains an internal couple, a psychic structure that mediates the capacity for important and intimate relationships. The internal couple is based on the person's experience of the parental couple relationship, modified by knowledge of other couples and by previous experience in adult intimate relationships. The single mother may present to her child her image of herself in relationship to a man, whether she is actually in a relationship to a man or not. The father does the same in terms of his relationship to a woman. It is not a single version of an internal couple that is presented but a wide range of possibilities. This happens in the ordinary course of events as a single parent talks about other couples, remembers her parents, or shares her hopes and fears for her child's development and capacity to relate. Thus, it is entirely possible for a single parent to present a full range of possibilities for the child's capacity to be in a loving and sexual relationship as an adult.

This is also possible if the parent is homosexual. Does the internal couple that such a homosexual parent presents include a full range of possibilities for development or is it skewed more toward a homosexual couple, just as the heterosexual parents' internal couple is skewed toward a heterosexual couple? Research implies that homosexual couples may present the full range of options to their children. Homosexual couples also carry within them internal couples based on their experience of their birth parents as a couple.

HOW DO YOU UNDERSTAND HOMOSEXUALITY?

Nowadays, homosexuality is understood not as pathological, but as one of the potential patterns for human sexual development and sexual object choice. As one of the outcomes in human development, it is, of course, influenced by the primary objects. The influence of the child's experience with both parents and the quality of their relationship is important to the choice of developmental path. The parents present to the children a broad spectrum of internal objects, inclusive of their sexual aspects, for relating. These are relevant to the developmental pathways that include heterosexuality, homosexuality, and bisexuality.

Homosexuals may seek treatment for discomfort with their homosexual orientation or, more commonly, with other aspects of their life or relational abilities. If the treatment is intensive and thorough, it will involve exploration of early life experiences, including those that were formative in the development of gender and sexual object choice. This does not imply a bias as to the preferred outcome any more than when comparable exploration is conducted with a heterosexual patient.

IS OBJECT RELATIONS THERAPY
APPLICABLE TO SUICIDAL EMERGENCIES?

If a person's life is at risk, the capacity for trust and the risk of suicide have to be assessed, and appropriate plans for management of the risk situation have to be implemented immediately. Here, object relations therapy provides for a safe holding context within which the centered therapy relationship can form. If we can understand what contributes to various patients' suicidal ideation, we can begin to move them from being a danger to themselves toward understanding the relational element in their depressive panic. We view the suicidal impulse in the ways shown in table 22.1.

Making the unconscious constellation conscious helps the patient to give up the suicidal ideation.

HOW CAN IT HELP IN MANAGED CARE SITUATIONS?

In a health maintenance organization or managed care situation, we do not have the luxury of taking as long in therapy as is optimal for the patient. Some therapists adjust to the reality of the four-session contract by intervening more actively in the hope that if the therapist does more in the limited situation, the patient will get better faster. We have found that this does not bear out in practice. It is more useful to spend the time giving the patient a way of thinking and working with a psychodynamic approach that shows how much needs to be done and how it could be accomplished, than to try desperately to do a little in too short a time. Time is better spent educating the patient in what can be done than in deluding him and the sponsoring agency into thinking that four sessions is going to be enough for anyone except a basically healthy person in short-term developmental crisis.

For instance, in the student mental health field, young patients face the anxiety of beginning school away from home, forming and breaking intimate and sexual relationships, resolving roommate disputes, meeting the challenge of academic crises, and coping with changes in their parents' situations. Married students may seek help for marital tension due

Table 22.1.   The Object Relations of Attempted Suicide

- An attack on the internal object with which the self is identified
- An attack on the self to spare the object
- An attack on the object with which the self is destructively fused
- An attempt to separate the self from the object

to overwork or academic pressure, or for adjusting to the increased emotional and financial responsibilities of having a child. Others may need help in adjusting to a physical illness. Here, a brief approach that focuses on the challenge that has temporarily overwhelmed the adaptive capacities of the individual or family often enables the patients to move back to their previous level of good adjustment within one to three sessions. If patients discover that there are longer-term issues underlying these crises, they can consider what kind of help they would need for a more thorough readjustment. The patient and therapist together can consider alternate possibilities, including low-fee therapy outside the health maintenance organization or counseling center. This often enables the patient to decide to make the required economic and emotional investment, even when that investment will not be supported by an insuring institution.

IS INTENSIVE OBJECT RELATIONS THERAPY ONLY FOR THE RICH AND THE WELL-EDUCATED?

Of course, long-term therapy calls for a financial commitment. As more therapists are becoming trained in the object relations therapy method, more of the agencies that offer reduced-fee counseling are able to offer object relations therapy as part of their therapeutic armamentarium. Psychoanalytic institutes offer low-fee psychoanalysis to motivated applicants who qualify for fee reduction. Object relations therapy is not only for the well-educated. The potential patient does require a degree of psychological-mindedness to communicate with the therapist in the language of object relations, but we have found that psychological-mindedness does not correlate directly with intelligence, level of education, or cultural background. There are some patients among the rich, the well-educated, and the privileged who are unable to work in an object relations method and require a more educational approach. Similarly, there are patients from disadvantaged communities, with limited language capacity or intellect, who work well on relationships and feelings and feel grateful for insight. They may welcome this new vista on understanding their lives and make more use of it than do some more sophisticated patients.

OBJECT RELATIONS THERAPY SOUNDS SO COMPLICATED, MUST IT TAKE A LONG TIME?

We tend to think of object relations therapy as a long-term method going on over years rather than months. It is, however, a way of working and thinking about clinical situations that can be quite helpful for short-term work (see chapter 18 on Brief Therapy).

NOTES

This chapter gives an object relations bird's-eye view of various conditions such as alcoholism, addiction, suicide, eating disorders, learning disorders, psychosis, and sexual paraphilia. We consider the object relations approach to homosexuality and affairs. We conclude with thoughts on the relevance of object relations theory to short-term therapy and managed care.

Intrapsychic and institutional dynamics (Main 1957, Stanton and Schwartz 1954).

Affairs (D. Scharff 1982, D. Scharff and J. Scharff 1991).

Perversion/paraphilia (Freud 1905b, Joseph 1989, Sachs 1923).

Psychosis (Kernberg 1975, Ogden 1982, Searles 1965, Volkan 1976)

Eating Disorders (Ravenscroft 1988, Selvini Palazzoli 1974).

Psychosomatics (McDougall 1989, 1995).

Sexuality (Scharff 1982, Glassgold and Iasenza 1995, Levine 1992).

Results of sexual trauma (J. S. Scharff and D. E. Scharff 1994),

Family therapy for psychosis (Lansky 1981).

Hysteria (Breuer and Freud 1895).

"Need adapted approach" (Alanen et al. 2000).

(23)

THE ROLE AND EXPERIENCE OF
THE OBJECT RELATIONS THERAPIST

WHAT ARE YOUR VALUES AS
OBJECT RELATIONS THERAPISTS?

We value insight, psychological-mindedness, respectful listening, and affective attunement. We value making the unconscious conscious by experiencing it in the countertransference and then revealing it to the patient in an interpretive mode. We do not value symptom relief without in-depth reconstruction. We value maturation and growth and the developmental process. We value process and review.

HOW DO YOU VIEW SYMPTOMS?

We see symptomatology as a compromise between unacceptable ways of relating and the demands of current relationships. Therapy consists in making the unconscious conscious to recover lost, repressed parts of the self and so to make more of the self available for interaction with and modification by external objects.

HOW DO YOU ADDRESS THE PEOPLE IN
THERAPY WITH YOU?

When we are working with people in consultation, we usually use surnames. In families, we call parents by their surnames and the children by their forenames. In couple therapy, we use surnames in the opening phase of therapy, but as we get to know the couple, who naturally are calling each other by their first names, we tend to use the more informal form of address within the session, although in communicating on the telephone we tend to revert to the more formal form of address.

DOESN'T THE USE OF THE TERM "PATIENTS" GO
AGAINST THE NONAUTHORITARIAN STANCE OF
OBJECT RELATIONS THERAPY?

Not in our view. As physicians, we think of ourselves as working with patients. There is no pejorative connotation to us in the use of this terminology. It is simply analogous to social workers or counselors working with clients, or teachers working with students. The likelihood of transfer of an authoritarian role relationship from earlier experience with physicians of the body needs to be considered and interpreted, but that does not negate the possibility of a collaborative stance. Personal respect and integrity transcend the boundaries of terminology.

HOW IS THE THERAPIST DIFFERENT IN THE
EARLY, MIDDLE, AND LATE PHASES OF THERAPY?

The main distinguishing feature is the therapist's capacity to work with the patient. In the early phase, there is a greater tendency for the therapist to be as resistant as the patient is to uncovering anxiety-provoking material. This is not a devious or pathological collusion. Therapists are simply caught up in the defensive process. Unless they are affected in this way, they are unable to know what they and the patient have to work beyond. In the middle phase, we see that both therapist and patient have an increased capacity to analyze resistance and to move into areas of greater anxiety. In the late phases of therapy, we see a more collaborative, whole object relationship between therapist and patient with fewer, shorter-lived reversions to primitive relating to the therapist as a part-object.

HOW ARE OBJECT RELATIONS EXPERIENCED IN THERAPY?

The internal object relationships of the patient or patient group operate as a kind of map or script of relationships to be recreated with the therapist. These recreated relationships in therapy are re-editions of the original relationships to the object of infantile dependency. A relatively conscious and mature or collaborative relationship that corresponds to the ideal or good-enough object relationship enjoyed by the central ego governs the quality of the therapeutic alliance that will be enlivened by or assaulted by the unconscious internal object relationship of the exciting or rejecting sort, respectively. As the therapist contains the expression of these repressed object relationships, the patient is enabled to modify and rework their more troublesome aspects.

CAN YOU GAVE AN EXAMPLE OF AN OBJECT RELATIONSHIP EXPERIENCED IN INDIVIDUAL THERAPY?

Mr. Donald, an architect, would have preferred to see a male therapist, he told me (JSS). He did not like my office furnishings, the neighborhood of my home office, or my high fee. I should live where he did, charge the same fee per hour as he did, and redecorate my office in leather. He attacked my attempts to link his feelings about me to his history. I was left feeling rather destroyed and unable to think of what to say next, or remember what I had just said. It was as if I was not there. When I learned later of his relationship with his mother, I was able to see what he had been re-creating in the transference. She used to insist that he go shopping with her, and since he looked like her, she used to try hats on him to see if they would suit her face. He hated these shopping trips and would rather have been playing soccer with his friends. As he felt as a child, I felt coerced, turned into the opposite sex, my autonomous, thinking self temporarily annihilated. He was giving me to feel as he had felt as a child in relation to his mother. I experienced a concordant countertransference, concordant with his self in relation to him as the annihilating maternal object. The repressed object relationship was re-created in the transference. There was also evidence of just enough central ego functioning in relation to me as a good-enough object that he continued to attend his sessions, pay the full fee promptly, and contribute to a therapeutic alliance sufficient to support the emergence of this and other repressed object relationships.

DO YOU ALWAYS HAVE COUNTERTRANSFERENCE?

Yes. Countertransference and transference are constantly operating. Most of the time, however, countertransference remains unconscious and is experienced simply as a feeling of being in tune with the patient. At moments, however, it obtrudes. The therapist becomes conscious of a countertransference response that is puzzling or jarring or in some way. It interferes with the unconscious automatic piloting mechanism that keeps the therapist in tune and on track. Attending to the countertransference creates a reflective space between the experiencing and observing parts of the therapist. Here the therapist finds the space for process and review to figure out how experience in the here-and-now with the patient reflects the patient's unconscious object relations set.

HOW DO YOU KNOW THAT YOUR COUNTERTRANSFERENCE ISN'T "JUST YOU AND YOUR PROBLEMS"?

It is you. It is always you, but it has been stimulated in response to the patient. You want to check, however, that you do not always import a typical and repetitive countertransference based on your own neurotic conflicts. The only safeguard against this is to ensure that you have been adequately treated in your own personal therapy or psychoanalysis. You also subject your own reactions constantly to process and review. If you discover that the countertransference has been contributed more by your own problems than by a feeling response in reaction to the patient, then it is best to simply admit it to yourself and work on it, rather than imposing it on the patient and insisting that the patient deal with an interpretation that you arrived at from a false basis. You will learn that your own areas of weakness can become the very places where you will be most acutely receptive to patients' transference difficulties. With knowledge, experience, and treatment these areas of weakness can be turned into strengths.

IS PSYCHOTHERAPY FOR THE THERAPIST ALWAYS REQUIRED?

Few of us have the maturity to conduct reliable therapy without our own experience of therapy. Even when therapists are basically healthy, their work will acquire more depth if they have also had the experience of exploring their unconscious object relations from the patient's side of the therapeutic relationship. Object relations therapy calls for therapists to use their own internal responses as a set of clues to what the patient brings to them. They cannot read the clues unless they are sure of the validity of their responses. Experience in personal therapy provides the baseline for knowing themselves well enough so that they can have confidence in knowing when something foreign to their internal reality has been experienced because of the encounter with the patient. We encourage all our trainees to have a substantial experience of personal therapy or psychoanalysis, even when it is not felt to be necessary for their personal life.

WHEN WORKING WITH COUPLES AND FAMILIES, HOW DO YOU DECIDE TO WORK TOGETHER IN COTHERAPY AND HOW DOES COTHERAPY CHANGE YOUR WAY OF WORKING?

We tend not to work together in cotherapy. We find that we can usually do the work alone as well as with a cotherapist, and this is more economical. Sometimes, however, a family will be particularly difficult; for instance, when there is more than one hyperactive child, a cotherapist may be found necessary to support the holding environment. At other times, we choose to work in cotherapy for the opportunity of learning from a colleague and experiencing the transference within the cotherapy relationship rather than in the intrapsychic realm as occurs when one is working alone. Cotherapy is useful in training couple therapists.

Cotherapy changes the way of working by changing the focus of the countertransference. In cotherapy, the countertransference is experienced within the cotherapy relationship. We find ourselves dealing with our cotherapist according to a particular object relationship pattern that reflects a repressed object relationship operating between the couple or members of the family. This can usefully be demonstrated to the family or couple when the cotherapists talk about their experience and relate it to the family. When the cotherapists are married, as we are, the therapists' own marital issues are stirred by the task of allowing the transference to resonate in the cotherapy relationship. As a married cotherapy pair, we must agree to confront our own internal couple so that the couple in therapy can distinguish their internal couple that they have projected into us. This process and review tends to take longer and be more complicated than for the cotherapy team that is not married. So for economy of time and money and to save ourselves and our families from the upset of the intrusion of work into the family life space, we usually choose not to work in cotherapy.

(24)

THE DEVELOPMENT OF
THERAPEUTIC CAPACITY

HOW CAN YOU BEAR TO
WORK THIS CLOSELY WITH PEOPLE?

Ours is difficult work, if we do it properly. It throws us into the farthest recesses of our own personality and it makes us confront parts of ourselves that we find problematic. We can bear the work only if we have sufficient support for doing it. By this we do not mean current support as much as resources already built into ourselves. These resources come from previous clinical experience and from supervision, peer supervision, consultation, and therapy. We choose to be therapists because of our own internal object relations set: We need to repair objects that we feel our neediness and aggression have damaged. To some extent then, in return, it is gratifying to us to be somewhat hurt in our work life and to recover from it and to heal the parts of ourselves that we see in our patients. When, through therapy and continued clinical experience, we become healthier and have less need to make this kind of reparation, we can go through a period of boredom in our work. This is a moment where some therapists may quit or experience burnout. It is important to recognize that this is a phase in the growth and development of the therapist. We encourage therapists to seek help to get over this so as to be able to keep working, now from a new basis in healthier, more adaptive functioning instead of from the previous masochistic position.

WHAT DOES WORK AS AN OBJECT RELATIONS THERAPIST DO TO YOU?

It can wear you down from time to time. It can get inside you so that, if you do not sufficiently metabolize your work, you may go home and start treating your family as your patients have treated you. Sufficient time to process experiences is absolutely crucial and should take place in the office and not in the back-home setting. At the same time, object relations therapy affords work that constantly challenges you. It requires and facilitates your continued personal growth. The gratification of being a therapist lies in finding yourself gradually more capable of dealing with a wider range of problems. There is no danger of feeling, as a surgeon we knew once felt, that you have already done so many of the same kinds of procedures that there is nothing new anymore. The human personality is infinitely more subtle and demanding than the body. It requires greater agility, ingenuity, and capacity for tolerating ambiguity. Good therapy is a challenging experience from which both patient and therapist can grow.

HOW DO YOU TAKE CARE OF YOURSELF SO THAT YOU CAN DO THIS KIND OF WORK?

Again, individual and peer group supervision are essential, until the therapist feels able to work alone. Even then, the wise therapist will seek consultation for difficult situations in order to maximize effectiveness. Most therapists need an experience in personal therapy or psychoanalysis, even when this has not been necessary for them to enjoy their own life and love relations. Only in this way can they summon up more repressed aspects of their own personalities and press them into therapeutic service. The therapist must also actively develop an intimate and social life so that no patient or client bears the burden of being the therapist's major gratifying object. Otherwise, the therapist is too afraid of the abandoning object that the patient will become as soon as the patient is well enough to leave the therapist, in which case improvement and progress may be seriously compromised.

WHEN YOU SAY SUPERVISION, DO YOU MEAN THROUGH THE ONE-WAY SCREEN?

No. We do not use the one-way screen, because even though using it supervisors can see and hear what is being said and done, they cannot know the therapist's internal experience. Supervisors get to know that only by working with the self-report of the therapist and by monitoring the resonance of the therapist's experience of the patient within the supervisory relationship. The supervisor offers a psychological space to the therapist in which supervisor and therapist together can explore the therapist's unconscious responses to the patient or patient group under discussion.

WHAT IS INFANT OBSERVATION AND HOW DOES IT IMPROVE CLINICAL SKILL?

At a twice monthly infant observation seminar, therapists meet to discuss carefully recorded observations of a baby being cared for at home. Each clinician has been visiting a mother-baby pair weekly over a period of two years, with the goal of simply observing what takes place, and they do nothing to intervene as they would do in their role as therapists. In the seminar, they take turns reading their observations. Most important of all, they report and deal with their own feelings that are aroused during the observation task. In discussion with a consultant, the seminar group develops hypotheses about the infant's emerging psychic structures.

Learning firsthand about a child from infancy to toddlerhood gives a vivid understanding of early development, which is useful in work with adults who are struggling with conflict dating from that time of life. Infant observation also prepares the clinician for sitting with experience patiently over time, not trying to force change, but containing anxiety in the transference—a crucial skill for allowing interpretation to arise from shared experience, which is most effective for fostering growth.

WHICH RESEARCH TOOLS ARE COMPATIBLE WITH OBJECT RELATIONS THERAPY?

Infant observation is a naturalistic form of research, but the observer is not asking prescribed research questions, and so there is no test associated with this form of research. The Object Relations Test (O.R.T.) developed in London by Herbert Phillipson involves the standardized scoring of reactions to images somewhat like those of the better known Rorshach and Thematic Apperception tests. The O.R.T. required updating and had not been in use until Martin Shaw in the United States issued an approved, revised version. This test reduces a person's narrative responses to strings of key words, which when scored according to a manual give a profile of the person's object relations. Drew Westen applied a Q-sort procedure to the Thematic Apperception Test to measure four dimensions of object relations—malevolent and benevolent affect, need-gratifying and respectful investment in others, understanding of social causality, and differentiating of self and other. He found that object relationships develop in a multifaceted progression motivated by affiliation and attachment, and also by gratification of the drives. In addition to using the Thematic Apperception Test, other tests cited by Westen are the Picture Arrangement Test, the Rorschach, Bell's Object Relations Inventory, Burke's comprehensive Object Relations Profile, and Piper's Quality of Object Relations Test. Tests in areas related to object relations include the Ainsworth Strange Situation to measure infant attachment, the Adult Attachment Interview, Benjamin's protocol used in coding social and family interaction, and Birtchnell's Interpersonal Octagon representation of how humans relate in terms of closeness/distance and upperness/lowerness. These and other tests are referred to more fully and cited in the chapter on research in *Object Relations Individual Therapy.*

WHERE CAN THERAPISTS GO FOR REFUELLING?

In addition to personal therapy and supervision, therapists who work in depth need a place to nourish themselves by sharing experiences, finding encouragement, and studying the latest theories and techniques. At a time when society is offering little support for intensive treatment, therapists need to create an oasis. That's why we created the International Psychotherapy Institute, a learning community where therapists from around the country gather about five times a year for intensive study modules using a method that we call the Group Affective Model. Members present concepts and illustrate them with clinical material, and then meet in small groups to discuss their personal reactions to the new ideas. In the process of discussion, the group finds that the concepts are displayed in the group interaction. This experience of the concepts in action enables therapists to study them in real time, internalize them, and then apply them in clinical work, with greater conviction of their value.

HOW DO YOU COPE WITH TERMINATION?

You cope with termination by thinking of it from the first day. The end of every session presages termination. Attention to the end of the session deals with issues of separation and reminds therapist and patient of the day when they will part. When the patient is ready to terminate, the therapist will go through a process that runs in parallel with that of the patient. Therapist and patient together will mourn the loss of the treatment opportunity, even while they rejoice together that it is no longer necessary.

A steady source of referrals is certainly a help.

HOW DO YOU DEAL WITH PATIENTS OR CLIENTS AFTER THERAPY IS COMPLETED?

We do not seek personal relationships with patients or clients after therapy. Nevertheless, we may meet former patients as new neighbors, parents at our children's schools or soccer games, party guests, and professional colleagues. In some of these situations, we may want to welcome a relationship on a new basis, but we remain sensitive to the influence of the previous therapeutic relationship. We know that former patients continue to think of us in our therapeutic role and experience us as an internal presence integrated into their psychological structure that, even if metabolized, exerts the influence of an internal object. Even the well-analyzed transference is potentially there, although no longer applicable, and the former therapist no longer has the authority to address its resurgence. The therapist who has not anticipated this revival of the transference may have to do some post-therapy self-analysis to accommodate to the shift to a role without the usual tool of interpretation.

Under no circumstances do we want to have intimate, emotional, or sexual relationships with current or former clients, including those who become our colleagues or students. Our influence is such that we can never be sure that there is not a transference relationship determining the nature of their interest in us. If we feel drawn to make an exception, we need to reexamine our countertransference to the patient and to the termination. It is important that we seek our social, intimate, and sexual relationships among the many people who have not consulted with us professionally.

This does not mean that we refuse to speak to former patients or clients. If we meet in a situation of professional colleagueship or social acquaintanceship, we want to behave naturally and unobtrusively with them, always following their needs. We do not allow our own longing, curiosity, or any remaining discomfort to lead us into seductive, rejecting, or impersonal behavior that is hurtful.

In agreeing to a contract for offering therapy and in accepting payment for our services, we make a commitment to subordinate our own interests in order to be the necessary therapeutic object for the patient. Our investment in the therapeutic process is our compensation for the personal loss that we must take for the patient's sake.

NOTES

Infant observation (J. Scharff and D. Scharff 1998; Williams 1984; Magagna (in press).

Nurturing the therapist's self (J. Scharff and D. Scharff 2000).
Object relations research (Shaw 2002; Westen 1990).
Measures of relationships (Morrison et al. 1997a, 1997b).
Complex attachment in couples (Clulow 2001; Fisher and Crandell 1997).
Coding social and family interaction (Benjamin 1996).
Interpersonal octagon (Birtchnell 1993).

(25)

A GUIDE TO FURTHER READING

WHAT ARE THE BEST THINGS TO READ FIRST?

The introductory readings that we are about to recommend are fully referenced in the reference section that follows. Briefly, here is what we have found most helpful.

We suggest starting with David Scharff's edited volume, *Object Relations Theory and Practice*, a collection of papers by the major contributors selected and integrated by him. Then read his introduction (written with E. F. Birtles) to Ronald Fairbairn's *Psychoanalytic Studies of the Personality*, Hanna Segal's *Introduction to the Work of Melanie Klein*, and Donald Winnicott's simple book, *The Child, the Family and the Outside World*. All of these books are quite accessible and readable. Segal's and Fairbairn's texts are focused on object relations theory whereas Winnicott's is a good overview of his approach to development and family life. A short, simple volume called *Love, Hate and Reparation* by Melanie Klein and Joan Riviere puts Kleinian theory in everyday language.

The most succinct introduction to Klein and Fairbairn can be found in David Scharff's *The Sexual Relationship: An Object Relations View of Sex and the Family*, Appendix A. An expanded simple introduction to the British object relations theorists is in David and Jill Scharff's *Object*

Relations Family Therapy, chapters 3 and 4. An excellent concise overview is given in John Sutherland's article, "The British object relations theorists: Balint, Winnicott, Fairbairn, Guntrip." A good summary of the major contributions to object relations theory is included in Judith Hughes's book, *Reshaping the Psychoanalytic Domain: The Work of Melanie Klein, W. R. D. Fairbairn and D. W. Winnicott*. We also recommend N. Gregory Hamilton's basic text *Self and Others*.

HOW CAN I FIND OUT MORE ABOUT FAIRBAIRN?

Fairbairn's papers, including "A Synopsis of the Author's Views Regarding the Structure of the Personality," are collected in his book, *Psychoanalytic Studies of the Personality*. His paper "Observations on the nature of hysterical states," written later than that book, is reprinted with other unpublished papers in *From Instinct to Self*, edited by David Scharff and Ellinor Fairbairn Birtles. See also David Scharff's edited *Fairbairn, Then and Now,* and for an update on the current applications of Fairbairn's theory, see *The Legacy of Fairbairn and Sutherland,* edited by Jill and David Scharff. For a quick review, look at Fairbairn's one-page "Synopsis of an object relations theory of the personality" in *The International Journal of Psycho-Analysis*. Fairbairn's ideas are modified to include the regressed ego in Harry Guntrip's *Schizoid Phenomena, Object Relations and the Self*, of which pages 288–331 are particularly helpful in clinical practice. If you want to know more about the man and his life, John Sutherland's short biography, *Fairbairn's Journey to the Interior,* is fascinating.

WHERE CAN I READ MORE WINNICOTT?

A readable account of the development of Winnicott's ideas in their philosophical context is to be found in Adam Phillips's *Winnicott*, a small, scholarly volume that does justice to the complexity and ambiguity of Winnicott's whimsical theorizing. A useful, less complicated statement of the concepts appears in Simon Grolnick's *The Work and Play of Winnicott* and Robert Rodman's *Winnicott: Life and Work*. Turning to the original, Winnicott's work is spread through many papers that are collected in two volumes called *Collected Papers* and *The Maturational Process and the Facilitating Environment*, both of which you might enjoy dipping into. A more advanced, better-integrated collection of Winnicott's ideas appears in *Playing and Reality*, his last major book before his death.

WHERE CAN I FIND MORE KLEINIAN THEORY?

Melanie Klein's discursive writing style can be difficult for the student reader, who will get a better grasp of the concepts from reading Segal. If you are interested in reading the original, we suggest that you start with "Notes on some schizoid mechanisms" in *Envy and Gratitude and Other Works* and "A contribution to the psychogenesis of manic-depressive states" in *Love, Guilt and Reparation*. The Kleinian concepts of projective and introjective identification are explored and summarized in Jill Savege Scharff's book *Projective and Introjective Identification and the Use of the Therapist's Self*, chapters 2, 3, and 4.

Like Klein's, Wilfred Bion's work is fascinating for the advanced reader, but it is extremely difficult to understand in the original. If you are ready for the challenge, begin with *Learning from Experience*. Fortunately his ideas on groups, knowledge, psychosis, thought, transformations, and psychoanalytic practice have been simplified and summarized by Leon Grinberg and some of Bion's other students in a little book called *Introduction to the Work of Bion* and more recently in *The Clinical Thinking of Wilfred Bion* by Neville and Joan Symington. His group theory is presented in Margaret Rioch's excellent exposition in *Psychiatry*.

CAN YOU EXPAND ON THE APPLICATION OF OBJECT RELATIONS THEORY TO COUPLES AND FAMILIES?

British object relations theory is applied to marital dynamics in Henry Dicks's classic, *Marital Tensions*; to couple and family therapy in David and Jill Scharff's books, *Object Relations Family Therapy*, *Object Relations Couple Therapy,* and *Treating Relationships* (in press); and to sexuality in David Scharff's *The Sexual Relationship*. Original papers by Roger Shapiro and John Zinner, who applied object relations theory in their pioneering family research, appear in Jill Scharff's *Foundations of Object Relations Family Therapy*.

The interrelation of intrapsychic and interpersonal forces at work on the development of the self as it relates to its objects is explored in David Scharff's *Refinding the Object and Reclaiming the Self* and in an advanced text, *Object Relations Individual Therapy* by Jill and David Scharff.

All of the abovementioned books are fully cited in the bibliography under the headings "Object relations theory" and "Application of object relations theory to couple and family therapy."

HOW CAN I MAKE A DEEPER STUDY OF OBJECT RELATIONS?

The advanced reader who is already familiar with the basics and wants to make a broader or deeper study of object relations theory and related psychoanalytic subjects may choose many readings from the annotated reference section. Here we would like to highlight a few. Of the various relevant contributions, we have found most useful the writings of Christopher Bollas, Patrick Casement, Nina Coltart, Betty Joseph, Stephen Mitchell, Thomas Ogden, Michael Parsons, Harold Searles, Hanna Segal, and books edited by Elizabeth Spillius. Alan Schore's research on neural development and affect regulation and Steve Suomi's ethological research on primate behavior are highly relevant to the object relations therapist and well worth reading.

To guide you to your particular area of interest, we have grouped the references in ten categories: object relations theory of individual and group, application of object relations theory to couple and family therapy, integration of object relations theory with other approaches, American object relations theory, transference and countertransference, self psychology, Freudian theory, attachment theory, chaos theory, and other relevant contributions.

BIBLIOGRAPHY

OBJECT RELATIONS THEORY OF
INDIVIDUAL AND GROUP

Balint, M. (1968). *The Basic Fault.* London: Tavistock.

Bick, E. (1968). The experience of the skin in early object relations. *International Journal of Psycho-Analysis* 49:484–86.

——— (1986). Further considerations on the role of the skin in early object relations. *British Journal of Psychotherapy* 2:292–99.

Bion, W. R. (1959). *Experiences in Groups.* New York: Basic Books, 1961.

——— (1962). *Learning from Experience.* New York: Basic Books.

——— (1967). *Second Thoughts.* London: Heinemann. Reprinted London: Karnac, 1984.

——— (1970). *Attention and Interpretation.* London: Tavistock.

Bollas, C. (1987). *The Shadow of the Object.* New York: Columbia University Press.

——— (1989a). A theory for the true self. In *Forces of Destiny: Psychoanalysis and Human Idiom.* London: Free Association Books.

——— (1989b). *Forces of Destiny: Psychoanalysis and Human Idiom.* London: Free Association Books.

——— (1992). *Being a Character.* New York: Faber and Faber.

——— (2000). *Hysteria.* London and New York: Routledge.

Bowlby, J. (1969). *Attachment and Loss. Vol. 1: Attachment.* London: Hogarth Press. New York: Basic Books.

——— (1973). *Attachment and Loss. Vol. 2: Separation: Anxiety and Anger.* London: Hogarth Press. New York: Basic Books.

——— (1980). *Attachment and Loss. Vol. 3: Loss: Sadness and Depression.* London: Hogarth Press. New York: Basic Books.

Casement, P. (1991). *On Learning from the Patient.* New York: Guilford.

Coltart, N. (1992). *Slouching Towards Bethlehem.* London and New York: Free Association Books and Guilford Press.

Dicks, H. V. (1967). *Marital Tensions: Clinical Studies Towards a Psycho-analytic Theory of Interaction.* London: Routledge and Kegan Paul.

Fairbairn, W. R. D. (1944). Endopsychic structure considered in terms of object relationships. In *Psychoanalytic Studies of the Personality,* pp. 82–135. London: Routledge and Kegan Paul, 1952.

——— (1952). *Psychoanalytic Studies of the Personality.* London: Routledge and Kegan Paul. (Also published as *An Object Relations Theory of the Personality.* New York: Basic Books.)

——— (1954). Observations on the nature of hysterical states. *British Journal of Medical Psychology* 27:105–25.

——— (1958). On the nature and aims of psycho-analytical treatment. *International Journal of Psycho-Analysis* 39:374–85.

——— (1963). Synopsis of an object-relations theory of the personality. *International Journal of Psycho-Analysis* 44:224–26. Reprinted in *From Instinct to Self: Selected Papers of W. R .D. Fairbairn, vol. 1,* ed. D. E. Scharff and E. F. Birtles, pp. 155–56. Northvale, NJ: Jason Aronson.

Greenberg, J. R., and Mitchell, S. A. (1983). *Object Relations in Psychoanalytic Theory.* Cambridge, MA: Harvard University Press.

Grinberg, L., Sor, D., and Tabak de Bianchedi, E. (1975). *Introduction to the Work of Bion,* trans. A. Hahn. Strath Tay, Scotland: Clunie Press.

Grolnick, S. (1990). *The Work and Play of Winnicott.* Northvale, NJ: Jason Aronson.

Guntrip, H. (1961). *Personality Structure and Human Interaction: The Developing Synthesis of Psychodynamic Theory.* London: Hogarth Press and The Institute of Psycho-Analysis.

——— (1969). *Schizoid Phenomena, Object Relations and the Self.* New York: International Universities Press.

——— (1986). My experience of analysis with Fairbairn and Winnicott. In *Essential Papers on Object Relations,* pp. 447–68, ed. P. Buckley. New York: New York University Press.

Hamilton, N. G. (1988). *Self and Others: Object Relations Theory in Practice.* Northvale, NJ: Jason Aronson.

Heimann, P. (1950). On counter-transference. *International Journal of Psycho-Analysis* 31:81–84.

Hinshelwood, R. (1994). *Clinical Klein.* London: Free Association Books.

Hinshelwood, R. D. (1991). *A Dictionary of Kleinian Thought.* Northvale, NJ: Jason Aronson.

Hopper, E. (1991). Encapsulation as a defence against the fear of annihilation. *International Journal of Psycho-Analysis* 72(4): 607–24.

—— (2003). *The Fourth Basic Assumption in the Unconscious Life of Groups and Group-like Systems.* London: Jessica Kingsley.

Hughes, J. M. (1989). *Reshaping the Psychoanalytic Domain: The Work of Melanie Klein, W. R. D. Fairbairn & D. W. Winnicott.* Berkeley: University of California Press.

Joseph, B. (1989). *Psychic Equilibrium and Psychic Change: Selected Papers of Betty Joseph,* ed. M. Feldman and E. B. Spillius. Number 9 in The New Library of Psychoanalysis. London: Tavistock/Routledge.

Klein, M. (1935). A contribution to the psychogenesis of manic-depressive states. In *Love, Guilt and Reparation and Other Works 1921–1945,* pp. 262–89. London: Hogarth Press, 1975.

—— (1946). Notes on some schizoid mechanisms. *International Journal of Psycho-Analysis* 27:99–100. And in *Envy and Gratitude & Other Works, 1946–1963.* London: Hogarth Press and the Institute of Psycho-Analysis, 1975. New York: Dell, 1977.

—— (1948). *Contributions to Psycho-Analysis 1921–1945.* London: Hogarth Press.

—— (1952). Some theoretical conclusions regarding the emotional life of the infant. In *Envy and Gratitude and Other Works 1946–1963,* pp. 61–93. London: Hogarth Press and The Institute of Psycho-Analysis, 1975.

—— (1955). On identification. In *Envy and Gratitude and Other Works 1946–1963,* pp. 141–75. London: Hogarth Press and The Institute of Psycho-Analysis, 1975.

—— (1975). *Envy and Gratitude and Other Works 1946–1963.* London: Hogarth Press and The Institute of Psycho-Analysis, 1975.

—— (1975). *Love, Guilt and Reparation and Other Works 1921–1945.* London: Hogarth Press. Reissued 1975, Delacorte Press.

Klein, M., and Riviere, J. (1967). *Love, Hate and Reparation.* London: The Hogarth Press and The Institute of Psycho-Analysis.

Little, M. (1951). Counter-transference and the patient's response to it. *International Journal of Psycho-Analysis* 32:32–39.

Main, T. F. (1957). The ailment. *British Journal of Medical Psychology* 30:129–45.

Meltzer, D. (1975). Adhesive identification. *Contemporary Psychoanalysis* 11:289–310.

Mitchell, S. A. (1988). *Relational Concepts in Psychoanalysis: An Integration.* Cambridge, MA: Harvard University Press.

Money-Kyrle, R. (1956). Normal counter-transference and some of its deviations. *International Journal of Psycho-Analysis* 37:360–66.

Murray, J. M. (1955). *Keats.* New York: Noonday Press.

Ogden, T. H. (1982). *Projective Identification and Psychotherapeutic Technique.* New York: Jason Aronson.

—— (1986a). Internal object relations. *The Matrix of the Mind,* pp. 131–65. Northvale, NJ: Jason Aronson.

—— (1986b). *The Matrix of the Mind.* Northvale, NJ: Jason Aronson.

—— (1989). The autistic-contiguous position. In *The Primitive Edge of Experience,* pp. 47–81. Northvale, NJ: Jason Aronson.

—— (1989). *The Primitive Edge of Experience.* Northvale, NJ: Jason Aronson.

Parsons, M. (2000). *The Dove That Returns: The Dove That Vanishes.* London: Routledge.

Phillips, A. (1988). *Winnicott.* Cambridge, MA: Harvard University Press.

Racker, H. (1968). *Transference and Countertransference.* New York: International Universities Press.

Rioch, M. (1970). The work of Wilfred Bion on groups. *Psychiatry* 3:56–65.

Rodman, F. R. (2003). *Winnicott: Life and Work.* Cambridge, MA: Perseus Books.

Sandler, J. (Ed.) (1987b). *Projection, Identification and Projective Identification.* Madison, CT: International Universities Press.

Scharff, D., and Birtles, E. (1994). *From Instinct to Self. Selected Papers of W. R. D. Fairbairn. Vol. 1. Clinical and Theoretical Papers.* Northvale, NJ: Jason Aronson.

Scharff, D. E. (1982). *The Sexual Relationship: An Object Relations View of Sex and the Family.* London: Routledge and Kegan Paul.

—— (1992). *Refinding the Object and Reclaiming the Self.* Northvale, NJ: Jason Aronson.

—— (Ed.) (1994). *Object Relations Theory and Practice.* Northvale, NJ: Jason Aronson.

Scharff, D. E., and Scharff, J. S. (1998). *Object Relations Individual Therapy.* Northvale, NJ: Jason Aronson.

Scharff, J. S. (1992). *Projective and Introjective Identification and the Use of the Therapist's Self.* Northvale, NJ: Jason Aronson.

—— (2001). Case presentation: the object relations approach. *Psychoanalytic Inquiry* 21(4): 469–82.

Scharff, J. S., and Scharff, D. E. (2000). *Tuning the Therapeutic Instrument: Affective Learning of Psychotherapy.* Northvale, NJ: Jason Aronson.

—— (Eds.) (2005). *The Legacy of Fairbairn and Sutherland.* London: Routledge.

Searles, H. (1965). *Collected Papers on Schizophrenia and Related Subjects.* New York: International Universities Press.

—— (1979). *Countertransference and Related Subjects—Selected Papers.* New York: International Universities Press.

—— (1986). *My Work with Borderline Patients.* Northvale, NJ: Jason Aronson.

Segal, H. (1964). *Introduction to the Work of Melanie Klein.* London: Heinemann.

—— (1981). *The Work of Hanna Segal.* New York: Jason Aronson.

—— (1991). *Dream, Phantasy and Art,* ed. E. B. Spillius. Number 12 in The New Library of Psychoanalysis. London: Routledge and Kegan Paul.

Shaw, M. (2002). *The Object Relations Technique: Assessing the Individual.* Manhasset, New York: O.R.T. Institute.

Skolnick, N., and Scharff, D. E. (1998). *Fairbairn, Then and Now.* New York: The Analytic Press.

Spillius, E. (1988a). *Melanie Klein Today Volume 1: Mainly Theory,* ed. E. B. Spillius. Number 7 in The New Library of Psychoanalysis. London and New York: Routledge and Kegan Paul.

—— (1988b). *Melanie Klein Today Volume 2: Mainly Practice,* ed. E. B. Spillius. Number 8 in The New Library of Psychoanalysis. London: Routledge and Kegan Paul.

—— (1991). Clinical experiences of projective identification. In *Clinical Lectures on Klein and Bion.* Ed. R. Anderson. Number 14 in New Library of Psychoanalysis. London: Routledge and Kegan Paul.

Stadter, M. (1996). *Object Relations Brief Therapy.* Northvale, NJ: Jason Aronson.

Stewart, H. (1990). Interpretation and other agents for psychic change. *International Review of Psycho-Analysis* 17:61–69.

—— (1992). *Psychic Experience and Problems of Technique.* Number 13 in The New Library of Psychoanalysis. London and New York: Routledge.

Sutherland, J. (1963). Object relations theory and the conceptual model of psychoanalysis. *British Journal of Medical Psychology* 36:109–24.

—— (1980). The British object relations theorists: Balint, Winnicott, Fairbairn, Guntrip. *Journal of the American Psychoanalytic Association* 28:829–60.

—— (1989). *Fairbairn's Journey into the Interior.* London: Free Association Press.

Tustin, F. (1980). Autistic Objects. *International Review of Psycho-Analysis* 7:27–38.

———— (1981). *Autistic States in Children*. Boston: Routledge and Kegan Paul.

———— (1984). Autistic shapes. *International Review of Psycho-Analysis* 11:279–90.

———— (1986). *Autistic Barriers in Neurotic Patients*. New Haven, CT: Yale University Press.

Winnicott, D. W. (1945). Primitive emotional development. In *Through Paediatrics to Psycho-Analysis*, pp. 145–56. London: The Hogarth Press, 1975.

———— (1951). Transitional objects and transitional phenomena. In *Through Paediatrics to Psycho-Analysis*, pp. 229–42. London: Tavistock, 1958. Reprinted by the Hogarth Press, 1975.

———— (1956). Primary maternal preoccupation. In *Through Paediatrics to Psycho-Analysis*, pp. 300–305. London: Hogarth Press, 1965.

———— (1958). *Through Paediatrics to Psycho-Analysis*. London: Tavistock, 1958. Reprinted by the Hogarth Press, 1975.

———— (1960). The theory of the parent-infant relationship. In *The Maturational Processes and the Facilitating Environment*, pp. 37–55. London: Hogarth Press, 1975.

———— (1963a). Communicating and not communicating leading to a study of certain opposites. In *The Maturational Processes and the Facilitating Environment*, pp. 179–92. London: Hogarth Press, 1975.

———— (1963b). The development of the capacity for concern. In *The Maturational Processes and the Facilitating Environment*, pp. 73–81. London: Hogarth Press, 1975.

———— (1964). *The Child, the Family and the Outside World*. London: Penguin Books.

———— (1965). *The Maturational Processes and the Facilitating Environment*. London: Hogarth Press.

———— (1971). *Playing and Reality*. London: Tavistock.

APPLICATION OF OBJECT RELATIONS THEORY TO COUPLE AND FAMILY THERAPY

Box, S. (1981). Introduction: Space for thinking in families. In *Psychotherapy with Families*, ed. S. Box et al., pp. 1–8. London: Routledge and Kegan Paul.

Box, S., Copley, B., Magagna, J., and Moustaki, E., (Eds.) (1981). *Psychotherapy with Families: An Analytic Approach*. London: Routledge and Kegan Paul.

Dicks, H. V. (1967). *Marital Tensions: Clinical Studies Towards a Psychoanalytic Theory of Interaction.* London: Routledge and Kegan Paul.

Framo, J. (1970). Symptoms from a family transactional point of view. In *Family Therapy in Transition,* pp. 12–57, ed. N. Ackerman, J. Lieb, and J. Pearce. Boston: Little Brown.

Klein, R. S. (1990). *Object Relations and the Family Process.* New York: Praeger.

Luepnitz, D. (1988). Psychoanalytic theory as a conceptual source for feminist psychotherapy with families. Chapter 12 in *The Family Interpreted: Feminist Theory in Clinical Practice,* pp. 168–95. New York: Basic Books.

Main, T. F. (1966). Mutual projection in a marriage. *Comprehensive Psychiatry* 7:432–49.

McCormack, C. (1993). *The Borderline Marriage.* Northvale, NJ: Jason Aronson.

Ravenscroft, K. (1988). Psychoanalytic family therapy approaches to the adolescent bulaemic. In *Psychoanalytic Treatment and Theory,* ed. H. Schwartz, pp. 443–88. Madison, CT: International Universities Press.

Scharff, D. (1982). *The Sexual Relationship: An Object Relations View of Sex and the Family.* London: Routledge & Kegan Paul. Reprinted 1998, Northvale, NJ: Jason Aronson.

—— (1992). *Refinding the Object and Reclaiming the Self.* Northvale, NJ: Jason Aronson.

—— (Ed.) (1996). *Object Relations Theory and Practice.* Northvale, NJ: Jason Aronson.

—— (2003). Couple and Family Therapy. Special issue. *Journal of Applied Psychoanalytic Studies* 1(3).

Scharff, D. and Scharff, J. (in press). *Treating Relationships.* Greenbelt, MD: Rowman and Littlefield.

Scharff, D., and Scharff, J. S. (1987). *Object Relations Family Therapy,* Northvale, NJ: Jason Aronson.

—— (1991). *Object Relations Couple Therapy.* Northvale, NJ: Jason Aronson.

Scharff, D. E., and Scharff, J. S. (2003). Using dreams in treating couples sexual issues. *Psychoanalytic Inquiry* 24(3): 468–82.

Scharff, J. S. (1989a). Play: an aspect of the therapist's holding capacity. In *Foundations of Object Relations Family Therapy,* pp. 447–61, ed. J. Scharff. Northvale, NJ: Jason Aronson.

—— (Ed.) (1989b). *Foundations of Object Relations Family Therapy.* Northvale, NJ: Jason Aronson.

—— (1992). *Projective and Introjective Identification and the Use of the Therapist's Self.* Northvale, NJ: Jason Aronson.

—— (1995). Psychoanalytic marital therapy. In *Clinical Handbook of Couple Therapy*, ed. N. Jacobson and A. Gurman, pp. 164–93. New York: Guilford.

—— (2003). Play in family therapy with young children. *International Journal of Applied Psychoanalytic Studies* 1(3): 259–68.

Scharff, J. S., and Bagnini, C. (2002). Object relations couple therapy. In *Clinical Handbook of Couple Therapy Vol. 3*, ed. A Gurman and N. Jacobson, pp. 59–86. New York: Guildford.

—— (2003). Narcissistic disorder. *Treating Emotional, Behavioral, and Health Problems in Couple Therapy*, ed. D. K. Snyder and M. A. Whisman, pp. 285–307. New York: Guildford.

Scharff, J. S., and Scharff, D. E. (1994). *Object Relations Therapy of Physical and Sexual Trauma*. Northvale, NJ: Jason Aronson.

—— (1997). Object relations couple therapy. *American Journal of Psychotherapy* 51(2): 141–73.

—— (1998). *Object Relations Individual Therapy*. Northvale, NJ: Jason Aronson.

—— (2003). Object-relations and psychodynamic approaches to couple and family therapy. In *Handbook of Family Therapy*, ed. T. Sexton, G. Weeks, and M. Robbins, pp. 59–81. New York: Brunner-Routledge.

Scharff, J. S., and Varela, Y. de (2000). Object relations therapy. In *Comparative Treatments for Relationship Dysfunction*, ed. F. Dattilio and L. Bavilacqua, pp. 81–101. New York: Springer.

Shapiro, R. L. (1979). Family dynamics and object relations theory: an analytic group-interpretive approach to family therapy. In *Foundations of Object Relations Family Therapy*, ed. J. S. Scharff, pp. 225–58. Northvale, NJ: Jason Aronson.

Stadter, M., and Scharff, D. E. (2000). Object relations brief therapy. In *Brief Therapy with Individuals and Couples*, ed. J. Carlson and L. Sperry. Phoenix, AZ: Zeig, Tucker, and Theisen.

Stierlin, H. (1977). *Psychoanalysis and Family Therapy*. New York: Jason Aronson.

Symington, J., and Symington, N. (1996). *The Clinical Thinking of Wilfred Bion*. London and New York: Routledge.

Williams, A. H. (1981). The micro-environment. In *Psychotherapy with Families*, ed. S. Box et al., pp. 105–19. London: Routledge and Kegan Paul.

Winer, R. (1989). The role of transitional experience in development in healthy and incestuous families. In *Foundations of Object Relations Family Therapy*, ed. J. S. Scharff, pp. 357–84. Northvale, NJ: Jason Aronson.

Wright, K. (1991). *Vision and Separation between Mother and Baby.* Northvale, NJ: Jason Aronson.

Zinner, J. (1976). The implications of projective identification for marital interaction. In *Contemporary Marriage; Structure, Dynamics, and Therapy,* ed. H. Grunebaum and J. Christ, pp. 293–308. Boston: Little, Brown. Also published in *Foundations of Object Relations Family Therapy,* ed. J. Scharff, pp. 155–73. Northvale, NJ: Jason Aronson.

Zinner, J., and Shapiro, R. (1972). Projective identification as a mode of perception and behavior in families of adolescents. *International Journal of Psycho-Analysis* 53:523–30. Also in *Foundations of Object Relations Family Therapy,* ed. J. S. Scharff, pp. 109–26. Northvale, NJ: Jason Aronson.

—— (1985). The use of concurrent therapies: therapeutic strategy or re-enactment? In *Foundations of Object Relations Family Therapy,* ed. J. S. Scharff, pp. 321–33. Northvale, NJ: Jason Aronson.

INTEGRATION OF OBJECT RELATIONS THEORY WITH OTHER APPROACHES

Bacall, H. A., and Newman, K. M. (1990). *Theories of Object Relations: Bridges to Self Psychology.* New York: Columbia University Press.

Fosshage, J. (issue ed.) (2001). Perspectives on an object relations clinical presentation: The process of change. *Psychoanalytic Inquiry* 21(4): 467–552.

Greenberg, J. R., and Mitchell, S. A. (1983). *Object Relations in Psychoanalytic Theory.* Cambridge, MA: Harvard University Press.

Mitchell, S. A. (1988). *Relational Concepts in Psychoanalysis: An Integration.* Cambridge, MA: Harvard University Press.

Slipp, S. (1984). *Object Relations: A Dynamic Bridge between Individual and Family Treatment.* New York: Jason Aronson.

—— (1988). *Theory and Practice of Object Relations Family Therapy.* Northvale, NJ: Jason Aronson.

AMERICAN OBJECT RELATIONS THEORY

Grotstein, J. (1982). *Splitting and Projective Identification.* New York: Jason Aronson.

Jacobson, E. (1954). The self and the object world: vicissitudes of their infantile cathexes and their influence on ideational and affective development. *Psychoanalytic Study of the Child* 9:75–127.

—— (1965). *The Self and the Object World.* London: Hogarth Press.

Kernberg, O. F. (1975). *Borderline Conditions and Pathological Narcissism.* New York: Jason Aronson.

—— (1976). *Object Relations and Clinical Psychoanalysis.* New York: Jason Aronson.

—— (1980). *Internal World and External Reality.* New York: Jason Aronson.

—— (1987). Projection and projective identification: developmental and clinical aspects. In: *Projection, Identification, Projective Identification,* ed. J. Sandler, pp. 93–115. Madison, CT: International Universities Press.

—— (1991). Aggression and love in the relationship of the couple. *Journal of the American Psychoanalytic Association* 39:45–70.

Mahler, M. (1968). *On Human Symbiosis and the Vicissitudes of Individuation.* New York: International Universities Press.

Mahler, M., Pine, F., and Bergman, A. (1975). *The Psychological Birth of the Human Infant: Symbiosis and Individuation.* New York: Basic Books.

Masterson, J. (1981). *The Narcissistic and Borderline Disorders: An Integrated Developmental Approach.* New York: Bruner/Mazel.

Meissner, W. W. (1987). Projection and projective identification. In *Projection, Identification, Projective Identification,* ed. J. Sandler, pp. 27–49. Madison, CT: International Universities Press.

Rinsley, D. (1982). *Borderline and Other Self Disorders.* Northvale, NJ: Jason Aronson.

Sandler, J. (1980). *Internal World and External Reality: Object Relations Theory Applied.* New York: Jason Aronson.

—— (1987a). Projection and projective identification. In *Projection, Identification, Projective Identification,* ed. J. Sandler, pp. 93–115. Madison, CT: International Universities Press.

—— (Ed.) (1987b). *Projection, Identification, Projective Identification.* Madison, CT: International Universities Press.

Volkan, V. (1976). *Primitive Internalized Object Relations.* New York: International Universities Press.

TRANSFERENCE AND COUNTERTRANSFERENCE

Heimann, P. (1950). On counter-transference. *International Journal of Psycho-Analysis* 31:81–84.

Jacobs, T. J. (1991). *The Use of the Self.* Madison, CT: International Universities Press.

Racker, H. (1968). *Transference and Countertransference.* New York: International Universities Press.

Scharff, J., and Scharff, D. (1998). Geography of the transference. In *Object Relations Individual Therapy,* pp. 242–81. Northvale, NJ: Jason Aronson.

Searles, H. (1979). *Countertransference and Related Subjects: Selected Papers.* New York: International Universities Press.

——— (1986). *My Work with Borderline Patients.* Northvale, NJ: Jason Aronson.

SELF PSYCHOLOGY THEORY APPLIED TO INDIVIDUALS AND COUPLES

Kohut, H. (1971). *The Analysis of the Self.* New York: International Universities Press.

——— (1977). *The Restoration of the Self.* New York: International Universities Press.

——— (1982). Introspection, empathy, and the semi-circle of mental health. *International Journal of Psycho-Analysis* 63:395–407.

Lansky, M. (1981). Treatment of the narcissistically vulnerable marriage. In *Family Therapy and Major Psychopathology,* ed. M. Lansky, pp. 163–82. New York: Grune and Stratton.

Solomon, M. (1989). *Narcissism and Intimacy.* New York: Norton.

FREUDIAN THEORY

Breuer, J., and Freud, S. (1895). Studies on hysteria. *Standard Edition* 2.

Erwin, E. (2002). *The Freud Encyclopedia.* London and New York: Routledge.

Freud, A. (1946). The ego's defensive operations. In *The Ego and the Mechanisms of Defense,* pp. 30–70. New York: International Universities Press.

Freud, S. (1895). The psychotherapy of hysteria. *Standard Edition* 2:253–305.

——— (1900). The interpretation of dreams. *Standard Edition* 4:150–51.

——— (1901a). The psychopathology of everyday life. *Standard Edition* 6:53–105.

——— (1901b). On dreams. *Standard Edition* 5:633–86.

——— (1905a). Fragment of an analysis of a case of hysteria. *Standard Edition* 7:7–122.

——— (1905b). Three essays on the theory of sexuality. *Standard Edition* 7:135–243.

—— (1910a). The future prospects of psycho-analytic therapy. Five lectures on psychoanalysis. *Standard Edition* 11:141–51.

—— (1910b). A special type of object choice made by men. *Standard Edition* 11:165–75.

—— (1911). Formulations on the two principles of mental functioning. *Standard Edition* 12:213–26.

—— (1912). Recommendations to physicians practicing psychoanalysis. *Standard Edition* 12:111–20.

—— (1914). Remembering, repeating and working through. *Standard Edition* 12:147–56.

—— (1915a). Repression. *Standard Edition* 14: 46–58.

—— (1915b). Observations on transference love. *Standard Edition* 12:159–71.

—— (1915c). The unconscious. *Standard Edition* 14:166–204.

—— (1917a). Mourning and melancholia. *Standard Edition* 14:243–58.

—— (1917b). Transference. *Standard Edition* 16:431–47.

—— (1917c). Resistance and repression. *Standard Edition* 16:286–302.

—— (1920). Beyond the pleasure principle. *Standard Edition* 18:7–64.

—— (1921). Group psychology and the analysis of the ego. *Standard Edition* 18:67–143.

—— (1923). The ego and the id. *Standard Edition* 19:12–66.

—— (1924). The dissolution of the Oedipus complex. *Standard Edition* 19:173–79.

—— (1930). Civilization and its discontents. *Standard Edition* 21:64–145.

—— (1933). New introductory lectures on psycho-analysis. *Standard Edition* 22:3–182.

—— (1940). An outline of psychoanalysis. *Standard Edition* 23:144–207.

Scharff, D. E. (Ed.) (2001). *The Psychoanalytic Century: Freud's Legacy for the Future*. New York: Other Press.

ATTACHMENT THEORY

Ainsworth, M. D. S., Blehar, M. C., Waters, E., and Wall, S. (1978). *Patterns of Attachment: A Psychological Study of the Strange Situation*. Hillsdale, NJ: Lawrence Erlbaum.

Bowlby, J. (1969). *Attachment and Loss, Volume I*. New York: Basic Books.

Clulow, C. (2001). *Adult Attachment and Couple Psychotherapy*. London: Routledge.

Fisher, J., and Crandell, L. (1997). Complex attachment: patterns of relating in the couple. *Sexual and Marital Therapy* 12(3): 211–23.

Fonagy, P. (2001). *Attachment Theory and Psychoanalysis.* New York: Other Press.

Kirkpatrick, L. A., and Davis, K. E. (1994). Attachment style, gender, and relationship stability: a longitudinal analysis. *Journal of Personality and Social Psychology* 66:502–12.

Main, M., and Goldwyn, R. (in press). Interview based adult attachment classification: related to infant-mother and infant-father attachment. *Developmental Psychology.*

Morrison, T., Urquiza, A. J., and Goodlin-Jones, B. (1997a). Attachment and the representation of intimate relationships in adulthood. *Journal of Psychology* 131:57–71.

—— (1997b). Attachment, perceptions of interaction, and relationship adjustment. *Journal of Social and Personal Relationships* 14:627–42.

Slade, A. (1996). Attachment theory and research: implications for the theory and practice of individual psychotherapy. *Handbook of Attachment Theory and Research,* ed. J. Cassidy and P. R. Shaver. New York: Guilford.

Sroufe, L. A., and Fleeson, J. (1986). Attachment and the construction of relationships. In *Relationships and Development,* pp. 51–71. Hillsdale, NJ: Lawrence Erlbaum.

Stern, D. (1985). *The Interpersonal World of the Infant.* New York: Basic Books.

Suomi, S. J. (1994). Influence of attachment theory on ethological studies of biobehavioral development in nonhuman primates. In *Attachment Theory: Social, Developmental, and Clinical Perspectives,* ed. S. Goldberg, R. Muir, and J. Kerr, pp. 185–200. Hillsdale, NJ: Analytic Press.

CHAOS THEORY

Bertalanffy, L. von (1950). The theory of open systems in physics and biology. *Science* 111:23–29.Hillsdale, NJ: Lawrence Erlbaum.

Briggs, J. (1992). *Fractals: The Patterns of Chaos.* New York: Touchstone.

Field, M., and Golubitsky, M. (1992). *Symmetry in Chaos: A Search for Pattern in Mathematics, Art and Nature.* New York: Oxford University Press.

Galatzer-Levy, R. (1995). Psychoanalysis and chaos theory. *Journal of the American Psychoanalytic Association.* 43:1095–113.

Garland, C. (Ed.) (1998). *Understanding Trauma.* London: Duckworth.

Gleick, J. (1987). *Chaos.* New York: Viking Penguin.

Grotstein, J. (1990). Nothingness, meaninglessness, chaos and the "black hole": II The black hole. *Contemporary Psychoanalysis:* 26(3): 377–407.

Moran, M. (1991). Chaos and psychoanalysis: the fluidic nature of mind. *International Review of Psycho-Analysis* 18:211–221.

Palumbo, S. (1999). *The Emergent Ego.* Madison, CT: International Universities Press.

Prigogine, I. (1976). Order through fluctuation: self-organization and social system. In *Evolution and Consciousness: Human Systems in Transition,* ed. C. H. Waddington and E. Jantsch, pp. 93–126, 130–33. Reading, MA: Addison-Wesley.

Quinodoz, J.-M. (1997). Transition in psychic structures in the light of deterministic chaos theory. *International Journal of Psycho-Analysis* 78(4): 699–718.

Scharff, J., and Scharff, D. (1998). Chaos theory and fractals in development, self and object relations, and transference. In *Object Relations Individual Therapy,* pp. 153–82. Northvale, NJ: Jason Aronson.

OTHER RELEVANT CONTRIBUTIONS

Alanen, Y., Vehtinen, V., Lehtinen, K., Aaltonen, J., and Räkköläinen,V. (2000). The Finnish integrated model for early treatment of schizophrenia and related psychoses. In *Psychosis. Psychological Approaches and Their Effectiveness: Putting Psychotherapies at the Centre of Treatment,* ed. B. Martindale, A. Bateman, M. Crowe, and F. Margison, pp. 235–66. London: Gaskell.

Benjamin, L. S. (1996). *Interpersonal Diagnosis and Treatment of Personality Disorders.* New York: Guildford.

Birtchnell, J. (1993). The interpersonal octagon. In *How Humans Relate: A New Interpersonal Theory,* pp. 215–29. Westport, CT: Prager.

Bollas, C., and Sundelson, D. (1995). *The New Informants.* Northvale, NJ: Jason Aronson.

Chodorow, N. (1978). *The Reproduction of Mothering.* Berkeley: University of California Press.

Cozolino, L. (2002). *The Neuroscience of Psychotherapy: Building and Rebuilding the Human Brain.* New York: W. W. Norton.

Dare, C. (1986). Psychoanalytic marital therapy. In *Clinical Handbook of Marital Therapy,* ed. N. S. Jacobson and A. S. Gurman, pp. 13–28. New York: Guilford Press.

Erikson, E. (1950). The eight ages of man. In *Childhood and Society,* pp. 247–74. New York: Norton. Revised paperback edition, 1963.

Fonagy, P., Gÿorgy, G., Jurist, E. L., and Target, M. (2003). *Affect Regulation, Mentalization and the Development of the Self.* New York: Other Press.

Foulkes, S. H. (1948). *Introduction to Group-Analytic Psychotherapy: Studies in the Social Integration of Individuals and Groups.* London: Heinemann. Reprinted London: Maresfield Reprints, 1983.

Gilligan, C. (1982). *In a Different Voice: Psychological Theory and Women's Development.* Cambridge: Harvard University Press.

Glassgold, J. M., and Iasenza, S. (Eds.) (1995). *Lesbians and Psychoanalysis: Revolutions in Theory and Practice.* New York: Free Press.

Kaplan, H. S. (1974). *The New Sex Therapy: Active Treatment of Sexual Dysfunctions.* New York: Brunner/Mazel.

Langs, R. (1976). *The Therapeutic Interaction. Vol. 2: A Critical Overview and Synthesis.* New York: Jason Aronson.

Levine, S. (1992). *Sexual Life: A Clinician's Guide.* New York: Plenum.

Magagna, J. (Ed.) (in press). *Intimate Transformations.* London: Karnac.

Masters, W. H., and Johnson, V. E. (1970). *Human Sexual Inadequacy.* Boston: Little, Brown.

McDougall, J. (1989). *Theaters of the Body: A Psychoanalytic Approach to Psychosomatic Illness.* New York: Norton.

——— (1995). *The Many Faces of Eros: A Psychoanalytic Exploration of Human Sexuality.* New York: Norton.

Miller, J. B. (1991). The development of women's sense of self. In *Women's Growth in Connection: Writings from the Stone Center,* pp. 11–26. New York: Guilford.

Sachs, H. (1923). On the genesis of sexual perversions. *Internationale Zeitschrift für Psychoanalyse* 9:172–82, trans. H. F. Bernays, New York Psychoanalytic Library, 1964, as quoted in C. W. Socarides, "Homosexuality," in *The American Handbook of Psychiatry,* vol. 3., 2nd rev. ed., ed. S. Arieti and E. B. Brody, pp. 292–315. New York: Basic Books, 1974.

Scharff, J., and Scharff, D. (1998). Clinical relevance of research: object relations testing, neural development, and attachment theory. In *Object Relations Individual Therapy,* pp. 117–51. Northvale, NJ: Jason Aronson.

——— (2000). *Tuning the Therapeutic Instrument: Affective Learning of Psychotherapy.* Northvale, NJ: Jason Aronson.

Schore, A. (1994). *Affect Regulation and the Origin of the Self: The Neurobiology of Emotional Development.* Hillsdale, NJ: Lawrence Erlbaum.

Schore, A. N. (2003a). *Affect Dysregulation and Disorders of the Self.* New York: Norton.

——— (2003b). *Affect Regulation and Repair of the Self.* New York: Norton.

Selvini Palazolli, M. (1974). *Self-starvation: From the Intrapsychic to the Transpersonal Approach to Anorexia Nervosa.* Milan: Feltrinelli.

Siegel, D. J. (1999). *The Developing Mind: Toward a Neurobiology of Interpersonal Experience.* New York: Guilford.

Stanton, A. H., and Schwartz, M. (1954). *The Mental Hospital.* New York: Basic Books.

Strachey, J. (1934). The nature of the therapeutic action of psychoanalysis. *International Journal of Psycho-Analysis* 15:127–59.

Tomkins, S. S. (1995). *Exploring Affect: The Selected Writings of Silvan S. Tomkins,* ed. E. V. Demos. Cambridge, England: Cambridge University Press.

Westen, D. W. (1990). Towards a revised theory of borderline object relations: Contributions of empirical research. *International Journal of Psycho-Analysis* 71:661–93.

Williams, G. (1984). Reflections on infant observation and its applications. *Journal of Analytical Psychology* 29:155–69.

INDEX

complimentary identification, 150–54

concordant identification, 150–54

containment, 38, 43–44, 48–50, 63, 90; in therapy, 118

core affective exchange, 141, 145, 185–86

countertransference, 95, 113, 224–25; assessment, 121; contextual, 149; in cotherapy, 226; and dreams, 161; in family therapy, 179–82, 184–87; focused, 149; importance, 155; and play, 166; use, 124–25, 190–91. *See also* transference

couple relationships, 40–42, 85; affairs, 214–15. *See also* therapy

death instinct, 12–13, 43

defenses, 18; analysis, 138, 143–44; assessment, 120, 124–25

development, 31–35, 53–55, 83, 193–94; assessment, 118–19, 124, 126–27, 166–68; personality, 3–4. *See also* psychosexual development

dreams, 11, 102; assessment, 121, 125–26, 128–29; in therapy, 73, 76–78, 144, 157–61, 168–72

dynamic issues, 173–77

eating disorders, 210

ego, 6–7, 13, 15, 17, 20, 83; antilibidinal, 25, 29; central, 28–29; development, 105; internal saboteur, 25, 160; and introjective identification, 38; libidinal, 25–26, 29, 103; and repression, 24–25, 27–28, 50; and self, 30–31. *See also* structural theory

endopsychic structure, 11, 23–25, 30–35, 40–41, 56, 158

environment mother, 45, 46–47, 49, 149

experiential therapy, 111

Fairbairn, Ronald, 83, 105–7, 183; development of object relations theory, 3, 7–9, 16, 20–21; dreams, 158; hysterical conversion, 213; and normal development, 31–35; and psychosexual stages, 119; and self, 27–28, 29. *See also* endopsychic structure

fantasies, 14, 33, 37, 50, 60, 71–72; assessment, 121, 126; cultural, 165; infant, 4, 8, 53–54, 56; and play, 168; in therapy, 94–98, 102, 108, 138, 144–46, 161–65

fathers, 8

feminism, 111–12

fixation, 15

fractals, 81, 88–89, 91–92; individuals and families, 84–85; scaling, 84–85, 86, 91–92

free association, 17

Freud, Sigmund, 17–18, 63, 70, 193, 213; and abstinence, 146; as basis for object relations, 3–4, 7–8, 19–20, 25–26, 183; dreams, 157–58; perversions, 215; transference and countertransference, 94–95, 155. *See also* psychoanalytic theory; psychosexual development; structural theory; topographical theory

geography of transference. *See* transference